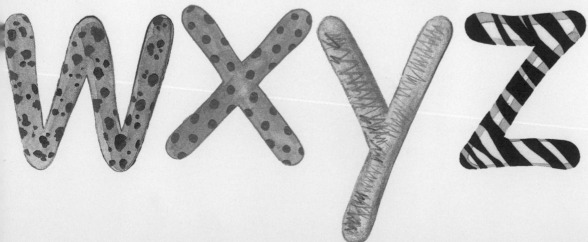

Written and illustrated by Loris Lesynski

Annick Press

Toronto • New York • Vancouver

© 2004 Loris Lesynski (text and illustrations)

Annick Press Ltd.
All rights reserved. No part of this work covered by the copyrights hereon may be reproduced or used in any form or by any means—graphic, electronic, or mechanical—without the prior written permission of the publisher.

We acknowledge the support of the Canada Council for the Arts, the Ontario Arts Council, the Government of Ontario through the Ontario Book Publishers Tax Credit program and the Ontario Book Initiative, and the Government of Canada through the Book Publishing Industry Development Program (BPIDP) for our publishing activities.

Cataloging in Publication Data

Lesynski, Loris
   Zigzag : zooms for zindergarten / written and illustrated by Loris Lesynski.

Poems.
ISBN 1-55037-875-9 (bound)
ISBN 1-55037-882-1 (pbk.)

1. Children's poetry, Canadian (English). I. Title.
PS8573.E79Z457 2004   jC811'.54   C2004-902072-2

Distributed in Canada by:
Firefly Books Ltd.
66 Leek Crescent
Richmond Hill, ON L4B 1H1

Published in the U.S.A. by:
Annick Press (U.S.) Ltd.

Distributed in the U.S.A. by:
Firefly Books (U.S.) Inc.
P.O. Box 1338
Ellicott Station
Buffalo, NY 14205

Printed and bound in Canada by Friesens, Altona, Manitoba.

The illustrations in this book were done in watercolor, colored pencil, and gouache. The text was typeset in Utopia, the titles in Lemonade.

Write to Loris Lesynski at Annick Press, 15 Patricia Ave., Toronto, Ontario, Canada M2M 1H9

www.lorislesynski.com

www.annickpress.com

ZIGZAG

Kindergarten Rocks!

Big kids, little kids,

girls and boys,

books and paints

and games and toys

    —kindergarten rocks!

Colorful mats, unusual hats.

Puppets, puzzles, balls and bats.

Numbers, letters—all of that's

    —why kindergarten rocks!

Zigzag

zigzag here and zigzag there
see some zigzags everywhere

zigzag edges on a paper bag

fences go in a zig and zag

zigzag notches on a front door key

the zigzag shape of a Christmas tree

zigzag string on a basketball hoop

see some zigzag noodles in my soup!

4

zigzag red and yellow stripes on a clown

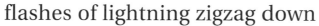

flashes of lightning zigzag down

snowflakes zigzag as they fall

... and what about the bounce

what about the bounce

what about the bounce of a Ping Pong ball?

Imagine some **bananas** in a zigzag bunch

or zigzag **sandwiches** just for lunch

zigzag **eyebrows?**

crayons, too

zigzag **stripes** on the zebra at the zoo

6

Up-and-down shoulders

back-and-forth feet

get your body going in a **zigga zagga** beat

zigzag elbows

zigzag toes

zigzag thumbs

... and a ziggy zaggy, wiggle waggle,

jiggle jaggy **nose**

7

Sit on Your Bottom

not on your elbows

not on your knees

sit on your bottom

please please please

TA DA!

not on your head

not upside down

sit on your bottom

and turn around

not on your nose

not on your chin

sit on your bottom

and let's begin

Lap

Where's my lap?

Where'd it go?

It was here a minute ago.

I know!

**I
STOOD
UP!**

Here's my lap,
back again.
It seemed to disappear and then

**I
SAT
DOWN!**

thumb thumb
finger fingers
palm palm CLAP
let your fingers hug
and have a cuddle
in your lap

Anything's a Drum

anything's a drum drum

a can can be a drum drum

tabletop's a drum drum

chair a double chum drum

drum drum anywhere, drum drum in the air

10

knees can be a drum drum
both of them a fun drum
hands are for a clap-drum
floor is for a tap-drum

drum drum anywhere, drum drum in the air

elbows-touch-each-other drum
head can be another drum
drumming in the air drum
drumming anywhere

drum drum anywhere

drum drum in the air, drum drum anywhere

drum

drum

drum

11

Hamster Rock 'n' Roll

The kindergarten hamster, round and round he goes,
running faster, faster on his little hamster toes.

Having fun, he loves to run in such a busy way.
But is he ever dizzy at the end of the day?

Paintbrush

paintbrush paintbrush
I love how you sway
I'd like to paint and paint all day
paintbrush paintbrush
I love how you swirl
together today
we'll paint the world
paintbrush paintbrush
tomorrow we'll play
it's time to wash you and
put you away

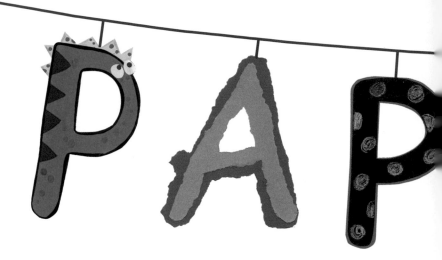

paper to paint on

paper to read

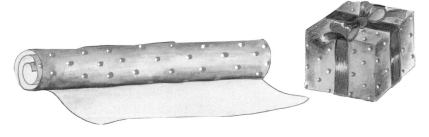

paper for presents

paper you need

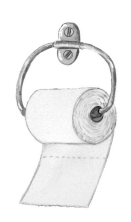

14

paper is flat, but glue and tape
can make it into any shape

if I were made of paper
and you were paper too,
we'd go to school in an envelope
and close the door with glue

15

Scissors

my scissors never listen

when I tell them what to cut

I try to cut a circle out of yellow paper but

    it

        looks

            like

                this:

my scissors never listen

when I try to cut a square

it comes out kind of crooked

looking something like a bear

    like

        this:

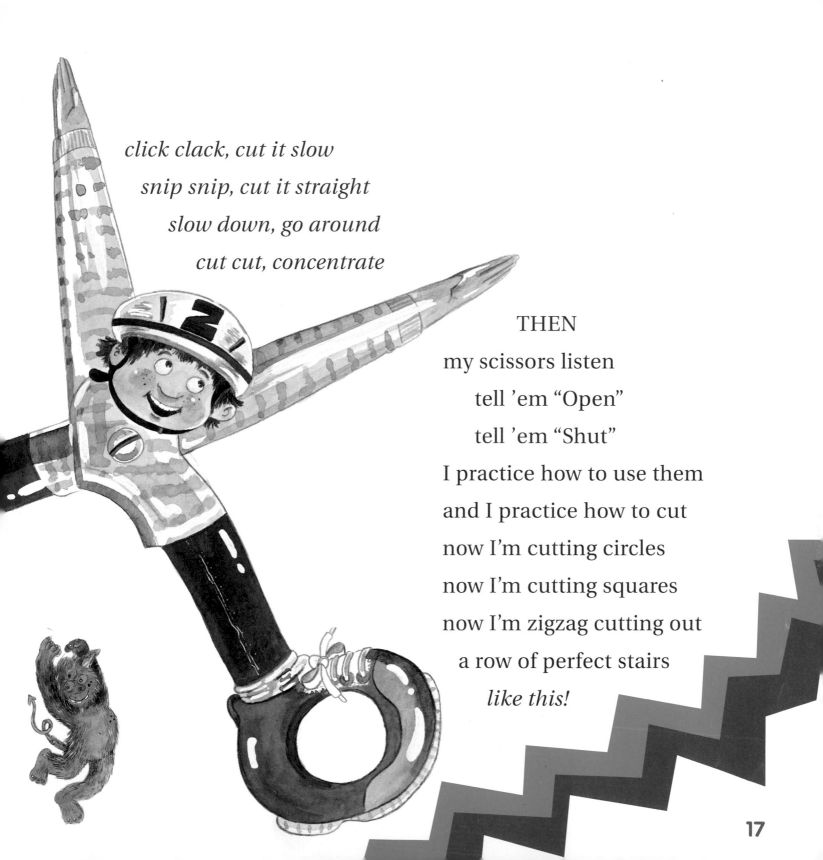

click clack, cut it slow
snip snip, cut it straight
slow down, go around
cut cut, concentrate

THEN
my scissors listen
tell 'em "Open"
tell 'em "Shut"
I practice how to use them
and I practice how to cut
now I'm cutting circles
now I'm cutting squares
now I'm zigzag cutting out
a row of perfect stairs
like this!

17

Stomp Up Steps

Stomp up steps
   stomp back down
      one stomp sideways
        one stomp around.

Sway up steps
   sway back down
      one sway sideways
        one sway around.

Tiptoe **up**
   tiptoe **down**
      one tip **sideways**
        one toe **around.**

S l o w up steps
   s l o w back down
      s l o w l y sideways
        s l o w l y around.

Zero

zero is nothing

zero is none

zero's not any

zero's no fun

a **zillion** is oodles

a zillion's a lot

a zillion is many

so many, too many

a zillion is probably more

than we've got

19

Monkeys on Monday

We're ...

monkeys on Monday,

toads on Tuesday,

wiggle worms on Wednesday, round then flat.

20

Birds on Thursday.

Elephants Friday.

The teacher says we're just like that,

like that.

21

The Alphabet

the alphabet has A in it

and X in it and K in it

it's why we like to play in it

and know just how it goes

letters, letters

everywhere,

in books, on T-shirts, underwear

the little bits of alphabet

together dance and then we get

a story ✔

a poem ✔

a joke ✔

a song ✔

a million zillion ways in which the letters all belong

Mrs. Zebra

Our teacher

Mrs. Zebra

likes

stripes

we try to find them

all the time

stripes

stripes on T-shirts

stripes on socks

stripes on books and

trucks and blocks

stripes we paint

stripes we draw

news of special stripes

we saw

stripes!

Zack Had a Cat

Zack had a cat

and the cat was white.

It whirled and twirled in the morning light.

Zack had a cat

and the cat was pink.

It sailed all day in the kitchen sink.

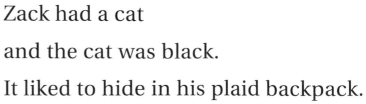

Zack had a cat

and the cat was black.

It liked to hide in his plaid backpack.

Zack had a cat
and the cat was red.
It named itself Tomato Head.

Zack had a cat that he painted blue,

then he made a mouse of playdough, too.

Oh, yes!

Zack had a cat as
yellow as the sun.
Which of the cats was
the favorite one?

You guess!

25

TEE HEE HEE

TEE HEE HEE
and *ha ha ha*
boo hoo hoo
and *lala lala* LA.
Whoopee!
Yippee!
Vroom vroom vroom!
School is over,
leave the room.

Yak yak yak
and sing and shout.
Time to let the noises out!

Cars Coming?

Kids are fast
but cars are faster.

    Look both ways or else disaster.

Kids are big
but trucks are jumbo.

    Running out is strictly dumbo.

Kids are cute
but wheels don't care.

    Check the traffic, see what's there.

Gumbo Baloney

Gumbo Baloney is the dog down the street.

Two sharp ears and four big feet.

Wet nose, one, and black spots, three.

I'd like him more if I didn't see

    so many

       so many

         so many

           TEETH.

What is mud? I do not know.
Where's it come from? Does it grow?
Mud is what it is, and so
all it is is
MUD.

A little earth, a little rain,
mixed together. What's its name?
MUD.

The garden when it's very wet,
and has no grass or flowers yet—
MUD.

The bottom of a puddle when
you jump right in and out again—
MUD.

Orange Popsicles...

Orange Popsicles, pink lemonade
    cupcake sprinkles in every shade
chocolate icing, cherry Jell-O
    beans of green and corn of yellow
the bread was white
    with blueberry jam
makes me wonder
    what color I am
                ... inside

Kitchen

Reeeeeeeeeeee ...

    friger-iger-igerator

    keep it cold

    I'll have it later

stove! *hot!* stove! *hot!*

  boil potatoes in a pot

(want to touch it? better not!)

  hot stove! stove *hot!*

soup cans, frying pans

cupboards full of food

sitting in the kitchen puts us

in a hungry mood

peanut butter, jam and honey, fill a spoon for me

after school the kitchen is the **nicest** place to be

Kindergarten Raps

Kindergarten

bindergarten

peppergarten

salt

smartygarten

partygarten

millymarten

malt

Follow me, wallow me, wallaby woe

follow me, mollow me

somebody's slow

hurry up giddy-up

get up and go

somebody's faster—*it's me!*

32

ABCD
HIJK
QRSTUV

THE RACE

Shortly after the laundry room discussion, Eva's pager went off and she hurried to the house of one of her patients in the next suburb. The family's infant son had been fine until a few weeks earlier, but then he fell suddenly and terribly ill. Eva was part of a team of doctors trying to keep him alive until he was old enough to be reconned. She didn't come home again until the next morning, and Phee could tell just by looking at her that the baby boy had died.

It was Sunday, the morning of Gryphon's big downhill race, so Phoenix and her sister were having an early breakfast while Oscar bustled about, trying to get out the door to deliver the sunrise sermon. Normally his lay minister did the early one and he did the later one, but he wanted to be there for Gryph's race, so he'd switched. All three of them fell silent when Eva walked in the door.

"We lost him. I'm just devastated." Eva dropped her purse and slumped into a chair at the table. "Those poor parents."

Phoenix glanced at her father. After Phoenix's first death Eva had quit her general practice and gone back to university to specialize in sick babies. Oscar had never objected, after that "discussion" in the park, not even once. He'd even supported the family with his modest minister's wages while she was at school, and had agreed to remortgage the house to secure her loan for starting up the neonatal clinic. But he hadn't agreed with her ideas. He still stood by the decision of the Congress. To this very day.

Oscar tugged his neatly trimmed beard. He was stuck at the coffee pot, thinking hard, his brow furrowed. One hand on the carafe, the other still tugging his beard. After a moment, he relaxed enough to pour the coffee and set it in front of his weary wife with a gentle kiss on the forehead. He placed his hands on her shoulders and gave her an affectionate—if somewhat distracted—squeeze.

"I'm sorry, Eva. I know you thought he'd make it. I had been praying."

"Thank you."

"I prayed too," Fawn piped up, whether or not it was true. At six, she had a little bit of a lying problem.

"Thanks, Fawn, honey."

"Will they have another one?" Phoenix stared at her bowl of cereal. The oat squares were soggy and separating. The milk was turning brown. She pushed the bowl away, suddenly sickened by it.

Would the reminders never end? Whenever one of Eva's babies died too soon, Phoenix felt as if her heart had been drop-kicked into the stratosphere. That could've been her fate. She too might never have lived to see her first birthday, let alone her fifteenth.

"I don't know," Eva said with a sigh. "I just don't know. Something changes in you when a baby dies. Permanent or not. A part of you dies too."

"We're blessed." Oscar bent and kissed Eva's hair. "Our Phoenix is still with us."

Eva closed her eyes and nodded, putting her other hand over Oscar's. Fawn decided this was a game and stuck her hand on top of the pile. Eva smiled and moved her bottom hand to the top, and then Oscar did the same, and then Fawn again, laughing, her red bangs falling across her face, until they were all slapping each other's hands and it was just Phoenix sitting there with the dead baby and her dead self on her mind.

Later, when they left for Gryph's race, Eva asked them not to mention the baby's death. Gryph had slept over at Saul's yet again, so had no idea about his mother's long, hard night.

"I don't want to spoil his special day," she said as they headed to the train. Fawn held one of her hands, and one of her father's. She skipped along, hardly seeming to be bothered by the sad news. Death had really not touched Fawn's own life directly, so Phee figured that it was hard for Fawn to actually connect it to herself. Not so with Phoenix. Her whole life—or what she could remember of it—she'd held each story of a baby gone before recon age as if they were bricks in her arms, weighing her down. She followed her parents across the green, giving her father a smile when he turned to wink at her.

"Okay, Phee?"

She nodded. He let Fawn skip ahead with Eva while he hung back to walk with Phoenix. "Are you sure?"

"Yes, Dad."

"It's understandable that this kind of thing would upset you." He took her hand in his. It felt awkward. She was too old, yet it felt good too, as if she were little again.

"I'm fine. Just sad about the baby."

"Me too," he said as they reached the train station. "And that's okay."

IT WAS ALWAYS STRANGE to enter Winter Park when it wasn't remotely cold out. It was the middle of June, and a beautiful hot sunny day outside. Phee was glad she'd stuffed a ski jacket in her pack, because as they made their way to the downhill section of the sprawling indoor winterized complex, she was freezing. The sun still shone through the clear roof, but the temperature inside was positively arctic.

Phoenix didn't sit with her parents and Fawn for the race. They were far up the bleachers to the left of the man-made hill, with a better view of the top half of the slope. Phoenix was down with Nadia and the boys, closer to the finish line.

"Did Gryph stay over at your place last night?" she asked Saul.

"You know he did. Why ask?"

"I don't know. Just wondering. He's hardly ever home anymore and—"

"And I"—Nadia cut Phee off and planted a kiss on Saul's lips— "would like you to myself every once in a while on a Saturday night."

"I'd like Gryph to myself every once in a while too," Huy joked. He'd been in love with Gryph since probably the fifth grade or, in other words, when he and the others realized he was "different," in that he liked boys. Or one in particular. Gryph.

"Gross," Neko said with a sneer.

Tariq silenced him with one of his looks. The boys didn't have a problem with Huy's being queer, and if Neko was going to last very long in their midst, he'd have to be okay with it too.

"Sorry," Neko muttered.

Another sharp look from Tariq prompted Neko to face Huy directly and apologize for real. "Sorry, Huy."

But Huy wasn't paying attention. He leaped up to watch Gryph as he shot out of the starting gate and cut down the slope. He was so fast that Phee could hardly keep her eye on him. He devoured the entire course with his customary precision, as if his snowboard were simply an extension of his body, and the hill was his alone and always had been. For almost the entire course.

Suddenly, mere seconds before he would've been an easy first across the finish line, he slowed. It was almost imperceptible, but Phee saw it in the sudden slackening of his form, a softening of his posture. Tariq caught it too—she could tell by the way his eyes shifted and he frowned. Huy was too busy cheering to notice. Neko and Saul didn't look as if they'd spotted the shift, and neither had Nadia. She was nestled under Saul's arm, inside the warmth of his jacket, and wasn't even watching the race.

"Come on!" Huy yelled, always Gryph's most enthusiastic cheerleader. He obviously thought Gryph still had it nailed. "Go! Go!"

"Go, Gryphon!" Neko pumped a triumphant fist in the air.

With a flat expression, Tariq watched Gryph carefully. He knew Gryph had blown it.

In the end, Gryph's delay had held him back just enough for the guy who'd been in second place to gain a tiny lead. Only seconds apart, the two of them crossed the finish line. Gryph took second place.

"No!" Huy yelled as the others grumbled.

"What just happened?" Phee marvelled out loud. "He had it! He had it all along! He gave it away. Did you see that?"

The winner, whooping with joy, threw his helmet into the air. The media members who had been flanked along the fence rushed him with their cameras.

Gryph gave a small wave to the crowd, and they erupted with cheers. No matter what, he was still their favourite. But not the winner. Not today anyway. What would Oscar say if Phee suggested that Gryph didn't care about winning anymore? Would that make him realize that something was wrong? That his son and proud winner would settle for anything less than best?

Chrysalis would not be okay with second best. Phee could see Gryph's Chrysalis agent making the phone call to his higher-ups from the VIP box, his posture communicating his disappointment keenly.

BUT GRYPH was a crowd-pleaser, nonetheless. A section of the crowd behind him, made up of mostly teenage girls, had placards that spelled out W-E L-O-V-E G-R-Y-P-H-O-N, and they did the wave with them, chanting his name. His fans clambered to get near him, pods ready for signing, digicams held high, snapping pictures blindly. A crush of more girls headed for him as he switched his goggles for his sunglasses. There were the TV crews, the journalists, more fans, his Chrysalis agent, his agent's assistant, his coach, his teammates. Everyone was always rushing to Gryph, as if he were just a mirage and would vanish before they could quench their thirst.

Gryph's agent said something to him, but Gryph, standing on tiptoes and scanning the crowd, only half listened to Lex.

"He's looking for you guys." Phoenix nudged Tariq, who was busy texting.

"Let's go, then," he said as he slid his phone into his pocket.

The group pushed through the crowd, Nadia clinging to Saul, her hand tight in his.

"I don't know why I let you drag me to these things." She frowned at Phoenix.

"You love it," Phoenix said, though she knew full well that Nadia did not love the cold of Winter Park, the unpredictable energy of crowds in general, or watching Phoenix's brother compete in any of the many sports he was a pro at. But she did love Saul, so she went where he went.

Closer now, Tariq locked eyes with Gryph over the sea of heads. They both nodded, just the slightest nod, but it said so much. Phee always marvelled at this, how the boys had an entire private language of looks and gestures. Gryph collected his snowboard, gracefully but firmly untangled himself from his adoring entourage, and slipped through the door leading to the corridor of change rooms in the basement of the complex.

"Saul, Huy," Tariq said. "You go ahead."

Nadia kissed Saul and reluctantly let go of his hand. "Love you, baby."

"Me too," Saul said with a blush, as he caught up with Huy, who was already bullying a path through the throng. This didn't come easily to Huy, who was gentle by nature and more concerned with the cut of his shirt than the task of being bodyguard, which is exactly why Gryph gave him the job. To harden him up. Years of this, and he was still the same soft-spoken sweetheart he'd been when he played with Phoenix and her dolls when they were kids. But he'd gotten bigger and bulkier—he could throw a mean right hook when necessary— and had traded pretending with dolls and tea sets for pretending to be meaner than he was. It was all a facade, though, for Gryph.

Phoenix and Nadia followed next, with Tariq and Neko bringing up the rear. The boys always sandwiched the girls like that, because Nadia hated crowds and got nervous if she was surrounded by strangers. It irked Phee that she was lumped in with Nadia, when she was more than capable of looking after herself. She didn't argue the matter, though, because it was a brotherly, protective gesture, and she had to admit that it felt nice to be taken care of.

THEY CHECKED IN with security and got their guest badges, then found Gryph's dressing room, the big one with the imaging wall and mini-bar and ambient stereo; it even had a little bedroom with an ensuite bathroom. Gryph was in the shower there, so his agent's assistant passed around hot chocolate and they sat down to wait. Saul pulled a flask from his pocket and poured a shot of whisky into his and Huy's drinks and Neko's too, though he was only fourteen. But he didn't spike Tariq's drink. He didn't drink alcohol. Tariq's dad drank to the point of oblivion most nights, and Tariq didn't want to end up like him. Gryph never drank either, because of the urine and blood tests, but the boys didn't bug him about it. Even though they ribbed Tariq on the subject often enough.

Saul poured whisky into Nadia's mug, but when he went to do the same to Phee's, she shook her head. She didn't want to drink if Tariq wasn't going to.

"Hey, Tariq, you have a budding clean and sober disciple over here."

"No." Phee blushed. It was true that she had a little crush on Tariq, but she'd melt into a puddle of embarrassment if he knew. "I just don't feel like it, is all."

Tariq glanced at her and shrugged, settling himself in one of the big easy chairs and surfing the music channels. Phee watched him. There'd been a small smile, hadn't there? When he shrugged?

PHOENIX REMEMBERED the time before Gryph was famous. Back then he changed with everyone else, in the sweat-stink dampness of the shared locker rooms. Now, his agent wouldn't sign him to a race or competition or commercial unless he was guaranteed his own private dressing room, stocked just so, with bowls of chocolate-covered almonds and a fridge full of mango juice and vitamin water. Gryph used to say that he felt weird about it at first, but really, who would turn down the warm, well-stocked comfort of this in favour of the cold, clammy stench of a communal change room? And besides, this way he could have his friends with him, whereas before they'd had to wait for him outside with everyone else.

The whisky episode over, Phoenix flopped down on the white leather couch beside Saul. Nadia was perched on his knee, leaning forward, her hands gripping a mug of hot chocolate.

"Saul?" Phoenix raised her eyebrows.

Saul was staring at the band of skin above Nadia's pants and below her top, or more specifically at the thin stretch of pink thong pulling against her dark, olive skin. He placed a finger on her spine and started tracing down.

"Saul!" Phoenix punched his shoulder.

Saul let his hand drop. "What?"

"Get a room, or get a grip. God."

"I almost spilled this all over my jacket!" Nadia licked a splash of hot chocolate off the back of her hand and twisted to glare at Phoenix. "Do you even know what this jacket cost? It's real fur around the collar, you know."

Gryph emerged from the bedroom, fresh from the shower, dressed in a pair of track pants, barefoot and bare-chested. He pulled his hair, dark and past his shoulders—much to Chrysalis's dismay—into a ponytail. He looked like a muscular rock star, with his gryphon tattoo along one forearm (their mother had been livid) and his nipple ring (even more livid) and his chiselled six-pack that had a legion of teenage girls wishing they could cop a feel. Phoenix looked at him and then quickly away, grimacing at the thought of how many girls wished they were in this room right now, within arm's reach of that famous six-pack. Never mind his fans, Phoenix could probably name a hundred girls just from school who would die to be in his company. But Gryph wasn't one for girlfriends. He went through girls as fast as he could down a meal, and bugged Saul for being with Nadia for almost two years. He called them Mr. and Mrs., while the girls lined up to hang off Gryph's arm, even if only for five minutes.

Gryph pulled on a T-shirt just as the door flung open and his and Phoenix's little sister hurled herself onto his back.

"Some kids from my class want to meet you. They're outside waiting. Come on!"

"Your wish is my command, Princess Fawn." Gryph slid his feet into a pair of flip-flops and piggybacked her to the door, where their parents stood just inside the room, looking as if they were just about to leave.

"You were amazing, hon." Eva tiptoed to kiss her tall son on the cheek. "Even if it looked as if you gave that other kid first place like some kind of present."

"There's my boy!" Oscar grabbed Gryph's hand and pulled him into a hug. "We're so proud of you, son. Good race. Good race. What happened at the end there? Looked as though you got distracted."

"He was just faster than me today, I guess." Gryph shrugged. "I'll get him next time."

"Not a doubt in my mind, son."

"Thanks, Dad."

Oscar nodded at the rest of them in the room. "How about a—"

"No!" they all said in unison, except the agent's assistant, who was newly back at work after being reconned from a fall while on vacation in Mexico. There was some talk about just how she'd fallen from a six-storey hotel balcony, but nonetheless, here she was. She used to be higher up than Lex, but she'd lost her memory during the recon and had to start back at the bottom. Gryph's agent put his phone call on hold and muttered to her, likely explaining that Oscar always offered to lead them in a prayer of thanks after every competition, and the offer was always unanimously declined.

It wasn't that Phoenix and Gryph didn't appreciate Oscar's bringing God into the whole equation, it was just that it was a little embarrassing when there were digicams and fans and friends around and you could never be sure who was watching. The last time Oscar led them in prayer, the boys and Nadia joining in reluctantly, a picture of the circle of them, heads bent, had landed on every podcast within five minutes, and the boys had run major interference for all the teasing. Having a sports celebrity among them made everything that much more public, which was perhaps the one and only downside of Gryph's fame.

Since then, no group prayers, though Oscar prayed enough for all of them. Eva put up with his piety, and even went through the motions, but she didn't believe in God. Phoenix's parents were the odd couple to the extreme that way. A doctor and a minister. Science and spirit. Fact and fancy.

Eva took Oscar's hand. "You can pray for all of us on the train on the way home, sweetheart."

"And I will, thank you very much." He kissed her forehead, and then plucked a reluctant Fawn off Gryph's back. "Let's go, kiddo."

"But I don't want to go! And he has to meet my friends from school!" Fawn wrapped her arms tighter around Gryph's neck. "He said he would. Right, Gryph?"

"You're choking him, honey." Eva pulled Fawn's little wrists, but she just held on, as the colour drained from Gryph's cheeks.

"So? He's got three recons!" Fawn leaned her whole six-year-old self into her grip. "Doesn't matter if I kill him."

"Fawn—" he croaked as he pulled her off and plunked her hard onto her feet. "That's not funny."

"Yes it was." Fawn stared at the floor. "And you do. Have three. Recons."

Oscar took her hand. "Fawn, you know better."

"I was joking."

Eva knelt and took her other hand. "No, you were being hurtful."

Fawn glanced over at Phoenix, who said, "I'm the last one you should be looking to for support in this one, brat."

"I was just joking!" Fawn looked at Saul, her favourite of Gryph's friends.

"Sorry, kid." He shrugged. "You're on your own this time."

"Recons are no laughing matter, even if you thought you were joking." Eva sighed. "Now come on, we're going home."

"I'm not going!" Fawn yanked herself away from her parents and ran to Gryph, locking herself around his leg this time. "I was only kidding. I'm sorry. I'm *sorry*, sorry, sorry, sorry, sorry—"

"I hear you, Fawn." Gryph swung her up onto his back and then said to their parents, "She can stay with us. I did promise to meet her friends."

Eva and Oscar glanced at each other, then once more at each of their children.

"It'll be fine," Phoenix said. "Don't worry."

"I cannot tell you how much I detest that platitude." Eva rummaged in her purse for Fawn's inhaler. "I think it should be banned. *Don't worry*. What a ridiculous thing to ask of a parent."

"Don't," Phoenix said as she put the proffered inhaler in her pocket, "worry."

"I"—Eva took Phoenix's face in her hands—"always will." She kissed her on both cheeks. "*Always*. Especially about you. Especially after this morning."

Again with the dead-baby reminder. And it wasn't restricted to just a few ways of dredging up Phee's past. It could be pretty much anything that sent Phee back into the murky stories of her death. Like the time she broke her leg the year before, rock climbing with Nadia and the boys, or when she had an asthma attack at the swim park, with her inhaler sitting at home, forgotten, beside her bed. Thankfully, Fawn had found Phoenix wheezing and wide-eyed, and she'd had her own puffer, and known what to do, so Phoenix had been okay. But if she died again, there was only one more recon. Most three-pers never had to be reconned, but Phoenix was down to her last one. And then after that, no more. A fourth death would be for real and forever. And she was only fifteen.

Fawn dragged Gryph out of the room to meet her friends just as the cart of food arrived from the canteen. The others set it out and dug in, while Phoenix backed up to the couch and sat, thinking about Fawn, and how she was her age when she'd died for the second time.

PICNIC

She'd died for the second time at the annual picnic for the West Sector One United Church, Oscar's church. The congregation had the park to themselves. It would've been similar to the picnics she'd been to since, starting with a sunrise sermon at the river's edge, and then a pancake breakfast, and then games for the children, and then lunch at tables with cheery cloths and colourful salads, baskets of buns, the smell from the barbecue wafting over the meadow to the river's edge.

Since that recon, every year at the picnic Phoenix had gone down to the river after her father's sermon. She stayed for hours, praying for her memory to return. The sound of children playing, birdsong, and the water rushing all surely part of the same soundtrack from nine years earlier, when it had happened.

Six years old. She'd been collecting rocks. That was no surprise. Phoenix still loved rocks. She was supposed to have been with Gryph, but she'd wandered off, and he was looking for her. After that, who knows what happened. She slipped? Fell? Thought she'd go for a swim? She could swim, her parents told her that, but the current from the river was too much for her.

The next thing she knew for sure was that Gryph saw her floating face down, the river carrying her south, toward the picnic meadow.

He ran along the bank, screaming, and then the adults came, Oscar and Eva at the front of an alarmed crowd. Oscar dived in for her.

"You had a yellow dress on," he always reminded her when he told the story. "And your hair was the colour of corn silk. You were like a piece of sunshine floating down the river. It was as beautiful a sight as it was tragic. I knew, even as I swam out to you, that your soul had gone again. It was like the first time, as if some of the air had left the world and we were all a little heavier for it."

And Eva, screaming, wading in to take her in her arms. "All I could think about was your tired little lungs filling up with water." Her mother had set her on the grass and tried to bring her back, pressing her little chest and breathing for her, until Oscar finally pulled her away. "And how I'd been eating potato chips while your heart beat slower and slower, until there was nothing, and how scared you must've been. I'm just so very, very thankful that you don't remember."

But Phoenix *wanted* to remember. She wanted to remember the time before, the years she'd lost, and even her death. She wanted to remember the fear she must've felt as she was swept down the river, just as much as she wanted to remember everything from before that moment. Riley, for example. The dog had been her constant companion, following her around, always keeping an eye on her. Maybe if he'd been allowed to come to the park that day he would've saved her, like a heroic dog out of the movies. But he'd overturned the barbecue the previous year and made off with a large steak, so was not welcome to come back.

Most of the pictures of her from that time showed her and Riley against various backdrops. Phoenix had seen the photos and the movies—she watched them all the time, trying to recapture pieces of her young self. No matter how hard she tried, she couldn't remember Riley at all. Worse, though, she didn't remember her mother or her father, or Gryph from before either. Or Nadia, even though they'd latched on to each other the first day of preschool. She didn't remember anything at all.

"PHEE?" Phoenix pulled herself away from the riverbank of nine years ago and forced herself to focus on Nadia, who was shaking her by the shoulder. "Phee."

"What?"

"Where'd you go?"

"Nowhere." Phoenix glanced at Fawn, sitting on the floor at Saul's feet now, reading to herself. Could Phoenix read before she died? She'd never asked her parents that. Fawn was an early reader. She could read picture books when she was four, but she still liked it best if someone read to her.

"Never mind." Nadia put a slender arm across her shoulder. "I know where you went. Same place you always go. We understand."

"No you don't, Nadia." There was no way she could understand. Nadia had never been reconned. Phee glanced at Lex's assistant. She was the only other person in the room who'd been reconned. In fact, she was only the seventh person Phee had met who'd been reconned at all. And the only one she'd ever met who'd lost her memory too.

"Yes I do." Nadia leaned against Phoenix's shoulder. "I understand."

Phee was going to let it go, because she loved Nadia and knew that she was only trying to be nice, but Saul piped up on her behalf.

"No, we don't understand, Nadia."

"Well, I *do*. I'm her best friend, after all. I know her better than any of you guys."

"That's true, but you're out of line, Nadia." Saul's tone was harsh. "You can't understand unless you've been through it."

"Oh, yeah?" Nadia stood, hands on her hips, poised to launch into it with Saul.

"Go for it, baby." He sat back, arms wide open. "How are you going to argue this one?"

Nadia growled at him. Fawn joined in, growling too. Nadia leaned forward, her hands on his knees. Her jacket was open, her low top offering a good view of her cleavage. "Saul!"

"Nadia!" He kissed her full on the lips and pulled her onto his knee. "It's a good thing we know each other's name, considering—"

"That there's a small child hanging on your every word?" Phoenix lifted Fawn onto her lap. She took Fawn's wrist and waved her hand. "Hello?"

"Read to me again, Saul?" Fawn teetered forward to pull another one of their grandparents' old children's books out of her pack. But Saul's eyes were locked on Nadia. "Phee?" Fawn thrust the book at her. "You read it."

The Velveteen Rabbit. Phoenix sometimes loved this story, and sometimes she hated it. This was one of the times she hated it. It made her feel funny in her gut, and reminded her of how she was different from her friends. As though she wasn't quite as real as they were, as though she was less of herself for having been reconned twice. As though she were her own second cousin—twice removed from herself, so to speak.

"Read!" Fawn ordered.

Phoenix opened the book, smoothing her hand across the pages. "'There was once a velveteen rabbit,'" she started. "'And in the beginning he was splendid.'"

CHARITY

A week after Gryph's snowboarding race, he joined Phoenix and Fawn in the garden as they packed squash and beans and spinach and tubs of raspberries into crates. He hadn't helped out much in the garden all year, whereas he used to like digging in the dirt and making things grow. Furthermore, she'd hardly seen him at home since the race.

"Thought you'd finally help?" Phoenix chucked a berry at him. "It's about time. Where have you been?"

He told Oscar and Eva that he was staying with Saul while his parents were out of town, but Phee knew from Nadia that Saul's parents hadn't gone anywhere. The boys still showed up for school every day, so she'd decided not to rat him out. But why the lie? What was he hiding?

Gryph bowed. "All in the name of being the Chrysalis poster boy."

"All in the name of getting wasted and scoring with countless girls with IQs to match their dress size, more like."

"Well, it's not their IQs I'm interested in, is it?" Gryph heaved a box of carrots onto the cart. "And the dresses come off pretty quick if I have anything to do with it."

"Why?" Fawn was suddenly at his side, munching on a dirty carrot.

"Never mind about Gryphon and dresses." Phoenix grabbed the carrot away. "What're you doing? You're six, right? Not three years old. Why are you eating a filthy carrot?"

"I washed it!"

"You wiped it on your shirt, Fawn." Phoenix poked the evidence with the carrot.

"That makes it clean!"

Oscar peeked around the side of the greenhouse. "The shuttle's here. Let's get going."

"I'll push the cart," Gryph said.

"It's the least you can do." Phoenix picked a handful of carrots and rinsed them thoroughly with the garden hose. "Mr. I'm-Too-Famous-to-Ever-Come-Home. What do you do all the time? You can't drink that much, and Saul would tell me if you were getting into trouble. I bet if I told Mom that you lied about Saul's parents going away, she'd freak."

"How come?" Fawn asked.

"Off you go, kiddo." Gryph took the carrots from Phoenix and thrust them at Fawn. "Why don't you hand these out to everyone? We'll meet you around front."

"What?" Phoenix looked away from Gryph's critical glare. "You're the one who—"

"Look at me, Phee."

Phoenix huffed, reluctantly turning her eyes back to him. She could tell by the set of his jaw that he was mad. Really, really mad.

"I didn't—"

"Don't ever say anything like that in front of Fawn ever again." Gryph's tone was even, but his eyes burned with a look that shrank Phoenix. "She's got a big mouth and even bigger ears. If she tells Mom, then I'm stuck here at home."

"So?" Phoenix kicked the dirt. She felt like Fawn, petulant and in the wrong, but earnestly self-righteous nonetheless. "What's so bad about that? What do you and the guys get up to that's so exciting, anyway?"

"None of your business." The look on Gryph's face softened, but into what? Disappointment? Frustration? Phoenix couldn't read it, but it unnerved her anyway. Not enough to stop her from pushing a little more, though.

"Drugs?" Phee asked. "Have you figured out a way to cheat the tests? Is that it? You're doing drugs? Because if you are, let me be the first to tell you that you've lost more brain cells than you can spare."

"Keep talking," Gryph growled. "Maybe you'll stop sounding like a clueless little twat eventually." Okay, so maybe Phee had pushed it a little too far. Gryph gripped her arm hard. "There's no way that I'm telling you anything. Why would I?"

"Because I'm your sister. And I worry about you." That sounded good, when the reality was that she was concerned but was honestly more curious than anything.

"You don't want to know." Gryph gave her arm a final fierce squeeze and then let it go. "So stop trying to figure it out."

"But if you're in trouble—"

"I'm not."

"Sounds like you are."

"Listen to me, Phee." Gryph brought his face right down to hers, his icy blue eyes locking on hers. "Put it out of your mind. Okay?"

Phee could think of a million responses to his request, but she knew full well the only one that he was willing to hear.

"Okay," she whispered.

"Then we have an understanding."

Phee didn't answer. It was hard enough to make the last response come out right, so she dared not try it again.

"Good. Because what I do is none of your business, Phee." Gryph turned the cart, his words sharpening. "And what my friends do is none of your business either. As for you, your job is an easy one. Even a retard can do it. Just keep your fucking mouth shut."

His words cut through her as if he'd stabbed her with the spade she held limply in her hand. She dropped it and gasped. "Gryph!" She ran after him. "Wait! I'm sorry!"

He disappeared around the side of the house with the cart, and when she caught up to him he was joking easily with the guards, handing the boxes into the cargo shuttle, as if nothing had happened. She stood off to one side, waiting for him to notice her, to say something, or to at least treat her as if nothing had happened. But he just ignored her, which hurt more than if he'd told her off again.

HOME FOR PHOENIX, Gryph, and Fawn was the gated community of the Shores. The luxurious houses were spread out along a pristine stretch of the Pacific Ocean, with reclaimed green space stretching on endlessly behind them. Security included an ironwork fence—custom-made by a renowned craftsman—that was electrified twenty-four hours a day. It hemmed them in on three sides and reached all the way down to the beach, where sensors anchored along the ocean floor took over. There was also a security guard at each of the two entrances, and remote-controlled closed-circuit cameras were everywhere.

The Shores was a three-per community, meaning that each individual was registered for up to three recons to be performed in the event of death between the ages of six months and sixty-five years. Oscar often muttered about the injustice of allotting the most recons to the highest-paid, most-educated, and heavily protected people, but he never muttered too loudly, because Eva had only to mention Phoenix's name, and he'd shut up. His ethics were complex and philosophically vast, but they all went on hold when it came to his own family.

And while they had plenty, others didn't have any food at all, which was why Oscar, ever the Good Samaritan, had the children work an enormous garden out at the back so that they could donate the food to one-pers and no-pers. The food was collected, along with other donations of food and clothing, at Oscar's church. Once a month, a social worker came with a cargo shuttle and a security crew from Crimcor. Everyone helped load it up, and then it zoomed off for the sister church that Oscar's congregation sponsored in a no-per zone.

OSCAR BROUGHT Gryph and Phoenix and Fawn on the ride to the church to have them help pack up the donations there. Once that was done, Oscar walked them to the train station.

"I'll be home for supper." He hugged each of them. "See you later."

"Bye, Daddy!" Fawn stepped onto his shoes, and he walked her a few steps like that, the two of them laughing.

"Later, alligator," he said. "In a while, crocodile." He stopped suddenly, and gazed off, with one of his looks.

"Dad?" Phoenix pulled Fawn off him.

"You know," Oscar said, as he fished in his pocket for his phone, "I've had an idea."

Gryph and Phoenix glanced at each other, eyebrows raised. When Oscar had an "idea," there was no telling what he was about to propose.

"Call your grandmother." Oscar handed his phone to Fawn. "Tell her we're dropping you off."

As Fawn chatted cozily with their grandmother, Oscar put an arm around each of his older children. "I'm going to take you with me today. It's time you see how the majority lives."

The majority meaning no-pers? Phee's stomach kicked up a flutter of nerves.

"We should check with Mom first." Phoenix had no interest whatsoever in seeing the squalor and lawlessness she'd heard so much about. "I don't think she'd let us go, Dad."

"We should get going now is what we should do," Oscar said. "Your mother is with a family who's more than likely facing the death of their only child. We won't disturb her. We'll be there and back in a jiffy, and the two of you won't even get out of the shuttle. This is a strong group of guards. It's the perfect time to go. Your mother knows I've wanted to take you two for some time now."

"But she doesn't want us to go, does she? She says—"

"She can appreciate *why* I want you to go, Phoenix."

"I'm in, Dad." Gryph glared at Phee, but not so that their father could see him. "Just take me if she doesn't want to go. If she's too scared to."

"It's not that I don't want to ..." If Gryph was going, Phee would too. Her curiosity was stronger than her fear. "And I'm not scared."

"Yes you are," Gryph taunted.

"I'm not!" She was, of course she was. She'd have been stupid not to be scared. But she wasn't about to let Gryph think that. "I just doubt that Mom would think it was safe."

"We'll be safe," Oscar assured her.

"How do you know, Dad?"

"We'll be in the shuttle. With security guards. And God." Phee started to roll her eyes, so her father changed gears. "And, well, safe is just as much a state of mind as it is a reality."

Phee eyed him again, arms crossed. She did want to go— especially to prove to Gryph that she wasn't afraid—but the sinking feeling in the pit of her stomach told her that it was a mistake.

"Don't worry." Oscar took Fawn's hand and they started back toward the shuttle.

"But how do you *know* if we'll be safe?"

"Phoenix! Are you crazy?" Gryph gave her a not-so-playful shove. "You'd turn down the chance to see a no-per zone for real and not just on TV?"

"No, I—" Curiosity was a powerful incentive. "I do want to go. But I—" She pushed her fear aside and forced a grin. She wouldn't be the fraidy cat. She'd let her curiosity and pride win this one. "I do want to go."

Gryph grinned too. "There's someone worthy of being my little sister. Feel the fear and do it anyway. Right?"

His shift in mood was like an elixir. She wanted more of it. Especially if he was going to act as if their fight in the garden had never happened. "Right. Only I'm not afraid."

"Yes you are." Gryph shoved her more playfully this time. "You're a terrible liar."

"Yeah, okay. So Phee is the nervous nail biter and Gryph gets to be the big bold brother."

"Sounds good to me."

"Okay, then." The sinking feeling hadn't vanished. She was still afraid. But Gryph was right. Sometimes in order to live your full life, you just had to feel the fear and do it anyway. He was the champion when it came to that. "Let's go."

THEY DROPPED FAWN at Eva's parents, and took off out of the Shores. Oscar and Gryph made easy conversation with the guards in their dark blue Crimcor jumpsuits and with the pilot and the social worker, but Phee was quiet. She sat on her hands so no one would notice the shaking. Her gut still twisted with anxiety, her ears buzzing with worry. *What if, what if, what if ...*

The shuttle zoomed over other three-per communities, and then inland over a two-per town, where the houses were closer together and the landscaping lacked a certain finesse and the shops and schools looked just a little tired and smelly, as if they were in need of a nice hot shower and would be shipshape afterwards. Then came a one-per town, with dirt lots turned into makeshift dumps, boarded-up shops, and housing projects built up in chaotic heaps, as if a toddler armed with play bricks had built it.

Ugly and desperate, but still so full of life. Mothers pushing babies on a swing set built from what looked like old machine parts and dangerous rope, hopeful flags of laundry hanging along wires strung between buildings, old people sitting in rickety chairs, smoking cigarettes, playing cards, boys tussling over a basketball. And the garden—Phoenix was surprised to see such an enormous and lush green square of abundance amid the concrete and garbage. A high fence framed it, and two burly men stood on either side of the only entrance, shotguns cradled in their arms.

"They've got guns!" Fear gripped Phoenix's guts. "Are they allowed?"

Her father shook his head.

"Aren't you going to report it?"

He shook his head again.

"But why not?"

"Think about it, Phee," Gryph broke in. "They're protecting the garden. They're just making sure they can feed their kids. Is that so wrong?"

"It's not wrong at all," Oscar said with a nod. "I would never stop someone from feeding their children, no matter what it takes."

"What if they shot at us for the food we've got?" Phee asked, keeping her eye on the men below, whose narrowed glares were locked on the shuttle as it passed overhead. "Even then?"

Gryph shrugged. "I wouldn't blame them."

"You wouldn't have a choice! You'd be dead."

"Okay, then, when I came back from being reconned, I wouldn't blame them."

"You wouldn't?" Phee's disbelief was obvious in her tone. "Come on, Gryph. Really?"

"I've got a life to spare," Gryph said with a smile. "Several, in fact."

"Speak for yourself," Phee grumbled. Since when did Gryph give a shit about one-pers? Since when had he become Mr. High-and-Mighty-Help-the-Less-Fortunate? She felt her father's arm on hers.

"Let me put it this way," he was saying. "If someone killed me for the loaf of bread I had in my hand in order to feed it to his starving child, I'd make sure that if it was my time to reach heaven, I'd tell God how I understood and forgave his desperate soul. And when that same man reached heaven—"

"It'd be hell, though, and not long after killing you," Phee said with a snort, "if Chrysalis found out." She could handle one person in her family lecturing her on ethics, but two was too many. "Murderers don't get reconned, in case you'd forgotten."

Oscar ignored her and continued. "When my murderer reached heaven, I'd sit him down and have him tell me about his children, and I'd tell him about mine. In heaven, the two of us could be friends in a way impossible here on earth."

"So?" Phoenix laughed. "Who'd want to be friends with anyone other than a three-per anyway?" She shot a glance at her brother.

Gryph had a disappointed frown on his face. "Take a look around you, genius."

"And then consider apologizing," her father added.

Aside from them, everyone on the shuttle—pilot, crew, social worker, and security guards—were two-pers. And they were staring at her. And not in a kindly way either. They'd heard her. Every single one of them had heard her.

Phoenix turned to the window again, embarrassed and confused. It used to be that she and her brother both thought their parents were weird for being so sympathetic with people who were less than three-pers. Eva with her "do no harm" mantra and Oscar with his "we're all God's children." Gryph and Phee used to joke about it even, how they wouldn't be surprised to come home for Thanksgiving dinner one day to find their house invaded by slovenly one-pers waiting for a free home-cooked meal, and filthy no-pers sleeping in their beds and wearing their clothes.

They were approaching the no-per zone now, and beneath them the chaos lurched out in all directions, distracting Phee from her thoughts. Directly below, little shacks and cramped shanties and hawker stalls lined the old freeway, which was now left to rare automobile traffic (Crimcor still patrolled in armoured trucks, for example), but mostly bicycles and pedestrians made use of it. Many no-pers made their homes under the protection of the overpasses, so children clambered over medians and played on the paved shoulders of the roadway outside their sad little huts. And then the eight-lane snake abruptly stopped in a heap of jagged rubble, grown over with brambles.

"Earthquake," Oscar explained. "Back when I was about your age. The freeway was never rebuilt."

The cargo shuttle started its descent, banking wide around a half-built housing project riddled with bullet holes and covered in graffiti. One entire wall had been blown out, revealing the tiny apartments, as if the building were a mangy dollhouse. People were living in it anyway, squatting in the squalor. A woman pulled aside a yellowed plastic sheet and stood at the edge, a baby on her hip. She yelled something at the shuttle, and then thrust her baby skyward at them. All the woman was wearing was a big T-shirt, and her baby wasn't wearing anything except a sagging rag for a diaper. The baby looked up with a blank, crusty stare. The woman was still screaming at them, but Phoenix couldn't hear what she was saying.

Phee turned to her father. "She wants food?"

"Maybe," Oscar said. "But more likely she wants us to take the baby. She probably can't care for him."

"Oh."

"Not so full of opinions now, are you?" Gryph said to Phee as they all watched the woman dangle the baby over the edge.

"No electricity. No running water." Oscar touched the window with his hand as the shuttle took the corner. "Those poor people. Imagine." He closed his eyes, his lips moving in silent prayer. The guards accompanying them snickered.

"Not here, Dad," Gryph said. "Come on."

Oscar finished and opened his eyes. "Prayer is for everywhere."

"You should get that on a shirt," one of the guards said, and all of them laughed. Phoenix saw Gryph bristle, ready to defend their father.

"There's the church," Oscar said.

As the pilot flipped on the landing lights and siren and lowered the shuttle onto an old parking lot, the back door to the church burst open and a jumble of people poured out, running for the shuttle, pushing each other, screaming, arms reaching up.

"Something's wrong," Oscar said. "There shouldn't be this many."

Below, a fist fight erupted between two men. A third picked up a plank of wood and swung it into the crowd, knocking over a mother with a toddler trying to hold on to her skirt and sending an old man face-first to the pavement.

"Go up!" The guard by the shuttle door pulled it open and trained his weapon on the crowd below, an angry belt of bullets spooling at his feet. "Take us up! Up!"

There was a sharp jolt as the pilot, startled, yanked the shuttle back into the air.

"What's happening?" Phoenix gripped her father's hand.

"These people shouldn't be here," Oscar said. "Something's gone wrong."

Phoenix gawked at the sight below. *Pandemonium.* It was a spelling-test word that she'd aced only last week, and exactly what this was. Pandemonium. The crowd churned and roiled as if it were a pot of boiling muck. The looks on their faces made Phoenix wince.

"Gross," she whispered, as a woman ripped her shirt off and shook her breasts at the shuttle, as if that would bring it down, as if that would get her fed. And then a man pulled himself out of the jumble and reached into his pocket, his eyes fixed on the shuttle. He lifted a handgun and pointed it skyward, his hands steady, his gaze a watery fury. Phoenix's breath caught in her throat. She coughed, suddenly breathless.

"Faster! Up! Up! Let's go!" The guard shoved Phoenix away from the window. "They're armed!"

"Do you blame them?" Gryph yelled at the same guard as he tried to pull Gryph away too. "Let me go!" Gryph wrenched free and kept watch over the chaos below.

"Gryph!" Oscar reached for his son, his eyes pleading.

Gryph reluctantly slid to the floor of the shuttle beside Phee as the guard at the door fired on the crowd.

Gunfire was returned from below as the shuttle banked sharply to the left, tipping Oscar to the floor too.

"Don't shoot!" Oscar pleaded. "Just take us out of here, please."

The gunman tossed Oscar a frown but lowered his gun.

Phoenix gasped, her asthma like a fist clutching her throat. She clung to her seat, her knuckles white, her lungs hot with the effort to breathe. She dug in her pocket for her inhaler and sucked the medicinal mist down her throat.

Within seconds, they were at a safe height.

"Wow." Gryph grinned as he lifted himself off the floor. "As messed up as that was, that was very, very cool."

The guards just stared at him. One of them shook his head, dumbfounded at Gryph's delight.

At last the fist at her throat relaxed, and Phee took a long, unsteady breath before speaking.

"Cool?" She kicked Gryph hard in the shin. "How can you say any of that was *cool?*"

"Maybe 'exciting' is a better word," Gryph allowed when he saw her expression. "The rush, I mean. The adrenalin, you know?"

"That same adrenalin gave me a friggin' asthma attack, Gryph!" That said, Phee turned on her father. "Gunfire? Riots? What the hell were you thinking? Why did you bring me here?" she screamed at him. "Are you stupid? What if I die? One more recon. That's it!"

"Well, how about that." Behind her, a guard scoffed. "Not really a three-per yourself, then, are you?"

Phee spun around. "Who said that?"

The guards all looked back at her with solidly blank expressions. One of them dared a shrug.

"Phee, honey. Please sit down." Oscar steered her to the seat beside his. He buckled himself in and then reached across Phoenix and buckled her in too. "I'm sorry, baby."

"You're sorry?" She hit his chest, and then hit him again with both hands as the shuttle sped out of the city just slightly faster than her pounding heart. "Why, Dad?"

"You shouldn't have brought her," Gryph said when Phoenix's tears finally made it impossible to speak. She leaned against her father and sobbed. She still smarted from the comment from the guard too cowardly to admit to saying it. "Not if you knew it was like this."

"But I didn't," her father said. "I would never put you children at risk."

"But you did!" Phee started in earnest again.

"But I had no way of knowing. In almost twenty years, they've never rushed the shuttle like that before." Oscar held Phoenix as she cried. "And I didn't recognize any of them from the church. I think someone must've leaked that we were coming, and the church couldn't stop them. I didn't know. Usually there's no problem."

"Still," Gryph said, "you shouldn't have brought her. She can't handle it, obviously."

Phee lifted her eyes to glare at her brother. She wiped her tears, wishing she could argue with him. But there was no point. He was right. She couldn't handle it. Not at all. What she wondered was why Gryphon could. How was he so different from her? Did he get off on adrenalin so much that danger excited him? Was it because he still had his three recons?

BACK AT THE SHORES, they collected Fawn and walked home along the waterfront path. The air was warm and fragrant with summer flowers and the salty sea, the sky was a cloudless blue, and the waves rolled up happily against the shore, but it was all lost on Phee. She felt dark and stormy and foul. Still shaken, she hung back from the others, refusing her father's invitation to walk with him.

"Why couldn't I come too?" Fawn tugged her father's jacket. "How come, Daddy?"

Oscar kissed her forehead. "Quiet, pet."

"But why not?" Fawn skipped ahead and then pirouetted so that she was walking backwards, facing them. "I'd be good. I'd help. I would!" She stumbled, and then turned so that she was walking normally, her back to them. "Next time, I'm coming too. You'll see.

I'm going to tell Mom you guys left me behind. It's not fair. She'll make you take me with you next time."

Gryph lifted his eyes and looked at Phoenix. This time, the darkness was gone. Replaced by something only slightly less chilling. Blame? Resentment?

"No one likes a tattletale, Fawn." Phoenix shoved her hands in her pockets. It had gotten colder suddenly, a chilly wind kicking up off the ocean. "Do up your jacket."

"Do this! Do that!" Fawn started skipping again. "Don't do this, don't do that!"

"Your mother—" Oscar covered his face with his hands. "What are we going to tell your mother?"

"The best thing would be to not tell her at all," Gryph said. "But little miss motor mouth Fawn is going to make that impossible."

"We're going to have to tell her anyway, Dad," Phoenix could hear the quaver in her voice. Truth was, she wanted her mother to know. She didn't want her father to get away with such a stupid decision. He should've known better. He was the parent, after all. Sometimes his optimism got the best of him, but ultimately he should've known better. "You screwed up, Dad. Own it. That's what you're always telling us when we do something wrong. Choose bravery, right? Choose truth."

"Fair enough." Oscar nodded. He walked a little farther, thinking. "You're absolutely right. I'll tell her. Of course I'll tell her. We have no secrets in this family."

Phee aimed another glance at her brother. He certainly had secrets. Lots of them. Gryphon stared back at her, challenging her. "I don't think you should tell her, Dad."

But Oscar shook his head. "Your sister is right. No secrets. Honesty is the best policy."

"You're sure you want to tell her?" Gryph raised an eyebrow. "You're really sure about that, Dad? We're okay. No one got hurt. Everyone got home safe and sound, right?"

"True." Oscar nodded. "But nonetheless I'll tell her."

Oscar walked ahead, giving Gryph the perfect opportunity to whisper harshly to Phoenix, "Way to go, baby."

Phee gave him the smallest of smiles. "I don't know what you're talking about, Gryph. We don't have secrets in our family. Right?"

With an exasperated sigh, Gryph sauntered off ahead of all of them, making a bee-line for home.

THE CHILDREN STAYED out of the way while Oscar made his confession when Eva came home. Moments later, she stormed upstairs and burst into Gryph's room, where all three of them were piled on his bed, reading to Fawn while they waited.

"Pack a bag. Each of you." She plucked Fawn off the bed and perched her on her hip, as if she were a baby. "We're going to Grandma and Grandpa's."

Gryph and Phoenix stared at her.

"Now!" Eva started crying, but quickly gritted her teeth and steeled herself, and the tears stopped. "Get off your butts and do what I tell you!"

"This is about you," Gryph said to Phoenix as Eva carried a protesting Fawn out of the room. "This kind of thing is always about you."

Phoenix threw a book at him. "Don't blame me for Dad's dumb move."

"He should've taken just me." Gryph pulled a backpack from his closet and started shoving clothes into it. "Then we could've kept it from her. If Fawn hadn't known where we went. If you hadn't insisted on telling Mom. Stupid idea, I might add."

"Should've, could've, would've. Talk to me after you've been reconned, Gryph. I'm sick of your bullshit." Phoenix slammed the door behind her. She hesitated in the hall, her heart pounding, waiting for him to come after her. When he didn't, it was almost worse.

Fawn's door was open. She was face down on the bed, bawling, as Eva thundered around, stuffing things into a suitcase, muttering to herself. "Go pack!" she yelled when she looked up and saw Phee just standing there, stunned. Phoenix tiptoed downstairs to find her father. He was slumped in a chair in the dark living room, his treasured old Bible balancing on his knee. He looked up and saw her in the doorway, but he didn't say anything. They looked at each other for a long moment, then Phoenix went back upstairs, her mind and heart in a tandem tailspin. What was happening to her family?

SYSTEM FAILURE

On Monday, Gryph and Phoenix walked to the train station in silence, with Fawn swinging between them, her knee socks already drooping at her ankles, her school uniform shirt untucked and buttoned up squint. She wasn't fazed by any of this. To her it was just a sleepover at Grandma and Grandpa's. A sleepover that might just go on and on and on.

"Me and Grandma's going to make cupcakes after school. And we're going to ice them with blue icing. And some purple too, maybe. Or red. I'm not sure. But I get to choose. But you have to be careful if you mix the colours too much because then it just looks like baby poo." Fawn laughed. "Did you hear me? I said baby poo. On the cupcakes."

"We heard you," Gryph said.

"But you didn't laugh."

"It's not funny," Gryph said slowly without looking at her. "That's why." Fawn fell quiet. This always shut her up, the way Gryph snubbed her. It worked for Phee too, his famous silent treatments. Come to think of it, it worked for everyone in the family. His friends too. He was the only one who could change the mood of an entire gathering just by being in a bad mood himself. Or a good one. He was big like that. He took up a lot of space, both physically and mentally. Not like Phee, who wanted to be as small as possible at all times. Preferably invisible.

Phoenix glanced back at her grandparents' house. Her grandmother stood on the porch, smiling and waving, as if nothing was wrong, as if she saw them off to school every day, when in fact this was a first. Some people want to be invisible, some want to play the denial game. Phoenix didn't want to go back there after school. She wanted to go home. She wanted everything back to normal.

Eva had joined them at the breakfast table, bedraggled and small, awash in one of her much larger mother's housecoats, her face a puffy tear-stained red. She'd managed to nurse a cup of coffee and then she'd folded her arms on the table and laid her head down and started crying again, only taking a breath to tell the three children to come back there after school. They would not be going home. At least not yet.

"But *when?*" Phoenix pushed her breakfast away, the jiggly eggs and grease-slicked bacon suddenly repulsive. This was all Phoenix's fault. How she wished she hadn't gone with Gryph and her father. "He didn't mean for it to happen like that! It's not his fault! He just wanted us to understand, Mom."

"*Understand,*" Eva said into the folds of the housecoat's arms, her voice muffled. "That's just it. You don't. You don't understand, Phoenix."

Eva's mother hugged her daughter, raising her eyes to the children in a silent suggestion that it was time to leave for school.

"KNOW WHAT, PHEE?" Fawn had given up on Gryph and had turned her attention to her sister. "Grandma started reading me *The Lion, the Witch and the Wardrobe* last night." Fawn swung hard, jerking Phoenix's arm back. "She's going to read me the whole thing. She says Grandpa read it to Mom when she was my age, but he can't because his brain is foggy. Grandma says that he read it to you too, but that was before you died that time in the park. So you don't remember neither."

"Can't you just be quiet for once, Fawn?" Phoenix yanked free of Fawn's hand, sending her stumbling forward.

"You pushed me!" Fawn planted her fists on her hips and glared at Phee. Then she switched to one of her perfected pained looks and appealed to Gryph. "She pushed me, Gryph!"

"I did not." Phoenix hurried ahead. "I can't stand you babbling on and on anymore. It's driving me crazy."

Thankfully, Gryph stayed with Fawn so Phee could march on ahead, fully engulfed in her misery. He was good for that, even now.

At the station, Gryph waited with Fawn until her train came, and then he signed for her with the children's monitor and joined Phoenix at the other end of the platform, where the train that picked up the high school students would stop.

"Don't take it out on her." Gryph shoved her. "She's just a kid."

"Take what out on her? I don't even know what's going on."

"Doesn't matter what's going on." Gryph shrugged. "Don't pick on her."

"Fine, Gryph. Whatever you say." Phoenix hugged herself. "I won't pick on her, if you won't pick on me. Deal?"

"Wow. Sometimes you can be a real bitch, you know."

Phoenix shrugged. "Takes one to know one."

Gryph laughed. "That's the best you've got?"

"Yeah, it is." Phoenix backed away. "Leave me alone, Gryph."

"Happily." Gryph wandered off down the platform to talk to a redhead who was new to the Shores. Phoenix rolled her eyes. The girl was smiling up at him, twirling her hair and batting her eyelashes like a living cliché. She got on the junior high train and waved at him until it was out of sight. At times like this, Phee wished her family had a private shuttle so she wouldn't have to take the train and endure the drama that surrounded Gryph every day.

"A bit young for you, don't you think?" Phoenix said, as Gryph rejoined her when their train pulled in.

"She was at the snowboard race," Gryph said. "And my last rock climbing competition."

"A groupie. How exciting for you."

Gryph shrugged. "I was just talking to her, Phee."

They got on last, and as Phoenix stepped on, the door shut too soon, catching her backpack. She yanked it free, and found a seat.

"Something must be wrong with the sensors." Gryph took the seat across from her. "Huh. Interesting." He watched the door at the other stops; it was definitely shorting out or something. Jackets, backpacks, even arms were getting stuck. Each time, they expected the intercom to announce that the car was being removed from service and they all had to get off, but it would seem that a cascade of security and safety measures had failed, leaving the doors of the car to work like jaws, snapping shut on the unsuspecting. Phee figured they were working on fixing it remotely.

Nadia and Neko got on at the first Bay View stop, and Phoenix told her what had happened the night before. She was only half listening, though, because she and Saul were texting back and forth, even though they'd see each other in minutes.

"It'll blow over," she said, smiling at whatever Saul had just texted her. "You'll see."

"I don't know, Nadia."

"It will." Nadia sent a reply off, her phone beeping to confirm it was sent. She looked up. "My parents fight all the time, and they always work it out."

"But your parents hate each other." The train slowed at Saul and Tariq's stop. "My parents aren't like that. They never fight."

"Don't worry about it." Nadia's phone rang. "Morning, handsome," she purred into it as she rose from her seat, craning over the other students to catch a glimpse of Saul. He was making his way to their car, phone at his ear. "See me, baby?"

He waved. She blew a kiss at him. Phoenix groaned.

Tariq came up behind Saul just then and tripped him, sending him sprawling. His phone soared through the air and over the edge, plummeting to the ground two storeys below the elevated tracks.

"What an asshole!" Nadia said. "He's going to have to pay for that phone."

Saul leaped to his feet and sprinted to catch up to Tariq. They scrapped playfully on the platform, like a couple of puppies, until the lights flashed and the recorded voice announced the train's departure. The two boys got up, and made one last dash for the car. They reached out as the door was shutting, which would normally trigger the sensors to reopen the door and delay the train. If the sensors had been working.

"This should be fun." Gryph stuck his hand over one of the security cameras. "Neko, get the other one."

"Don't you dare," Nadia said.

Neko glanced at Nadia, then back at Gryph.

"I'm not going to tell you twice, scrote. Do it."

Neko stood on a seat and covered the other camera.

"Saul!" Nadia screeched as the doors rhythmically tightened against his arm, trying hard to shut.

"Hey!" Tariq yanked at the door with his free arm as the train started moving.

Neko dropped his hand, eyes wide with fear.

"Camera, Neko," Gryph growled. "I'm warning you."

Huy gave Neko a shove and he obscured the camera again.

"Open the doors!" Phoenix yelled. "Stop the train!"

The other students on the train yelled for it to stop too, several of them frantically pressing the emergency buttons located at intervals along the wall.

"Don't worry," Gryph said, but only loud enough for Nadia and Phee to hear. "We'll open the doors before it's too late."

He was putting a show on for everyone else, Phee decided. He knew what he was doing. And for a few seconds, that seemed to be true.

Tariq and Saul jogged along the platform as best they could as the train sped up.

"*No emergency detected,*" the automated voice said. "*Passengers are reminded to access security only in the case of an actual emergency.*"

"It's true!" Nadia screamed, trying to push her way to the door. "Stop the train!"

"Open the doors," Gryph finally ordered, and as if he'd broken his own spell, students stormed the doors, trying to pull them open.

But the doors were jammed, still trapping the boys.

And the technical failure was system-wide, so the train kept gaining speed.

"We should be able to get the doors open." Gryph pushed his way to the door and pulled with all his might.

The end of the station was coming up, after which the train tracks launched into the air, high above the city.

"Recalibrating systems. Please stand by."

"Stop the train!" Nadia screamed. "Make it stop!"

"I'm trying!" Gryph and the others tugged hard on the doors, but they would not budge.

"This isn't funny, Gryph!" Outside, Tariq stumbled, banging on the train with his free hand. "Come on!"

"Help!" Saul screamed. Tariq's expression was one thing, but Saul's was another entirely. He reminded Phoenix of the people rioting below the shuttle in the no-per zone. Flooded with panic. Fear. Desperation.

Gryph saw it too. "I'm trying, Saul! Hang on!"

Phoenix pushed the alarm button nearest her again, but there was still no familiar ding.

With a primal growl, Gryph yanked on his side and Neko on his, along with the strength of anyone who could gain purchase on the steel doors. "Saul! Hang on!"

"Systems recalibrating. Do not access alarm until the system has been recalibrated."

"Stop the train!" Phoenix pounded on the alarm button anyway, as Nadia screamed and screamed, her face fixed with terror.

"Pull harder!" Gryph commanded. His face was white, and his arm muscles bulged from the effort.

Outside, Tariq and Saul stumbled and tripped, trying to stay on their feet. And then the look on Saul's face fell into sheer despair. Phee turned to see what he was seeing.

The narrow passage for the train to exit the station was not wide enough for Tariq and Saul to pass through as well. They would smash into the wall, likely leaving their arms inside the train as it sped onto the next station.

"Pull!" Gryph hollered, and then again as the door shifted a tiny bit. "Pull! Now!"

Everyone tugged hard, and finally the doors groaned open just enough for Tariq and Saul to fall free. They tumbled backwards and hit the platform hard, just as the train cleared the station.

"Thank God," Gryph said. "That was too close."

If Phee hadn't been reeling from what had just happened, she would've pounced on his words. How dare he declare his prank *too close*? How dare he thank God for fixing a mess he got himself into in the first place?

"Saul!" Nadia flung herself at the rear window, her hands pressed against the glass. Saul sat up and waved at her, giving her a shaky thumbs-up.

"Thank God!" Nadia crossed herself. Then she turned and slapped Gryph across the face. "You're such an asshole, Gryph!"

"Wow, Nadia. That's some bitch slap you've got." Gryph poked his tongue at his reddening cheek. "Look, I'm sorry, okay?"

"You want another one, asshole?" Tears streamed down Nadia's face. She raised her hand. "I can't believe you did that!"

"I got the doors open, didn't I?" Gryph raised an eyebrow. "Well?"

Nadia glared at him, her hand still poised, ready to slap him again.

"You sure you want to hit me again?" Whatever uncertainty and regret had softened Gryph when his friends were truly in trouble was diminished now as his face took on a familiar darkness.

"Absolutely." Nadia brought her hand back, but Gryph grabbed her thin wrist in midair and stopped her easily.

"Don't, Nadia."

The other students on the train were still watching, the atmosphere taken up by Gryph and his exploits. They watched with the same slack-jawed fascination that Fawn had when she watched television. This is what Gryph liked: the limelight.

"Let me go!" Nadia tried to wrestle free, but Gryph held tight, glaring at her.

"Let her go, Gryph." Phoenix took her other hand. "Come on, Nadia. Let's sit down."

After another long moment, Gryph let go. Nadia let Phoenix sit her down. Everyone on the train relaxed, shaking off the incident and resuming their usual morning routines of catching up with friends and trading homework answers. Nadia leaned her head on Phoenix's shoulder and cried as she rubbed the red marks Gryph had left on her wrist.

"He almost died!"

"But he didn't." Phoenix stroked Nadia's hair. "Saul didn't die. He's okay." She glanced over her shoulder at Gryph. He and Neko sat slumped in their usual seats, talking about something, looking for all intents and purposes as if nothing had happened. "He's okay."

Saul was okay. But what about Gryph?

The Good Gryph had been losing out to the Bad Gryph lately. Where was the proud champion athlete? The doting brother, loving son, fiercely loyal friend? More and more lately, there was only this dark, dangerous Gryph. And God help anyone who challenged him. Piss him off in front of his peers, challenge his leadership, and suffer the consequences. Nadia knew all this. They'd spent several recent sleepover hours trying to figure out how he could go from being the Gryph who'd patiently taught them how to ski on the bunny hill to being the Gryph who could pull something like the stunt on the train. Someone who would put his friends' lives in danger.

All of a sudden, Nadia sprang to her feet and stalked up to Gryph before Phoenix could stop her. Phoenix ran to her side and pulled her away.

"Come on, Nadia. Leave it."

"You know what, Gryph?" Nadia shook a finger at Gryph's smug smile. "You're not always going to get away with shit like this."

Gryph glanced around the train. Everyone's attention was back on Gryph. And he was happy to play to the crowd.

"They're fine, aren't they?" he said, the smile having slipped just a bit to reveal a snarl below.

"Let's go sit down, Nadia." Phoenix widened her eyes. "Please."

This was the worst Gryph, when he had a stage and the adrenalin in his system to strut across it, star of his own little drama.

"You do that, kids." Gryph brought his phone up to his ear. His eyes still on Nadia, who hadn't budged, he spoke into his cell. "You guys okay?" He nodded. "Cool. Pass the phone to Saul."

"Let me talk to him!" Nadia lunged for the phone, but Gryph held it out of reach.

"Saul?" Gryph turned his eyes to his lap as he spoke, and his tone dropped too. "You okay?"

Saul must've told him he was.

"Good. Sorry, man. I didn't think it'd be so hard to open the doors."

The two friends talked for another minute or so, with Nadia pleading for the phone until Gryph finally handed it to her.

DISCLOSURE

When the train pulled into the school station, Phoenix waited with Nadia for Saul and Tariq to arrive while Gryph steered Neko ahead of him into the building, heading for the stairwell where they normally met Huy every morning. By the time Saul and Tariq got there, Tariq was laughing about the whole thing, and Saul was too. He sounded okay, but when she got closer to him, Phee could see that he was deathly pale and shaking. Gryph must've said something to him about meeting him right away, because he let Nadia hug him only briefly, and then he pulled away.

"I'm okay, Nadia. Really."

"I was so scared! I thought you were going to die!"

Phee wouldn't have thought it possible, but Saul paled even more, his skin nearly translucent under his eyes.

"I didn't though, did I?"

"But still—"

"I'll see you later, okay?"

"Where are you going?" Nadia reached for him as he turned away. "You're shaking!"

"I'm fine. I've got to meet Gryph."

"Don't go!" Nadia got hold of his jacket and he stopped. "Saul, please!"

Tariq kept going, slowing only to toss Saul a warning look. "Don't be long, man."

Saul nodded, prying Nadia's hands off him. "I have to go, Nadia."

"Do you love me, Saul?"

"I love you, Nadia." Saul kissed her. "You know that."

"Then stay with me now," she said. "Just this once, choose me over Gryph."

"I'll see you later, you know that." He kissed her again. "But right now, I have to go."

"But you don't! Not really. Not after what just happened! You almost died!" She grabbed his trembling hand. "You can stay with me! Just this once."

"I know you understand, Nadia." Saul pulled away and walked backwards, toward the school entrance, where Tariq was waiting for him. "I know you do."

He turned and jogged away. He caught up with Tariq, and the two of them disappeared into the school.

Nadia sat down on the nearest bench and cried. "I can't do this anymore, Phee."

Phoenix sat beside her, Saul's tremors on her mind. She'd never seen him like that, but then he rarely got caught in one of Gryph's pranks. He was the one who held back, who played safe, who never took sides when any of the guys argued.

"His brave face is just for Gryph," Phoenix said. "He wanted to stay with you. But you know how boys are. Especially those boys. It's all about them. We're never going to know what goes on with those guys. We can only hope—"

"That they don't kill each other?" Nadia wiped her eyes with her sleeve. "That they don't kill someone else? They're all going to max out on their recons before they hit twenty! And then what?"

"Now you're exaggerating, Nadia. None of them have ever gotten that seriously hurt."

Nadia said nothing.

"I'm right," Phee said gently. "Aren't I? You're exaggerating. None of them have ever even come close to needing a recon."

"Not yet, maybe!"

"They take risks, but they're smart. No one's been hurt." Phoenix found an old tissue in her pocket and dabbed Nadia's tears away. "Gryph was timing it. He knew what he was doing. They've been friends forever, and not a single one of them has had a recon, right?"

Again Nadia said nothing.

"Right, Nadia?"

"Sometimes I really hate Gryphon," Nadia replied. "Chrysalis's golden boy. He thinks he's immortal."

"Well, we all are, in a way. To a point."

"How can you say that?" Nadia blew her nose. "You, of all people. You should get what I'm talking about. Okay, so if Saul dies, he gets reconned, okay, so he lives. But what if something went wrong during the recon? What then? What if I lost him forever?"

"And how often does that happen? Next to never, in all reality."

"Still, it could! And what if he lost his memory, like you?"

"Also highly unlikely."

"But what if?"

What if, what if, what if? Phee knew all too well the perils of letting her imagination run rampant. What if, indeed.

"He'd forget about me! He wouldn't remember *us*. He'd come back and I'd be a stranger to him! Just some random girl. What if he didn't fall in love with me again?" Nadia started bawling, her shoulders heaving the way they always did when she was gripped by a crying fit. "He wouldn't even remember our first kiss!"

"But he's okay, Nadia." Phoenix patted Nadia's back, her own thoughts spinning. "He's okay."

"You don't understand, Phee." Nadia gulped back a sob. "You've never been in love."

And you wouldn't understand either. You've never been reconned. Phee thought it, but didn't speak it. She had to bite her tongue, but she didn't say it.

PHOENIX STAYED WITH NADIA until she calmed down enough to go into class. She got late passes for the two of them and then saw Nadia to her room. On her way to her own room, Phoenix passed Clea, tall and lithe and the only girl who could make wearing glasses sexy. She didn't even need them. They were strictly for show—she'd had laser surgery when she was five. But she thought they made her look especially hot. And she was right.

"Pass?" Clea held out a manicured hand, her long nails a slick luscious pink.

Phoenix flicked it at her. It landed on the floor.

Clea folded her arms over her already supplemented breasts (her daddy was plastic surgeon to the stars) and looked down her carefully crafted nose at Phoenix. "Cute."

"You know, Clea." Phoenix picked up the pass. "If you want Gryph so badly, you should try a little harder with me. He never dates anyone I don't like."

"Aw, Phee, you don't like me?" Clea offered a practised little pout. "I'm devastated."

"It's true. I don't particularly like you at all."

"Maybe you should tell your brother that." Clea shrugged.

"I already have. Many, many, many times." Phoenix folded her own arms over her size-challenged chest. "Every chance I get, in fact."

"Mm. Is that right." Clea turned on her heel. "Maybe you should ask him why he let me go down on him in his dressing room at the snowboard championships, then?"

Phee's face twisted with disgust. "He did not." Phoenix glared at Clea's back. "I was there."

"So was I." Clea stopped. "In the other room."

"No way."

"Very cute, reading to your sister like that. *The Velveteen Rabbit* was one of my favourites. On pod, mind you. What loser still reads from actual books?"

Phoenix sucked in her breath. "Well, you'd know all about fake, wouldn't you?" With her hands, she bounced enormous imaginary breasts in front of her.

"And you'd know all about being brought to life by the magical nursery fairy, so to speak." With that, Clea turned once again, giving Phoenix the back of her as if she were giving her the finger.

PHOENIX FUMED ALL MORNING, searching for Gryph between classes. She could stand a lot of shit from Gryph, but not Clea. Doing Clea, or getting done by Clea, was in direct violation of the sibling code of ethics. Do not hook up with the other's version of evil incarnate. Simple rule, and Gryph had blatantly broken it.

He was nowhere to be seen. At lunch, Phoenix found Nadia, and the two of them went outside to the field to watch Saul's practice, even though Nadia was still sore at him for the morning.

"Then let's not go out there," Phoenix suggested. "If you're so mad at him."

"I still love him," Nadia said as they pushed out into the daylight. "Like I said, you don't understand, Phee."

ONCE OUTSIDE, Nadia flung her backpack to the ground and glared across the field to where Clea was leaning on Saul while she pulled on one of her cheerleader sneakers. Saul, dressed in his catcher padding, just stood there.

"What the hell is she doing?"

"Don't worry." Phoenix rescued the backpack before the contents spilled out. "She's into Gryph."

"Then why is she pawing Saul?"

"She's not pawing him." Phee couldn't believe she was defending Clea. "She's leaning on him. Trust me, Clea is into Gryph." Phoenix told her about Clea's earlier claim.

"Maybe so." Nadia kept her eyes on Clea. "But she used to be into Saul."

"Way before you," Phoenix said. "Get over it."

Gryph emerged from the locker room, a bouquet of baseball bats over his shoulder. Clea ran for him, practically bouncing. She threw herself on him, and he lifted her right up off her feet and kissed her.

"Fair enough," Nadia mumbled. "But just let me have my catty attitude today, okay?"

Saul was heading their way now, with a slow sort of waddle because of his padding. Nadia stood up with a flourish. "I can't talk to him right now. I'm still upset."

"Come on, Nad. Why don't you see what he has to say?"

"Tell him to call me." Nadia stood and grabbed her bag. "I'm going inside."

"Nadia—"

"Later, Phee." Nadia stalked off toward the school.

"Do you want me to come with you?" Phoenix called over her shoulder.

"No," Nadia stopped. "No, actually. I don't."

Phoenix turned her eyes up to the sky. "God? Oscar's daughter here. Help?"

Saul saw her leave, so he stopped to pull off his leg pads and then sprinted across the rest of the distance, leaving Clea and Gryph in a make-out knot behind him.

"Where'd Nadia go?"

"Inside."

"Is she still mad at me or something?"

"Yeah." Phoenix laughed. "Or something."

"Look, I couldn't stay with Nadia this morning." Saul sat beside her, toying with his catcher's mask, which rested on his lap. "You know that, right?"

"I know you chose the guys over Nadia. You always do. Even though she's been your girlfriend for almost two years."

"It's not like that!" Saul growled again. "I love Nadia, but my buddies are just as important. I'd be *nothing* without them. It's not a matter of either or. I have to have both. Nadia and the guys. Got it?"

"Got it," Phoenix said.

"But you don't really. You don't understand."

"Seems to be what everyone thinks of me today."

"But you don't." Saul let his catcher's mask roll off his lap. "Gryph and Huy and Tariq, and even Neko now ... we're more than friends. We're *brothers*. It's different from you and Nadia being best friends. That whole BFF crap is for girls. It's different for guys."

"Oh, really? How about you enlighten me?"

"It's just ... I don't know." Saul shrugged. "It's just different. You wouldn't understand."

"I have an idea." Phoenix shielded her eyes against the sun and looked at Saul. "How about you don't presume to know me, and I don't presume to know you. Sound fair?"

"Sure." Saul gave her a sardonic smile and stood. "That's a great idea." He started to walk away, but Phee called his name. He turned.

"What?"

"This morning," Phee said, "you were shaking really hard. I've never seen you like that before. Are you okay?"

"I came pretty close to having my head ripped off by a brick wall. You'd be shaking too."

"I guess."

"Right." Saul was looking everywhere except at Phoenix.

"But still, I've never seen you like that before. You're sure you're okay?"

"Yeah." Saul sighed. "I haven't been feeling so great lately, that's all."

"Maybe you should have my mom check you out."

"No!" Across the field, the coach called for Saul. "I mean, no thanks. I can't."

"Well"—Phoenix tried to meet his eyes, but he shifted his glance back across the field and rubbed his face again—"maybe get your own doctor to check you out."

"Mind your own business, Phee."

"Saul!" the coach hollered. "Get over here or get out of here!"

"Thanks for your concern and everything." Saul backed away, clutching his helmet. "But don't worry about me. Just go find Nadia and tell her that I love her. Try to make her understand."

"You just told me I didn't understand." Phoenix laughed. "So how can I make her understand? I'm just a girl, after all."

"I'm sorry I said that. I know you get it." Saul held up a hand, half wave, half dismissive gesture. "Just talk to her for me." He turned and sprinted across the field to his team.

NADIA CAME HOME with Phee after school and cried on her bed for several hours. In the brief moments when she wasn't crying, she was gripped by anger. At Saul, mostly, but Gryph too. When she finally had to go home, Phoenix steered a still-weepy Nadia toward the train station. They didn't talk much as they crossed the green. They climbed the stairs to the platform, and Phoenix turned to hug Nadia goodbye when she spotted Saul sitting on a bench down at the end. He stood when he noticed them. He lifted a hand in half a wave. Nadia took a couple of steps toward him, but then changed her mind and turned on her heel.

"What do I do?"

Phoenix gave her a little push. "Go talk to him."

"What do I say?"

"You've been together forever, so I think you can probably come up with something."

"No." Nadia emphatically shook her head. The gesture was not lost on Saul. With his arms open, he started in their direction. "You stop right there, mister!" Nadia pointed a finger at him. He did as he was told, standing still and jamming his hands into his pockets.

"You go talk to him first," Nadia whispered to Phoenix. "You go tell him how fragile I am and how badly he hurt me today. I want him to get it for once, you know? I want him to realize how his choices hurt me."

"And you think your theatrics will make him change his mind?"

Nadia shrugged. She pulled out a tissue, and after checking to ensure that Saul was still watching, she dabbed her tears and sucked back a loud sob. "Go. Tell him."

This time it was Nadia who gave the shove and Phoenix who stumbled forward. She went up to Saul and spoke before he could start. "Look, she loves you, blah, blah, blah. She sent me over here"— she gestured back at Nadia, who was watching while trying to look as if she wasn't—"so I could tell you a load of crap to make you think she's still mad at you, even though she's not. Not mad, anyway. Hurt and sad, yes. Proof in point: she spent the whole afternoon in tears on my bed. Or the bed at my grandma's, if we're being specific."

"Your grandma's?"

"Gryph hasn't said anything?"

Saul shook his head, eyebrows lifting into a question.

"Don't ask. Long story. Back to Nadia."

Saul shoved his hands deeper into his pockets and stared at his feet. His shoulders slumped forward. "I feel like a complete ass."

"Okay. Good start."

"Truth is ..." Saul glanced up at her, almost shyly. "I spent the afternoon crying too."

"What?" Phoenix glanced back at Nadia, who was churning the air with her hand, gesturing for her to speed it up. "You? Crying? I don't believe it."

"Look, there's something that I want to tell you. Something big. But you have to promise not to tell anyone. And I mean it. No one."

"Why me?"

"Because ..." He glanced at Nadia, then again at his feet. "Because I think you'll understand."

Phoenix laughed. "That's a first."

Saul stared at her, in no joking mood.

"Okay, why me? Why not Nadia?"

"I can't tell Nadia."

"Why not?"

"It'll make sense when I tell you. I can trust you—"

"But not Nadia?"

Saul ignored the comment. "You're a true friend, Phoenix. And I hope you still will be after I tell you."

"I will, Saul. Of course I will."

"You might. You might not. You won't know until after you hear what I have to say."

"Then say it, already." The conversation was going around in a frustrating little circle, one that made her stomach clench. Clearly, he had a secret. A big secret. Phee wanted to know it, of course, but there was a part of her that cautioned against her curiosity.

"I will. First, though"—Saul's eyes pleaded with her—"you have to promise not to tell Nadia."

"I can't promise that. She's my best friend. I'd be lying to your face if I told you I wouldn't tell her. You know all about best friends. You pick yours over your girlfriend all the time."

"Maybe I shouldn't."

"Exactly."

"And maybe, just this once, you can promise to keep something from her."

"No can do," said Phee.

"Even if her knowing what I tell you would destroy her? Hurt her?"

Phee felt a shiver creep up her spine. What did he want to tell her that was such a big deal?

Saul read her silence as a refusal to keep a promise. He pulled his hands out of his pockets and ran them over his face. He looked tired. Drained. What was his secret? Cancer or something? In love with someone else? What? Her curiosity could not let it go.

"What if I do promise?" She heard herself say this and immediately wanted to take it back. Her curiosity had gotten her in trouble before. She wished she could just leave well enough alone, but she couldn't. She wanted to know what he was holding on to. What was pulling him down, weighing on him so heavily?

"For real?"

Phoenix nodded.

"You wouldn't tell?"

"Promise, Saul."

"I'm going to tell you"—Saul leaned forward—"but keeping it secret is a matter of life and death. I know that you get what that means, Phee. That's why I think I can tell you. That's why I think I can trust you."

His seriousness unnerved her, so she went for a joke. "Well, we all know you're not gay." She laughed. Saul didn't. "Okay, that fell flat. So what is it?" Phoenix glanced over her shoulder again. Nadia was starting toward them, walking slowly, ever the injured princess.

"I'm a one-per."

"She's coming this way, Saul. Get on with it."

"I just told you."

"Told me what?" She'd heard him, but her brain had refused to process his words.

"I'm a one-per." He leaned closer still, his voice barely a whisper. "No one knows. Except you now."

"You ... you can't be." He'd been Gryph's best friend since kindergarten. He lived in a three-per community, went to a three-per high school. It made no sense. He might as well have been talking gibberish.

Nadia was getting closer. Panicking, Phoenix gripped Saul's arm and marched him in the opposite direction.

"Where are you going?" Nadia flung her arms down at her sides and stamped a foot as a train pulled up and a swarm of commuters flooded the platform.

"Just a sec, Nadia!" Phoenix lifted a hand. "Hang on."

As suited and briefcased men and women bustled past them to the escalators, Phoenix stood on tiptoe to be eye to eye with Saul. She jabbed him on the chest with each word she said.

"Tell me that you're lying."

"I'm not lying. God's honest truth." Saul raised one hand and placed the other over his heart. "I solemnly swear."

Phoenix jabbed him once more, this time hard. "If you think this is funny, you're wrong, Saul."

"I'm dead serious, Phoenix. I swear."

"Then how do you live in this sector? How can you go to our school? Your family is registered as a three-per, right?"

"Officially, yes. We have an assumed identity. It's a long, long story, and I wouldn't get into it here, even if it was safe to. But I can assure you I won't get caught unless I land at Chrysalis for a recon. They'd find out when they checked my DNA. So this morning, when it was such a close call, I kind of freaked out. That's why I was shaking so bad."

"But Saul—" Phoenix's stomach flung itself against her rib cage. He had to be making it up. There was no way he could be telling the truth. But ... but if he was? If he really was only a one-per, she did not want this knowledge. And how could she not tell Nadia? He'd been lying to them all along. He wasn't who he said he was! All these years, thinking he was one of them, only to find out he'd just been some low-life pretending to be like them. Phoenix was going to throw up. It had to be a joke. "All I can say is that this better be your sick, twisted idea of a prank. You can go tell Gryph and the guys that they got me good. Ha, ha. Very funny."

"Wait!" He gripped her wrist hard as she turned to walk away. "You promised you wouldn't tell! You can't go back on your word. And you can't tell Nadia. You can't. You promised!"

"How can you expect me to keep this kind of secret?" Her unease leaped from her stomach to her head and pounded at her temples. "If you're even telling the truth." She wanted to give it back. She did not want to know this. She couldn't know this! She shouldn't.

"She's coming." Saul glanced over the crowd at Nadia's black head bobbing in their direction. "You promised, Phee. Don't forget. I know you won't betray me like that."

"Me betray *you*?" She rolled her eyes. "I can't believe you'd even say that after what you've just told me."

"You promised."

"I heard you. I get it, okay?"

"Okay." Saul's reply was tiny, just a nervous whisper. "Thank you."

Nadia dodged between commuters as the crowd thinned and the platform finally cleared. She stopped a short distance away and planted her hands on her hips. With a practised swish of her head she sent her long, dark curls behind her shoulders.

"Well?"

Saul stepped forward and pulled her to him. "I'm sorry, Nadia." He looked at Phee as he said it. "I'm so sorry."

Of course it made sense for him to apologize to Nadia for his behaviour earlier, but to Phee there was no doubt that he was apologizing to *her*. Or regretting his decision to tell her his secret.

Nadia, with a quick wink in Phoenix's direction, clasped her hands behind Saul's neck, leaned up, and kissed him long and hard, pressing herself against him in a way that was not exactly appropriate for the train station.

Sure enough, the sax solo was interrupted and a tinny voice recited the rules and regulations against loitering while the thin blue light scanned across their faces, matching them up to their profiles.

"Nadia Balkashan, Saul Morrisey, and Phoenix Nicholson-Lalonde, you have been identified as being in violation of loitering bylaw C58, section one. Proceed to the nearest exit immediately or tickets will be issued to your parental accounts, with fines due within forty-eight hours."

"They missed the train," Phoenix said as the happy couple pulled apart. "And I live in this sector. You should know that."

There was a pause as the system processed the information. *"Phoenix Nicholson-Lalonde, proceed to the nearest exit immediately. Saul*

Morrisey and Nadia Balkashan, the next train will be arriving in three minutes and twelve seconds."

"I better go," Phoenix said as the familiar countdown started. She had one minute to get off the platform or the loitering ticket would be waiting in her parents' inbox online by the time she got home.

Nadia pecked her cheek and hugged her. "Thanks, Phee."

"... thirty-four, thirty-three, thirty-two ..."

Saul gave her a quick hug too, whispering as he did. "No matter what you think about me, no matter what you think about any of it ... you promised."

"... eleven, ten, nine ..."

"Run!" Nadia laughed as Phoenix made a dash for the stairs. Phoenix took them two at a time. At the bottom, she leaned against the wall and tried to calm down. She had to slow her breathing. She sat on the bottom step and dropped her head into her lap.

"In through the nose," she told herself. "Out through the mouth." She dug in her pockets but knew she didn't have her inhaler with her. This was no time for an asthma attack. If her parents had known about her asthma before she'd died the second time, they could've requested that her recon include a built-in ventolin response system. But the asthma had only really cropped up since she was ten. So in the absence of her puffer, she'd have to calm herself down.

Breathe in. Breathe out. Inhale, exhale.

She could hear the train draw into the station above her, the musical chime of the doors sliding open. The footsteps of another wave of commuters hurrying home. She scooted to the edge of the step to get out of the way, but she couldn't quite stand just yet.

Saul. *Saul.* A one-per!

It wasn't possible.

Was it?

But *how?*

How could this have happened?

How could his family get away with living in the three-per sector?

Was his whole family one-per, or had they taken him in?

Her father had a friend, a missionary who worked in the no-per zone and who had sneaked an orphan home to raise as his own. The child fell off a cliff while on a field trip at school and was whisked to the hospital where Chrysalis came to do a check of his DNA profile in preparation of his recon. The results, of course, exposed him as a no-per. They took him off life-support almost immediately. Oscar's friend went to jail. And there he remained, over a decade later.

No wonder Saul freaked out that morning when Gryph pulled that stunt with the train doors. What an idiot. If she were only a one-per, she wouldn't hang out with Gryph and the boys. She'd keep to herself. Wary of danger. If she were a one-per she'd never tell anyone. Not ever.

She caught herself. *If* she were a one-per? She was a one-per in actuality, if not status! She might've been born a three-per and live in a three-per world, but she had only one left now. Still, she tried to make sense of it all. "I'm not really."

"Not really what?"

Phoenix turned at the sound of her father's voice. He stood behind her, protecting her from the mass of people pushing down the stairs.

"Daddy!" Phoenix leaped up and hugged her father. She pulled back and frowned at him. "How long were you standing there?"

"Long enough to know that you're worrying about something, as usual." They started down the steps together, Phoenix's arm linked with her father's. "Do you know that you've always done that, nodded and shook your head and furrowed your brow as if having a very serious conversation with an invisible friend. God, maybe?"

"Maybe I should be talking to God." Phee already felt better even just being in her father's company. "But I was only having a very serious conversation with myself."

"About what?"

What Saul had told her, of course.

"Nothing, really."

"'A very serious conversation with myself,'" Oscar quoted her in a funny falsetto before returning to his fatherly voice. "Such a conversation is rarely about nothing."

"Just stuff."

"I'm good at 'just stuff.'" Oscar leaned in conspiratorially. "And 'nothing really' too. It's part of my job."

"I don't need a minister, but thanks."

"I meant part of my job as your father."

"Really, Dad. It's just boy stuff." And it truly was, in a way. "Nadia and Saul. You know. Same old."

"Suit yourself," Oscar said with a wink. "But you know where to find me if you change your mind and want to talk."

They were crossing the green now, the lush grass so inviting that Phee kicked off her flip-flops to feel the warm carpet of it underfoot.

"Brilliant idea, kiddo." Phee watched her dad as he undid his shoes and peeled off his socks. Could she tell him? Not so much as a father, but as a minister? Did that count as tattletaling? Ministers were like lawyers; they had to honour confidentiality.

But no. She knew in her heart that Saul would never forgive her if she told her dad. Even if he never found out, Phee worried that her guilt would be stamped across her face every time she saw him.

She'd promised Saul. And a promise was a promise, plain and simple. And she knew her dad wasn't buying her "boy trouble" line, so she gave him something more believable.

"Actually, I was worrying about you and Mom," she finally said. "Your silly little spat, if you have to know."

"It's not silly." Oscar frowned. "And I fear it may not be little, either."

"But it'll blow over, right?" Phoenix squeezed her father's arm. "Come on, let's go home and I'll make us a pot of tea and you can tell me about how the ladies auxiliary committee simply cannot decide on what colour bunting to have for the strawberry tea."

"It's true," Oscar said with a sad little smile that had nothing to do with the ladies auxiliary. "Red or white, the debate rages on."

"They're only battling over two colours? Not green or blue or orange too? Purple? Silver? Pink?"

"Helen Whitting is not going to budge." She and her father fell into step together. "She's already purchased enough red bunting to decorate the entire sector. The mistake was putting her in charge of shopping."

"Helen Whitting is a bully." Phoenix and her father made their way to the house across the green, both of them still barefoot. She imagined Helen Whitting—that's *Dr*. Whitting, if you please— tanned an unearthly orange hue after decades of fake 'n' bake salons; she was always perfectly coiffed, her lipstick always matched her slacks, which were always pressed and always capris ending halfway down her calves, revealing her liver-spotted legs and a blurry tattoo of a butterfly on one ankle from a time when she must've been far more interesting than she was now. It was working: Saul's shocking revelation was growing smaller and smaller behind her, as if she'd left it like a backpack bomb, abandoned on the bottom step of the train station. She concen- trated on the tickle of grass underfoot, the perfume from the lilac bushes that lined the green. "Therefore, I vote for white bunting."

FAMILY MEETING

That night Phoenix dreamed a different version of the events on the train platform. She dreamed that Saul hadn't cornered her. She dreamed that he hadn't told her about being a one-per. The dream was so real that it was almost boring, except for how good it felt to wake up thinking it hadn't happened. But then it was almost as if it truly hadn't.

Saul acted as if he hadn't told her. Maybe he regretted telling her, or maybe he wasn't sure what to say next about it. Either way, Phoenix didn't care. She'd just as soon put it out of her mind anyway.

At school the next day he didn't even say hello, and after when they all went to the mall he didn't talk to her. Usually she and Saul competed at Mortal Kombat, but he stayed on the other side of the arcade with Tariq, playing NASCAR with Nadia hanging off him the way a prep wears a sweater draped over his shoulders. A couple of times, once when he headed for the bathroom and then again when he was standing at the concession buying hot dogs for him and Nadia, Phoenix thought he might come up to her and say something. Each time her heartbeat raced and she scrambled to think of what to say to him. But both times, he passed her with a glazed-over look on his face. She knew that he saw her, but rather than meet her eye, he deliberately looked right through her and carried on past her without even slowing his pace.

That was fine with her. She could play the denial game. She was even good at it, and was improving her skills this whole week with the debacle that was her family's current situation. Eva would not talk to Oscar, while Oscar was waiting for her to make the first conciliatory gesture. Stalemate.

"Just tell Mom to call him." Phoenix was playing two-person Deer Hunter with Gryph. She hated this game, but was pretty good at it. Not as good as Gryph, though. But that was just the way it was. He was the always the winner, she the runner-up, if she was lucky. She levelled her sight on an eight-point buck in the cyber-distance and pulled the trigger. The bullet sailed up and over the deer, startling it. As it took off, Gryph nailed it. The holographic deer fell with a thud that shook the platform they stood on.

"Just stop shooting if you're not going to concentrate," Gryph said as they turned north in the forest. "Save your bullets. Stay behind me."

"Or tell her to come over and see him," Phee said. "She'd give up then, seeing how miserable he is. And lonely. He is sorry." Phee shot her gun at another deer in the distance, missing grandly this time. "You know he's sorry. I know he's sorry. She knows it too."

"I said stop shooting," Gryph said as the deer took off at a run.

Gryph pulled the trigger. The rifle shot blasted in her headset. The buck on the ridge reeled back.

"Too low," Phoenix said. "And too near the rump."

"Yeah?" Gryph cocked the rifle. "Well, you suck, so don't tell me how to play." He let the deer—fake, yes, but three-dimensional and realistic in every way, and whose suffering still hit Phoenix hard—stumble down the hill until his knees buckled and he collapsed onto the forest floor with a heart-wrenching whinny.

"Come on, Gryph. Shoot him." Phoenix had the holographic deer in her sights but knew Gryph would be mad if she shot his deer. He'd yanked off her visor and shoved her to the floor when she'd dared step on his game before. That had most certainly been a Bad Gryph day. She lowered her gun. "Please, Gryph. Come on. Put him out of his misery."

Gryph held his gun tight, butted against his shoulder. His head was tilted, eye to the scope. "It's pretend, Phee. Buck up." He glanced up at her and winked. "Get it? Buck up?" Turning his attention back to the writhing deer, he repeated, "It's just a game, Phee. Chill out. Always with the drama. You and Mom."

Gryph walked, and Phee followed out of habit. He stopped just shy of the animal and looked down at him. So did Phee. The deer was panting. Blood seeped from Gryph's first shot, which had landed in his gut, under his flank. The deer looked up at them, his big brown eyes moist and cloudy.

"Shoot him, Gryph."

"It's weird that death is final in a game, but not in real life." He kept his eye on the deer as he spoke. "This is what it's supposed to be like. Forever. Bloody, painful, and final."

It's not real, Phoenix told herself. It's only pretend. But the virtual game was so real that she could practically smell the deer's fear. "Just shoot him. Please."

"What do you think it's like?" He glanced at her now. "Death?"

"Better than his suffering, that's for sure." Phee raised her own gun. "And if you don't shoot him, I will."

"He's mine."

"Then do it, already!"

"It's a bizarre thing ..." Gryph stood at close range, set his crosshairs between the deer's wide, blinking eyes, and pulled the trigger. With a spray of blood, the buck's head flung back, and then he was still. "We've conquered death, but it's still such a mystery." He paused. "You really don't remember anything at all? From when you were dead?"

Instead of answering, Phoenix raised her visor and tugged off the headset. "I'm done." Gryph had never played like this. Dirty, mean. Cruel. She couldn't stand it.

"The game's not over!" Gryph paused it with a tap of his foot.

Phoenix stabbed the rifle back in its slot, which cancelled her game.

"Why'd you do that? Neko would've finished."

"All you care about is this stupid game and waxing poetic about a dying holographic deer when our family is crumbling for real."

"Again with the drama."

"It's not drama. It's real!"

"Why don't you go home, Phee," Gryph said with a shrug, "if you're so concerned about everything."

"I'd like to go home, only it doesn't exist right now!"

"You're overreacting, as usual. Give it a rest. It'll all work out."

"And you're underreacting, as usual."

"You're done? But—" Neko came up behind her, about to protest the parked rifle. She glared at him over her shoulder.

"I don't want to hear it, Neko." To Gryph, who'd resumed the game, she said, "It's easy for you—you're hardly there. And you won't be there at all, come September. But I'm there every day, for several more years. And Fawn has another decade, at least. You should be doing your part to keep the family *together*."

"It'll all work out," Gryph said again, eyes on the inside of his visor, back in the make-believe world of the game. "You should get your priorities straight. Some things matter more than others, Phee. Some things *are* actually a matter of life and death, and this one is not."

"What do you mean?"

Gryph didn't answer her. She backed away without saying anything more. What did he mean? Was that a cloaked reference to Saul? Did he know? Or did he only mean that Eva's reaction to their visit to the no-per zone was out of proportion? That she overreacted. The way Phee so often did, in his eyes.

Phee texted Nadia that she was leaving. Nadia, still hanging off Saul on the other side of the arcade, replied with a single "K." She didn't even look up, let alone come over and see if Phee was okay or why she was leaving in such a hurry. They were supposed to leave together, she and Nadia. She didn't know about the other boys for sure, but Saul and Gryph were going in the other direction, each having lied to his parents about staying at the other boy's house. She'd asked where they were going, but they didn't say. They never did, and it always pissed her off. Well, Nadia could find her own way home for once. Phee wasn't going to wait.

THE PORCH LIGHT WAS ON for her at her grandparents', along with almost every other light, giving a warm glow to the house. She walked right past it though, across the green to her own house, dark, except for one light. She found Oscar in his study, reading at his desk.

"Fawn phoned," he said as a greeting.

"Yeah?"

"She's called a family meeting."

"*Fawn* did?"

Oscar put his book down. *Neuroscience and Theology.* "She did indeed."

"Wow." Neither Gryph nor Phee had ever called a family meeting. That was such a parental thing to do. Or a Fawn thing, so it would seem. "She's a ballsy kid."

"She is. So, family meeting. Tomorrow morning."

"Great!" Bizarre that a six-year-old could put an end to the stalemate, but so be it. Phee hugged her father. "Everything will go back to normal, right?"

"I hope so, kiddo." Her dad kissed her forehead. "I hope so."

It had been less than a week since Eva had stormed out with her and her siblings, but it felt as if it had been a year. Most nights Phoenix stayed with Oscar at the house, partially because she missed her dad, and she missed their house, but mostly because she wanted to demonstrate to Eva that she'd forgiven Oscar for taking her to the no-per zone, and if she wasn't mad, the rest of them shouldn't be either. She was the one whose life had been at stake. If she could forgive, why couldn't Eva?

"Dad didn't know," she told her mother the night before when she walked over to her grandparents' house to visit after dinner. "He'd never intentionally put us kids in danger."

"Doesn't matter whether he meant to or not." Eva collected the dishes from the table. Phoenix's mouth watered at the lingering smells of pot roast and cheesy scalloped potatoes. Back at the house the best she and Oscar could put together was a plain old grilled-cheese sandwich and heated-up tomato soup from a tin. And a plate of pickles, if they were feeling gourmet.

"*Homemade* pickles," Oscar boasted. But it made no difference. They both missed Eva and Fawn. And Gryphon too.

"Are you hungry?" Eva would ask. "I can fix you a plate."

And every time Phoenix would shake her head. "No thanks. Dad and I had a good supper."

"What'd you have?"

"Chicken fajitas." Phoenix lied every time, claiming they'd had chili con carne, or chicken parmesan, or lamb kabobs. All of which Oscar could make quite easily, when his heart was into it. He just wasn't inspired, and neither was Phoenix, so it was tinned soup most nights. A box of crackers and a stack of cheese slices. They even ordered pizza one night, even though Oscar normally swore against fast food and was quite creative when it came to making homemade pizzas. Caramelized onions, pulled pork, and feta cheese went into one of his specialties. But they actually had straight-up, oil-slicked ham-and-pineapple from the pizza shop on his route home. He'd picked it up and they ate it right out of the box, not even blotting off the oil, which pooled on the surface of the pie and dripped off their chins.

After the pizza she'd broken out with a faceful of zits, either from the crappy food or the stress, but either way enough was enough. She was looking forward to the family meeting and everything going back to normal.

SATURDAY MORNING DAWNED as a glorious day, as if prepping the world for the Nicholson-Lalonde family reunion. The sky was blue, birds were chirping, and the smell of flowers already warmed by the sun woke Phoenix up with a smile. Shortly afterwards, the front door slammed, and footsteps sounded on the stairs. Clunky and light at the same time. Unmistakably Fawn. With a grin, Phee pulled the covers up over her head and feigned sleep. Fawn flung open the door and pounced on Phee.

"I'm home, Phee!" She poked Phoenix under the blanket. "Wake up! We're having a meeting because I said so, and Daddy's making waffles, and Gryph is coming in a couple of minutes, so you should get up and come downstairs now."

"Uhn," Phee replied with an exaggerated snore.

"You're only pretending." Fawn sat on her chest. "I know it."

"You knew I was pretending?" Fawn squealed when Phee grabbed her and pulled her under the covers. "And still I caught you."

The girls wrestled for a while, Phoenix aiming for Fawn's ticklish spots in particular. Fawn giggled so hard that she finally screamed that she had to pee and fled the room in a hurry. Phoenix sat up and set her feet on the floor and stretched. Hopefully, today was the day her family got glued back together.

THE BREAKFAST TABLE was laid out as if it were Christmas morning. Tablecloth and fancy runner, places set with the good dishes, maple syrup in the fancy decanter and the juice in a crystal jug, napkins folded at each place, and atop each plate, save one, sat a tiny envelope—no bigger than a business card—with a name written on it in Oscars's neat block printing. Inside each was an apology.

"I'm sorry. I made a mistake. I shouldn't have taken you. I'm sorry for that."

"No need to apologize to me." Gryph flicked his envelope back at his father. "I thought it was awesome. Beats my boring life, that's for sure. I'd go again, right now."

"Boring?" Eva frowned at him. "You think a warm home and loving parents and a good education and a safe community are *boring?*"

"That's not what I meant, Mom. You're overreacting. Again."

"I'm not." Eva took her seat at the table, carefully keeping her tone in check. "I'm just curious why you think your life is boring."

"If I left my life up to anyone but me, it would be boring." Gryph half laughed. "But thanks to me"—and here he gave a little bow— "Mr. Gryphon Nicholson-Lalonde ... my life gets less boring every day."

Phoenix frowned at him. What did he mean by that?

"What exactly do you mean?" Her mother echoed her thoughts. Eva's hands were poised over her cutlery, as if preparing for a knife and fork quick draw against her son.

"Why do you think I enter all these competitions?" Gryph grabbed a trio of waffles with his fingers and arranged them on his plate. "Not because I have something to prove. Not because of the prize money." He carved a hunk of butter from the dish and plopped it on top. "I like the adrenalin. That's why. It makes me feel alive. And if you guys had your way, I'd be some chess champion or mathlete or something like that."

"What terrible parents you have," Eva said. "Oh, such horrible jailers. How unbearable for you." Abandoning the cutlery, Eva put her hand out in a silent, stern request for the butter instead. "It must be excruciating for you to put up with a loving mother and father who want to keep you safe, who want to see you grow up into a healthy man. And how confusing, to have us be such tyrants, yet still let you engage in your high-risk sports. What an oppressed life you must bear, dear Gryphon. Such burdens."

"I might wonder every now and then where I inherited my need for adrenalin from ..." Gryph gave his mother a thin-lipped smile and a cock of the eyebrow. "But there's no doubt where I get my sarcasm from."

Eva exhaled a short, frustrated breath from her nostrils. "I'm simply trying to understand why you resent us for wanting to keep you safe."

"Because I have three recons, that's why. Why else are they there if it means we all still live our lives so goddamned carefully?"

"Son—" Oscar started to admonish him for his language, but Gryph cut him off.

"Sorry, Dad. It just slipped out. But really, Mom." He finally passed Eva the butter she'd been waiting for. "Have I ever hurt myself?"

"Plenty of times." Eva held the butter but made no motion to help herself to any. Instead, she punctuated the air with the little dish while she talked. "You've had two broken arms, a broken leg. More sprained ankles than I can remember. You blew your knee out last winter. And let's not forget the time you fractured your skull."

"Minor stuff." Gryph shrugged. "I mean, I've never *really* hurt myself. Not badly. Not ever a life-or-death situation. Which is pretty amazing, considering the shit I get up to."

"Gryph—" Oscar once again took aim at his son's language.

"Sorry, sorry." Gryph laughed.

Fawn piped up. "You have to pay the swear jar."

"Twice," Phee added.

"All right, all right." With an impatient groan, Gryph whipped out a dollar and slapped it on the table. "Here's for the two, and two on credit. I just don't see what the big deal is ... even if I did get so badly hurt to need a recon, that's what they're there for. Right?"

"No," Eva said. "We are not free to squander the life we have in the first place. Recons are expensive and still have their risks, as your sister can attest to."

"Whatever," Gryph said with a shrug. "Fact remains, I've never really hurt myself. And even if I did, I'd be back to normal before you know it. I just don't see the big deal. When it comes to me, anyway. Phee, I get. Me, not so much. I've never even been sick a day in my life, never mind even coming close to needing a recon."

"Because you are blessed," Oscar said quietly. "Truly blessed."

"No, Oscar." Eva shot her husband a pointed look. "He's *lucky*."

"He is *blessed* ... with talent, strength, innate athleticism, bravery, ambition. And he is—I would argue—watched over by God."

"And what about Phee?" Eva's eyes darkened. "When she was just a baby? And then when she was six? Where was your God then? Clearly not watching over her!"

"Please," Phoenix whispered, her cheeks going red. She didn't want to be the reason for another fight. Not again. Not when it had been going so well. Phoenix glared at Gryph, who was oblivious to the tension, mouth full, concentrating on his breakfast. "Please?" she said again, turning her eyes to her parents. "Please don't make this about me."

"Phee, honey." Oscar reached for Phoenix's hand and gave it a squeeze. "It's not about you—"

"No?" Eva sighed, exasperated. "Oscar, if it's not about Phoenix, what is it about? There is only one person in this room who is only one recon away from true and everlasting death."

Fawn, who'd been following along with her mouth open, waiting to jump in with her two cents' worth, promptly clamped her mouth shut. Phee, likewise sensing their parents drifting away, off on their own, even as they sat there just inches away, dropped her eyes to her lap and debated the pros and cons of leaving the table. With a huffy flourish? A discreet slip? Or sit still and disappear, try to tune out her parents' squabbling.

"What is it about? You and me, and this family we both love so fiercely ..." Oscar trained his eyes on his wife. He reached for her hand and—Phee slumped with relief—Eva let him take it. "Even if we have different ideas about life and God and raising our children. And I love you. That's true too."

"And I love both of you!" Fawn piped up with impeccable timing. "And for one thing, this is *my* family meeting. So no fighting." She scrambled onto her knees on the chair and leaned across the table and took hold of her parents' hands. "Now hug and say you're sorry." With that, she sat back and dug into her syrup-soaked waffle. Phee grinned at her little sister. Future diplomat in training. She wanted to give Fawn a grateful hug, but her limbs still felt sluggish and wary. She wanted to say thank you, but her mouth felt as if it was stuffed with wool. When Fawn looked in her direction, Phoenix winked at her instead. Fawn winked back.

"And the other?" Oscar asked, eyes still on Eva.

"Huh?" Fawn looked up.

Eva smiled. Phoenix let out a breath of relief, and with it her anxiety receded a little. All of them, seated around the table as normal as could be, while the atmosphere in the room rolled and shifted back to normal, like a weather pattern only Phee could sense. "When you say 'for one thing' it's usually followed by 'and for another.'"

"Huh?" Fawn said with her mouth full.

"Don't talk with your mouth full," Oscar said.

"And don't say *huh*. Ask properly."

Fawn shrugged. "Okay."

Phoenix surveyed her breakfast plate. A lone waffle, quickly cooling, the butter collecting into gelatinous pools. Two slices of bacon, the fat dabbed off by her father beforehand. A wedge of orange, like a fake grin at the bottom of her plate. She didn't want any of it. She was categorically unhungry. In front of the window over the sink hung a mobile of colourful origami cranes, bobbing and spinning in the breeze, the thin bamboo sticks and thread holding it together staying untangled despite each bird's chaotic spin. Her family was that mobile, with secret folds and nothing to grab on to, each of them spinning in the wind, with useless paper wings.

RAVE

Yet again, Gryph came in second at the surfing competition. None of his friends minded, and Oscar and Eva couldn't have cared less if he'd come in fortieth, so it was only Phee and Lex who seemed concerned. Lex, clearly because his star was apparently fading, and Phee because she knew that Gryph had thrown away another win. He'd let the other guy take the best wave, and that had made all the difference. The old Gryph would've fought him for it.

The whole day had been weird anyway, starting with the family meeting, and then getting weirder when Gryph had brought Clea to sit with everyone and introduced her to their parents as his "girlfriend," which made Eva embrace her in a joyous flustered hug. The announcement made Phee fume. He could do way better than her. She'd glared at the back of Clea's head the whole afternoon, annoyed at how she sat so tanned and glowing among the rest of the pale, sunscreened group, like royalty deigning to sit among the paupers.

And then, the after party.

They were all dressed up, or the girls were anyway. The boys had put a little effort into the evening, exchanging their board shorts and T-shirts for pants and button-down tops. And cologne. All of them wafting competing smells. Gryph had told Phee and Nadia to dress "older," so they'd put extra care into their makeup in the hope of getting in without being hassled for being underage. Gryph and his buddies never had a problem, not even with Neko. But then Gryph was famous. Different rules applied to him.

The unofficial after party for the surf competition was a late-night rave being held in an old warehouse in the two-per district, and when Phee asked why it wasn't in a three-per zone, it was Clea—dressed like a supermodel in a tiny sheath dress and perilous heels—who set her straight.

"Better drugs," Clea said with a grin as they exited the train. "Don't you know that?"

"Sure I do." Phee fumbled for a fast answer that wouldn't make her look as naive as she felt. "But Gryph doesn't do drugs, so why should that matter?"

"Gryph's not the only one at the party, honey." Clea winked at her. Phee was surprised at how badly she wanted to slap her, as in some over-the-top girl fight scene in a bad movie. Thankfully, Gryph pushed between them, breaking the moment.

Gryph gave her a dirty look. "Keep your mouth shut if you're only going to ask stupid questions, Phee. Remember"—he took Clea's hand and steered the group across the train station to a set of dark stairs—"I didn't want you to come. And if Mom knew you were here, she would disown me."

"Newsflash, Gryph. You're not the boss of me."

"That's really mature, Phee."

She knew she really should shut up. Nothing she said came out right. Exasperated, Phee fell back to walk with Saul and Nadia. Saul had never barked at her like that, and he was way more tolerant of Phee's questions.

"Where are we going, exactly?"

"Dunno." Nadia shrugged.

"Saul?" Without thinking, Phee gave him a playful shove. "Where're we going?"

It was a long moment before he answered, during which Phee realized he hadn't actually talked to her since revealing his secret to her the other day. She'd miraculously and momentarily forgotten about all that, caught up in tonight's adventure as she was. Her plan had been to give Saul the wide berth he was so clearly claiming, but here she was now, getting into his face out of habit more than anything. But apparently Saul was okay with that, or didn't want to act like an ass in front of Nadia.

"It's an old surfboard factory. Down by the port."

"Really?" Nadia turned her heavily made-up eyes to him, the glitter on her cheeks catching in a square of light from a building as they passed. "Is that safe?"

"Safe enough." He levelled a quick, critical glance at Phee. "It's a two-per zone, Nadia. We're not slumming with the one-pers tonight."

"I was just asking." Nadia pulled her hand away. "I know you wouldn't take us into a one-per zone. That's just crazy." She cast a glance at Phee. "Not saying your dad was crazy to take you to a no-per zone."

"It's okay," Phee said. "He knows it was stupid."

"Let me make myself clear." Saul scanned the road ahead. "We didn't want you two to come at all, so if anything goes down, keep that in mind."

It was true they'd had to beg. But in the change room, after the competition, when Nadia found out that Clea was going with them, she freaked out on Saul until he relented. And if Nadia was going, Phee was going. She didn't care what Gryph had to say about it. She was not going to be the only one left behind. Everyone's parents had been told they were at one another's respective houses, and they all had their phones in case any of the parents checked in.

The old surfboard factory was at one end of the Cannery, an industrial district down by the docks that was made up of fish-packing plants and seafood distributors, a part of the city Phoenix had never had reason to explore. The stench of fish and rot had hit them right off the train, but as they got closer it was getting worse. Phee made a face.

"Perfect to keep Crimcor out of the way," Saul explained, laughing at her and Nadia, who was holding her nose with two pink-lacquered nails. "Makes sense, doesn't it?"

Nadia whined about the smell, feigning a theatrical retch every few steps. Phee ignored it as best she could, focusing her thoughts on why the guys had relented and let her and Nadia come along that night. Maybe they shouldn't have begged quite so convincingly.

PHEE WONDERED if it was Neko who had made Gryph agree to let the girls come. Neko was only fourteen, and Nadia always worried about him. Maybe he figured that if Nadia came along for once, she'd relax a little about Neko. Neko was walking up ahead with Tariq. When they passed under the street light, she saw Neko lean in to Tariq, hanging on his words. What were they talking about? Tariq said little at the best of times. And what would he have to say to Neko, anyway? Phee could hardly get Tariq to talk to her at all, but there he was, hands gesturing, clearly engaged in whatever subject he and Neko were talking about.

The street light at the next corner was dark, its globe smashed, the glass in shards on the pavement. They caught up with everybody else. Clea, the essence of glamorous spindly model, with her impossibly high heels, clung to Gryph's arm. She wasn't complaining, though. Her face was almost expressionless, her slight pout and half-lidded eyes making her look at once clueless and intriguing, and, as always, beautiful. She offered a little wave to the girls.

"She better not think we're ever going to be friends," Nadia said as they both gave a pissy little wave in return.

"Do you think she practises that look in the mirror?" Phoenix muttered to Nadia as the boys led the way down a narrow alley. The smell was far worse here, boxed in as it was by the tall brick buildings on either side. Phoenix's eyes practically watered.

"Spends hours and hours, is my guess."

"Sorry?" Clea said over her shoulder. "I didn't quite hear you, Nadia."

"It was nothing, Clea. Never mind."

Gryph shot her a look.

"What?" Nadia gave him a sneer. "We were complaining about the godawful stench around here."

"Let's go, guys." Saul cut in between her and Gryph and took Nadia's hand, redirecting her before she could give Gryph more reason to regret his decision to let them come along.

THEY HEARD THE AFTER PARTY long before they saw it. When they were still a block away Phoenix could feel the bass in her gut, thumping along her bones. Her heart quickened. She'd never been to a rave before. Half-terrified, half-delirious with anticipation, she followed the others to the end of the alley and up to the front of the line, where a burly man wearing shades—even though it was dark—unhooked the chain across the door, greeted Gryphon with a discreet nod, and let them all in, no cover charge, no waiting. Just like that, they were in. And the smell was gone. Phee glanced up at a pair of enormous extractor fans near the ceiling. She gripped Nadia's hand and squeezed.

"That's better."

"Thank *God*, is all I can say. I was going to puke."

It was even darker inside than out, except for the pulsing lights that burst from strobes and lasers choreographed to the heavy bass. There was no dance floor per se, but the whole place was wall to wall with writhing bodies, sweat illuminated by the light show, hips grinding, eyes sparkling. Phoenix was transfixed. The music was not just *music*. Phee had never heard anything like it. It pulled at her very soul. More an emotion than entertainment. There was no way her body wasn't going to move. She slid along with the others to the far side of the massive warehouse, where a bar took up one wall.

After checking with Nadia, Saul leaned toward her and yelled over the music. "Do you want a drink?"

"What's Nadia having?"

"Some girly fruity thing with an umbrella and vodka."

"Tariq's okay with that?"

"He doesn't have to know."

"Oh. Okay. Uh ..." Quite frankly, Phoenix already felt drunk on the atmosphere, the music. The beat. "I'm okay for now, but thanks."

"No way," Nadia said. "Come on, get something." She grabbed Saul's wrist as he turned to talk to the bartender. "Get her what I'm getting."

"I'm okay for now. Really." Phoenix just wanted to dance. She wanted to be right in the middle of that sea of people, cresting with movement as the music did the same. "Come on. Let's dance."

"No thanks." Nadia pulled away. "You go. I'll come find you in a bit."

EVEN THOUGH she was there against Gryph's wishes and with no promise that he'd look out for her, she still felt obliged to tell him where she was going. When she did, he just nodded. "Text me if you get lost. I'll make sure to find you before we leave. And don't leave your drink unattended. Your *water*, I mean. Because you're not drinking, right?"

"Right."

"I mean it about the drink. People will put all kinds of stuff in it if you're not watching. Roofies, Special K. You name it."

"Got it." Phoenix gave him a double thumbs-up.

"Good." He turned away, dismissing her.

With that, Phoenix was on her own. She slid between writhing bodies to a spot between the speakers. There wasn't even a second of awkwardness, she just started moving.

HOW MUCH TIME went by, she had no idea. There was no break between songs, nor were there any songs, really. Just a trancelike soundtrack, created by drum and bass and light, bodies in motion. And then Tariq was beside her, off in his own world, eyes shut, dancing as if he was born to it. It so surprised Phoenix that she actually stopped for a moment. He must have sensed her staring, because he opened his eyes and, without missing a beat, handed her a bottle of water.

"Thought I'd check on you."

"I'm brilliant! This is amazing!" She took a sip, and then a gulp, not having realized how thirsty she was until that very moment. He said something, but she couldn't hear.

"What?"

"I said ..." Tariq took the bottle and leaned in so close that she could feel his breath on her ear. She shivered at the sensation, her arms rippling with goose bumps. "You suit this place."

And all of a sudden, despite the shivers, she was even hotter than she had been. She could feel her cheeks flare with red as Tariq took a swig of water. The music slowed, shifting into something Phee recognized. Under the bass crept an adagio her father played on the piano, but now it stretched into something massive. What would Oscar think of this place? She wanted to tell her father all about it. She wanted to bring him here, show him. How the music was prayer and exaltation at the same time. How the closest thing she could compare it to was *religion*. God himself. In shadowy rebel form, here among the shadows and secrets in long-forgotten alleyways. And it was clearly transformative, because here was Tariq, not only paying attention to her but *talking* to her.

"What?" she yelled again, realizing he was saying something else.

"I said you're a great dancer."

When she actually registered what he'd said, she managed a garbled thanks, and then immediately felt as if she'd accumulated a collection of unruly limbs. And on top of that, she had to go to the bathroom. She didn't want to ask Tariq where it was, though, so she told him she'd be right back and made her way toward the bar.

The others were gone. She scanned the crowd in the intermittent slices of light but didn't see the boys or Nadia. She headed for a glowing exit sign, figuring the bathrooms might be in that general direction. She was right, judging by the long line of girls formed outside a rusty door. She was of half a mind to go outside and pee in the alley, but not in a two-per zone, not at night, and not with thousands of inebriated partiers around.

It felt like forever before she was next in line. She glanced back at the mass of writhing bodies. Would Tariq still be dancing? Behind the rusty door was a small reeking bathroom with three doorless stalls. The third toilet was overflowing, the floor a slick puddle of putrid water. Hovering above a filthy seat, she peed as best as she could manage and then washed her hands, or rinsed them under the cold water. There was no soap, and nowhere to dry her hands, so she flapped them as she headed back out, only to find Nadia ten people behind the front of the line, Saul beside her, keeping her company.

"Hey!" Phee grabbed her in a hug. "Isn't this amazing?"

"As in amazingly crowded, noisy as hell, and stinking of sweat and booze and smoke? And I don't care what the guys say, I swear that I can still smell fish."

"The music!"

Nadia shrugged. "It's okay, I guess."

"Okay?" Phee gripped her best friend's shoulders and gave her a little shake. "This is way, *way* beyond okay! It's miraculous. Can't you feel it? Really feel it? Like in your soul?"

"Whatever." Nadia pulled away. "Maybe I'd be enjoying myself a little more if I could go pee. Like, right now. And if you hadn't abandoned me."

"I didn't! I told you I was going dancing."

"That was three hours ago, Phoenix."

"Really? Three hours?"

"Really. I've been stuck with Clea the whole time. We're making an art out of snubbing each other."

PHOENIX HUNG OUT with Nadia in the lineup, even though she really wanted to go back to the dance floor and Tariq. Saul stuck around for a few minutes, one hand shoved in his pocket, the other slung protectively around Nadia's bare shoulders. He would not look at Phee, and no matter how she tried to get him to talk to her, he would only nod, or shrug, and even then only when Nadia pushed for a response. The line moved slowly. Saul grew visibly impatient, looking around, not even pretending to listen to Nadia as she prattled on about Clea.

"She cannot dance," Nadia said. "You should've seen her. All swishy hips and finger snaps. Lame. Right, Saul?"

He shrugged, eyes searching the crowd.

"You're not even listening." Nadia twisted out from under his arm.

"You're right. I'm not. Sorry." Saul gave her a distracted kiss on the cheek. "I'm going to go find Gryphon. You okay here with Phee?"

Nadia pouted. "I guess."

"You'll stay with her?" Finally, he looked right at Phoenix. "Until I get back?"

Phoenix could only nod. She wanted to ask him so many questions but knew he'd brush her off. The only reason he was even deigning to look at her was to make sure she wouldn't leave Nadia alone in such a big crowd. Now was not the time.

THEY FOUND THE BOYS—Tariq included—and Clea at the far end of the warehouse, sitting on a banquette. Clea was wedged between Saul and Gryphon, laughing, one hand on Gryph's knee, the other reaching for her drink. Phoenix watched Nadia home in on Clea's thigh, which was pressed up against Saul's. He wasn't even talking to her, or even leaning in her direction. He had his head bent toward Tariq, his hands describing whatever he was talking about.

"Saul!" Nadia assumed her pissed-off position: arms folded, hip jutted out, chin cocked.

"Hey, baby." He looked up and grinned. Why could Phoenix see that he was totally infatuated with her, and yet Nadia was so quick to doubt? He climbed over Tariq and Neko, toppled an empty beer bottle and a candle, and, once standing, pulled Nadia to him in a warm embrace. Phee smiled. That should calm her best friend a little. Nadia looked so perfect in his arms, and he took such delight in her. Seeing them in their familiar embrace, Nadia with her back against his torso, her head leaned against his chest, his muscular arms embracing her sparrow-like form, she resolved once again not to tell Nadia about Saul's secret. Especially when he so plainly wanted to forget that he'd ever told Phoenix about it in the first place. She would forget about it too. Or try to.

WITHOUT BEING ASKED, Tariq and Neko got up to make room. At first, Saul gently ushered Nadia in front of him, but that would've meant she'd end up beside Clea. She pulled him aside and ushered Neko and Tariq back in first. They slid along the banquette, and then she slid in too. There was only space for one more, and Saul—always the gentleman—gestured for Phoenix to take it.

"I'm going to go dance some more." She surveyed the group, cozily squished against each other on the plush red seat. She winked at Nadia. "You okay, hon?"

Nadia nodded. With a glance at Clea, she pulled Saul's arm across her shoulders and snuggled in.

Phoenix wove her way back onto the dance floor. She closed her eyes and let the music fill her veins until she felt as if her heartbeat and the bass were one and the same. When the beat shifted, and she had to find her rhythm again, she opened her eyes and there was Tariq, watching her, a small smile on his lips. Arms folded, he wasn't dancing, just staring. With an embarrassed gasp, Phee spun away so he couldn't see her face, but he grabbed her arm and turned her back to him.

"Where're you going?"

"Nowhere." Phee was breathless from the dancing. She could feel the pulse at her wrist throbbing under his grip, pulsing against his palm. "Why?"

Tariq let go of her hand to gesture behind him. "Time to go."

"You came to get me?" Phee hollered over the music as it kicked back into a drum and bass frenzy.

"What?"

"You didn't come to dance?"

He shook his head, not in reply to her question, but to indicate that he couldn't hear her. He took her wrist again and led her out of the crowd to where the others were standing around, bleary-eyed and wan-looking, all of them.

"What time is it?" Phee asked as they collected their jackets.

Her question was answered when Gryph pushed open the heavy doors to the alley, and the pale wash of early morning met them with a damp, chilly embrace. And fish stench, of course. Within moments, Phee was freezing, the sweat she'd worked up dancing turning cold. She shivered. Tariq took his jacket off and draped it over her shoulders. Phee had to stop in her tracks, she was so blown over by his gesture. Clea and Nadia were wearing Gryph's and Saul's jackets too. It was a boyfriend sort of thing to do. She finally found her voice amid all her excitement.

"Th-tha-thanks, Tariq."

Tariq shrugged. "No problem." He walked beside her, and they made their way to a squat little diner near the station. A neon sign buzzed atop the roof: "The Balmoral." Phee had to laugh, though, because the B and the first l were burnt out, so the sign read "The a mor al." The amoral. How appropriate.

It was packed with ravers crammed into the little booths and taking up every stool at the counter. Only one waitress was working, along with the line cook, and the two of them looked dismayed as Phee's group made their way in. It was a funny sight, all the colourful costumes of the ravers, against the tired mint green and dull chrome of the wilted diner. Gryph waved to a guy wearing devil horns and a red fun-fur hoody at the back booth, and soon he and his friends settled their bill and vacated so that Gryph and the others could sit. Gryph never waited long for anything, or so it seemed. Phee wondered if that would change if he kept on coming in second. Or third. Or worse.

The waitress was older than Phee and Gryph's grandmother, and took their orders for hot chocolate and breakfast specials all around. As they waited for their food, the girls started to yawn—even Clea looked a little drained—and soon Nadia was asleep, her head resting on Saul's shoulder. Their food came, but Nadia continued to sleep.

"You have hers." Saul slid the plate across to Neko. "You're the scrawny one."

When everyone was done, Gryph paid for them all while Saul roused Nadia enough to get her walking, and they were on their way back into the morning, which was at least a little brighter and warmer now.

"I'll see Nadia and Phee home," Saul said when they arrived at the train station. By now, Phoenix was yawning too, and feeling the stretch and ache in her muscles from having danced all night long. Even sleepy, she hoped Tariq might offer to come along, but he didn't, and soon Saul and the girls were getting on one train, and the others were getting on another.

"Where's everyone else going?" Phee asked through a yawn. "Neko should go home too."

"They're taking Clea home, and then we're staying at Huy's," Saul said. "His parents are away."

"Oh." Phee yawned again.

The three made their way to Nadia's house, where Nadia stood on her front walk, half asleep and leaning against Saul.

"I'm going in," she said thickly. "I'm exhausted." Saul helped her up the steps but didn't go inside. Nadia's parents weren't fond of him to begin with, and certainly didn't want to find him in their house at this early hour. "Phee?"

"Yeah—"

Saul grabbed her arm. Phee gave him a curious look but told Nadia to go on ahead without her.

"You have to be tiptoe quiet," Nadia said through a yawn. "You wake my parents and I'll kill you."

When Nadia closed the door gently behind her, Saul turned on Phee. He grabbed her shoulders hard. "Have you told her?"

"No!"

"Then why is she acting all weird lately?"

"Saul, I haven't told anyone." She could see the worry in his eyes. "Not a soul. I swear. Nadia's not acting any more weird than normal."

He let go and sighed. "You better not have said anything."

"I haven't."

"You have to promise."

"I already did!" Phee brought her voice back down to a whisper. "I won't tell. Honest. So there's no point in avoiding me. Acting like a jerk doesn't make any difference. It'd be nice to have the old Saul back."

"I'm sorry."

"You should be."

"Well, I am. Okay? Are we good?"

"Sure."

"Good ..." Saul paused. "Because I didn't exactly tell you everything."

"No. No way, Saul. Don't tell me anything more. I don't want to know."

He told her anyway, oblivious to her protests. "I already used my one recon."

Phee was suddenly wide awake. She straightened. "What?" She leaned in, not wanting him to have to speak above a whisper. "What did you just say?"

"Remember when I went back east to visit my grandparents? When Gryph and I were in Grade 8?"

Phee nodded. Her gut churned. She wished he would stop talking, but at the same time she was compelled to know more.

"My grandpa didn't die. He's still alive."

"*You* died."

Saul nodded.

Phee sat down on the steps, stunned. He was done. He didn't have a recon left! Her head swam with all the implications. Saul sat beside her and whispered in her ear. "You can't tell anyone. Especially not Nadia. Okay?"

"Of course not." Phee covered her face with her hands and nodded. "I won't."

Behind them, the door opened and Nadia reappeared. "Aren't you going to meet up with the guys?"

Saul leaped to his feet. "I am."

Nadia glowered at him. "Then you better get going."

She let him kiss her but didn't return it. Instead, she fixed Phee with a nasty glare, and when he'd gone down the steps, she shut the door in Phee's face. Phee knocked as lightly as she could. The door swung open again.

"First Clea and now *you?*"

"Get a grip, Nadia." Phee laughed to cover her nervousness. She was afraid to speak to Nadia at all for fear of blurting out Saul's secret. "Your raging jealousy act is getting a little old. Me and Saul? As if!" With that, she pushed past Nadia and made her way up the stairs to her best friend's bedroom at the end of the hall, careful to avoid the creaks she knew intimately. Nadia padded along behind her, less careful, and still fixated on Saul and Phee's private moment on the front steps.

"Let it go, Nadia." Phee stripped off her clothes that smelled of smoke and sweat, and pulled on a pair of pyjamas she'd fished out of Nadia's drawer. "You're being an idiot. Go to sleep. We only ever talk about you. You, you, and only you. Okay?" She was angry at Nadia for her foolish assumption, but more so because she'd cut short any opportunity to ask Saul the details about his secret life.

Nadia stood there for another long moment, an annoyed look on her face. Her room was done in pinks and creams, and there she stood in wobbly heels and a short black dress and glitter dusted along her arms and a flock of bangles on each wrist. "You're right. I'm being stupid."

"Yes. Yes, you are. Now go to sleep."

With a nod and a yawn, Nadia got into her pyjamas and crawled into bed, and within moments she was asleep beside Phee. Phee listened to her best friend's steady breathing, trying to match her own with it. But she couldn't calm down, let alone sleep. She was worried. About everything. Gryph and his dangerous trajectory. Saul and his illegal status. Thank goodness sleep finally took her against her will, because her mind would've careered on like that forever. When she did finally sleep, she fell into a dream of that pulsating music. She was back on the dance floor, with Tariq. At last, a respite from her worries. She wanted the dream never to end.

DISCLOSURE

She got kicked out of her dream when the baby next door—whose open nursery window was right across from Nadia's—started wailing just after eight, which meant that Phee had had about two hours of sleep. After that, Phee lay awake, thinking while Nadia sprawled across most of the mattress, her arm flung over her head, snoring heavily. This, of course, made her think of Saul, and how he made fun of Nadia's snoring. Saul. Dear Saul. And his secret. Saul had no recon left. Phee figured he'd told her only so that she'd realize how serious the situation was, how important her discretion. She wouldn't tell a soul. And she wouldn't ask him about it. She'd behave as if he'd never told her at all. It was a heavy, dark secret, and she could respect that.

She and Nadia met the boys for a late brunch at a restaurant across the street from the arcade. It was a popular pancake house, and it was a weekend, so the place was full of families with children laughing and crying and running around, high on the sugar from their Belgian waffles. At Phee's table everyone was tired from the late night, so the talk was minimal, the coffee refills plentiful.

"Salt," Gryph mumbled. And Phee passed him the salt.

"Ketchup, please." Saul nodded down the table at the red bottle. Phee slid it to him, careful not to give him any sort of funny look. How could he just carry on, life as usual, dousing his scrambled eggs with ketchup? She was finding it hard. She had so many questions. How had he died? Who had reconned him and where? How could he pass as a three-per?

Phee watched Saul eat his breakfast. He held a piece of toast in one hand and used it to shovel up his eggs. What about his parents? They both had doctorates in the sciences and the two of them were working as consultants for a regional task force on ... on what? Phee tried to remember. Something about microbes in air particles. Was that a lie too? Were they even his real parents? What was his home life like? She'd never been to his house. But Nadia had, and Gryph. She'd ask him about it. Discreetly, of course.

HER CHANCE CAME when she and Gryph made their way back to the Shores later that day for a family supper. Her auntie Trish and uncle Liam and their three-year-old twin boys were coming up from Brampton, where they lived in a three-per suburb of other IT executives. It was Eva's father's eightieth birthday. Oscar was bringing in lobster from the East Coast, which he'd done every year for over a decade. She and Gryph were walking through the mall, taking a short cut.

"What's Saul's house like?"

"What do you mean?" Gryph was distracted, keeping his eyes on something ahead of them. Phee stretched up, trying to see what he was looking at, but she didn't notice anything remarkable. The mall was busy with shoppers and weekend traffic, but as far as she could see, nothing out of the ordinary.

"I mean, like ..." But Phee wasn't sure what she meant. She didn't want to say anything to tip him off to her curiosity. "Is it neat and tidy?" She had this idea that one- and two-pers lived dirtier lives. After all, the more valuable a citizen, the more recons you were assigned. Which meant, conversely, that less educated, less valuable people didn't know well enough to keep a nice home. Or, further-more, didn't have the means to pay someone else to keep it tidy for them.

"Of course it is. Mr. and Mrs. Morrisey both work from home."

"Well, that doesn't mean they keep a nice house—"

"Look, Phee … go over there if you don't believe me. I'm telling you, Saul's mom is a neat freak."

"What's she like? Does Saul look like her?"

"What kind of dumbass question is that?"

"I was just asking." Phee heard the nerves in her voice, the way it tightened and went higher.

"Why?"

"Because."

"Because why?" Gryph gave her a look, a warning. "Saul is my best friend. Not yours. He is none of your business, in fact. So stop with the questions."

"Okay," Phee said. She'd pushed it too far, and by Gryph's reaction, she'd hit on something.

"Good." Suddenly, Gryph stopped mid-stride. Phee craned to see what he was so fixed on, and finally she did. His eyes were locked on a boy up ahead at the electronics store. He glanced around to be sure that the clerk was distracted, and then he clearly and obviously slipped something off the counter and into his pocket.

"He just stole something," Phee marvelled. "In plain sight!"

"Hey, you! Stop!" Gryph took off after him. "You stay here, Phee," he called over his shoulder.

Screw that. Phee ran after him, straining to keep up to his athlete's pace. The boy ran ahead of them both, checking frantically over his shoulder every few steps, only to find Gryph on his tail.

The crowd of shoppers cut away to let Gryph through. "Someone stop him!" Gryph yelled.

The thief looked over his shoulder again and, on seeing Gryph neatly closing the distance, deked off to the right and broke into a flat-out run. But he was no match for Gryph, who easily caught up and tackled him, and they both fell to the floor. Phee was panting, feeling the familiar asthmatic tightness in her throat when she finally caught up. The two boys tussled on the polished-tile floor, the sound of the waterfall at one end of the food court drowning out the thief's protests. While Gryph might've been the stronger sprinter of the two, he didn't have much experience with fighting. The boy managed to wrench one hand free and punch Gryph hard in the temple. Gryph shook his head, dazed.

The boy seized the moment and slipped out from under Gryph. He sat on him and punched him in the temple again.

"Stop!" Phee cried as the boy leaned all his weight on Gryph's throat with a forearm. "Help!" Phee spun around, not sure what to do. "Over here!" She waved her arms at the two mall security guards running down the concourse. She turned back to Gryph, just as the kid pulled something from his pocket with his free hand. He lifted it up and it caught the light. A knife!

"Gryph!" she screamed, pointing helplessly. "He's got a knife."

"I see it! I see it." Gryph dug his chin under the kid's arm and shoved him off. Another heave and he flipped the smaller boy and was on top again. He pinned the boy's arm with the knife under one knee and sat on his chest. A crowd gathered, curious.

"Let us through," one of the security guards ordered.

"Let me go, asshole!" The boy, enraged and embarrassed, gave one last mighty shove, knocking Gryph off balance just enough to get his arm free. Still pinned under Gryph, he stabbed blindly at him, landing two or three good jabs.

Gryph toppled to the floor, and the boy scrambled to his feet, practically backing right into the security guards. They grabbed his arm and twisted it until he dropped the knife.

"Gryph!" Phee fell to her knees beside her brother. "You're hurt!"

"It's not bad." Gryph pulled his hand away from his stomach. His fingers and palm were red with wet blood. She pushed aside his hand and lifted his shirt. Just above his navel, a wide, oozing cut arced across to his rib cage.

"Oh, my God, no!" Phee shouted. "Call an ambulance!"

IT SEEMED LIKE FOREVER but it was probably only moments before Phee heard the sirens as the ambulance shuttle drew up outside. She stepped aside to let the medics attend to Gryph's gash. Phee called her parents and told them to meet her and Gryph at the hospital.

"I'm not going to the hospital," Gryph growled as the paramedic doused his wound with an antiseptic solution. "Tell them I'm fine."

"You're not fine."

Phee was right. Because he was still a minor, he couldn't refuse, and the paramedics insisted that he needed to be stitched up at least, if not further checked for internal damage. They also insisted that he be carried out on the stretcher, despite his objections. People were taking pictures faster than the security guards could stop them, and by the time they reached the ambulance, the images had already been uploaded to the local media.

"I can walk at least." Gryph made to stand, but the paramedic pushed him back onto the cot.

"Help us keep our jobs here," he said with a glance to the enormous TV screen mounted at the street corner. There was Gryph, larger than life, his bloody stomach for all to see.

"Then could we get out of here at least?"

Phee didn't think he sounded all that annoyed at the media attention, which was odd. This sort of thing was not okay with Chrysalis. They liked him to appear when and where they wanted so that he could say exactly what they wanted. Gryph managed a smile and made a peace sign before he lay back and let himself be strapped onto the stretcher.

The crowd cheered. Phee glanced up, and there she was on the massive screen, hurrying alongside the stretcher. She pushed her hair behind her ears and tried to ignore it, but then the commentary boomed from the towering speakers.

"Bringing you live, up-to-the-minute reporting on the shocking public attack of Chrysalis-sponsored star athlete Gryphon Nicholson-Lalonde, this is KPL News, where every second counts."

The crowd—with cellphones held aloft like lighters at a concert, trying to get a picture of Gryph—followed them to the ambulance. The security guards cleared a path for the paramedics to manoeuvre the stretcher back into the ambulance shuttle. As Phee climbed in behind him, she could hear the faceless newscaster drone on. *"Details are still coming in, but eyewitness accounts describe Nicholson-Lalonde as a hero caught in a brave act."*

"All for what?" Phee demanded as the doors shut behind them and the shuttle pulled away. "What did he take?"

"It wasn't about what he took." Another wince as Gryph tried to straighten his knees. "It's the principle of the matter."

"Keep them flexed," the man said as he took out a bag of fluid and an IV catheter.

"What was it?"

"A game."

"All that? For a stupid game?" Phee sighed, exasperated. "You can't be so reckless, Gryph! Do you *want* to be reconned?"

"I'm fine, aren't I?" Gryph paled as the paramedic took his arm and lined up the IV needle against his vein. "He's a thief. He shouldn't be allowed to get away with it."

"This'll only hurt for a moment," the paramedic said as he inserted the needle.

Gryph clenched his teeth and winced. Phee sat back on the bench, mystified, as the ambulance took off, the siren wailing.

Not that long ago, Gryph was careful not to do anything that might jeopardize his career stats or his contract with Chrysalis. This was unprecedented, putting himself in harm's way. She had to wonder about all those nights he didn't spend at home, and what he got up to. If it was anything like this, she didn't want to know.

OSCAR AND EVA arrived—along with Fawn, and Eva's father—minutes after Gryph was ushered into the trauma bay.

"Is he okay?" Eva asked, rushing past Phoenix on her way to the nurses' station.

"I think so," Phee said. "How come Granddad's here?" She pointed at her grandfather, already wandering aimlessly down the corridor, trailing his fingers along the wall.

"Your grandma's off getting things for the party," Oscar explained when Phee pointed. "I couldn't very well leave Fawn and him alone together, and we both wanted to come. You keep an eye on them both while we find out what's going on."

Oscar joined Eva at the nurses' station, while Phee steered her grandpa back to the waiting area, where Fawn had already made fast friends with two boys just a little younger than she was. Fawn had them following her under the banks of seating, pretending to be a pirate leading her prisoner sailors underground.

Shortly afterwards, Gryph's agent arrived from Chrysalis, with his assistant bustling behind him. Lex homed in on Phoenix and immediately started in with the questions.

"What happened? And why on earth did you let people tape it?"

"Why did I let people—"

"Never mind, the damage is done." Lex wasn't interested in hearing Phee's answers. He answered himself. "We get notified of any online uploads that mention Gryphon. In fact, that's how we found out; it's all over the lync. Why didn't you call us?" Again, he didn't wait for Phee's reply. "Never mind, we placed a media ban straightaway, thank God. Took a good half-hour to get the judge on board, but we don't want Gryphon's little adventure broadcast more than is unavoidable."

"Why not?" Phee broke in. "You can't expect people not to talk about it. The mall was packed. Everyone was taking pictures."

"Chrysalis has a reputation to uphold." Lex stiffened. "And so does your brother. This sort of ... of ... 'stunt' is not the kind of attention befitting a champion athlete sponsored by the largest and most important entity in this nation."

"He caught a criminal," Phee deadpanned. "Can't your media people spin that in your favour?"

"I'd rather they didn't have to, but they will."

What Lex wasn't saying, but Phee knew full well, was that he was worried that a publicized injury might affect the judges' decisions at the X Games. Every sponsor for every athlete invited to the X Games did its best to keep its athletes' images spotless and shiny leading up to the event every year. Considering that Gryph was the gold-medal winner for the past two years running in four events ranging from motorcross to skateboarding, Chrysalis had a lot at stake.

Lex's phone rang, so he dismissed her with a wave of his hand. Phee spotted Lex's assistant by the coffee machine and went to talk to her.

"What do you think of this?" Phee asked. "Is it as big a deal as Lex is making it out to be?"

"Well"—she turned to Phee and gave her a big polished smile— "Chrysalis openly requires its athletes to keep a low profile between competitions."

"That sounds like a line from the policy book." Phee laughed. "It's Aggie, right?"

"Yes." She looked up from arranging the tray of coffees in front of her. Still with the plastered-on smile. "Short for Agatha. And it is a line from the policy book. You caught me."

"Here, let me help you." Phee took the tray.

"Thank you."

"So, how's it going? Being back at work?"

Aggie shrugged. "It's a little easier. Every day."

"I don't know if they told you," Phee said, "but I lost my memory too."

"Lex mentioned it." Aggie's eyes sparkled with interest. "Do you get bits here and there sometimes? Like flashes?"

"I think so." Phee nodded. "But they're so fleeting that I mostly can't hold on to them. And I sometimes wonder if I'm just making it up. Splicing stuff from what people tell me and pictures and movies. I can't tell what is real memory and what isn't."

"Oh." Aggie's smile vanished. "I kind of hoped it got better with time."

"Me too," Phee said quietly.

Aggie worked her regulation smile back into place. "The coffee's getting cold."

"Aggie," Phee started, not sure where she was going with her thoughts. "Gryph's relationship with Chrysalis is okay ... isn't it?"

"Like I said, the coffee is getting cold." Aggie shook her head a little, as if silently admonishing Phee for trying to get information out of her by exploiting common ground. "Nice talking to you." She lifted the tray from Phee and went about distributing the drinks, coffee for Lex and Phee's granddad, hot chocolate for the kids. She left a hot chocolate on the tray for Phee. As if she were just a kid too.

WHEN EVA AND OSCAR emerged from the ER, they practically sagged with relief.

"They've cleared him for internal injuries and are just stitching him up now," Eva explained. "We should be able to take him home tonight."

Oscar bent his head, praying silently while Lex started organizing everyone. "We'll get you a Chrysalis shuttle to take you home. As for Gryphon, I'll want a statement to the press, either tonight or first thing in the morning, something we can use if we need to, and hopefully won't have to. I can have Aggie write up something we can splice for any occasion, if that's all right with you. And I'll speak directly to the doctor and his team to determine when Gryph will be well enough to resume his competition schedule—"

Eva raised a hand to cut him off. "In time for the X Games, you mean."

"Well, yes ... among other events."

"I can tell you right now that he will not be competing at the X Games this year."

"Mrs. Nicholson-Lalonde—"

"Now, now, Lex." Eva gave him a sly grin. "You know better than that."

"*Dr.* Nicholson-Lalonde, of course. I only mean to say that we'll be sure to get the attending physician's opinion on the matter as well."

"The attending physician's opinion is the same as this physician's." Eva squared her jaw. "And Gryph has said that he agrees. He does not want to compete. It's too soon. He wants to be able to do his best, and he can already admit that this will not be possible with only one month to recover."

"We'll have our own medical team examine—"

"You will not. I won't permit it."

While Lex reddened, Phee gazed at her mother with admiration. She could always tell when Eva was seething with anger because she grew calmer and more articulate the madder she became.

"If this is about his contract ..." Lex said in a near whisper.

"It most certainly is not." Eva's expression darkened. "This is about my *son*."

"Of course this is about your son, but surely you can understand that Chrysalis—"

"And furthermore," Eva continued, as if Lex hadn't spoken at all, "I am disappointed at your suggestion that my son has put himself in harm's way with the idea that he might get out of his contract with Chrysalis."

But he did want out of his contract.

It dawned on Phee that that was *exactly* what Gryph was doing.

He wanted out! That's why he was throwing away his wins lately, deliberately coming in second. He wanted Chrysalis to fire him. It made so much sense! But why? Why would he sabotage something so important to him?

Maybe it wasn't so important to him anymore.

Something had changed last year, and it had made Gryph think differently about Chrysalis. And life. He'd been more reckless than ever. He and the guys spent entire nights out getting up to mischief that Phee had no clue about. And he took more risks. He *did* put himself in harm's way. A year ago, he would never let himself get in the media spotlight for anything other than sports. Mind you, a year ago, he would never have let Phee come along to a rave either.

True or not, Eva wasn't about to let Lex make such accusations.

"We're done here. We'll arrange for a private shuttle," Eva said, stealthily changing the subject. "Or we'll take the train. If you need a statement from my son, you may come to our house in the morning to do so. You will use whatever he says in its entirety. No editing. And we will have our own recording to ensure that you do so. He is not your puppet, whatever you might think—"

"Eva, darling ..." Oscar set a steadying hand on his wife's knee.

"Let us see you home," Lex said, his expression even. "It's the least we can do."

"So that the media can see us riding in your corporate shuttle with the Chrysalis logo all over it? So that you can use even this— my son's hospital visit—in one of your ad campaigns? No," Eva said emphatically, "absolutely not. We'll make our own way home. No Chrysalis. No media."

"We have a family dinner tonight," Oscar explained, as if that had anything to do with it.

Lex ignored him, his eyes locked on Eva. "As you wish."

Eva glared right back at him. "Indeed."

"All right, everyone, let's all take a nice deep breath." Oscar demonstrated, his nostrils flaring as he did. He let out the breath with a roll of his hand in front of him. "We're all upset. It's been a shock to us all. I've prayed for calm and clarity—"

"Clarity?" Lex snapped at him. "Perhaps you and your wife and your son should all take some time to get *clear* about what his contract with us includes. He's developed quite the attitude as of late, and no one at Chrysalis is impressed. And as for his recent 'losses' ... What are we supposed to think?"

This time it was Oscar on the defensive. "What are you implying?"

Lex let a long, loaded moment go before he answered. "Your son is talented, of course, but he's nothing without our corporate support. Without our contract. It would be a shame if he chose to screw it up. Not to mention that that would also be a chargeable violation of his legally binding contract."

"Enough, Lex." It wasn't often that Oscar's cheeks reddened with anger, but they did now, colouring so suddenly that even Fawn noticed.

"Daddy, your face looks like a tomato—"

"Come on, Fawn." Phee swept her out of the way. "Let's go to the bathroom."

"But I don't have to!"

"Lex"—Oscar chewed his lip thoughtfully for a moment before continuing—"I think you and Aggie should leave now. My family would like to be alone."

"There was a time when you considered Chrysalis family." Lex talked as he snapped his fingers for Aggie to follow him. "And Chrysalis gladly returned such affection."

Phee's granddad appeared like a ghost behind Lex, who suddenly found himself face to face with the old man when he turned to leave. Lex drew in a surprised breath.

"Mr. Nicholson!"

"And who're you, Mr. Bigshot?" He peered at Lex with a sneer. "Who're you, making my girl angry like that?"

"If you'll excuse us." With his nose wrinkled, Lex minced his way around Phee's granddad. Her granddad did stink, as he'd started refusing baths a while ago. And right then Phee was glad for it and glad that Lex was getting a ripe noseful of rank old man.

"We'll be in touch," Aggie added with a cold smile before following him.

EVA STEERED HER FATHER back into the waiting area and sat him down. Phee plopped into the chair beside him.

"Well, that was fun." Phee elbowed her granddad gently. "Good on you, Granddad, standing up to Lex like that."

"Who?" He scowled at her.

"I want to go home now," Fawn said as she watched the two little boys leave with their mother. "I have no one to play with."

"I'll go check on how much longer it will be." Eva headed toward the ER doors.

Oscar gestured behind them at the admin counter. "I'll go get the paperwork done."

With her parents heading off in opposite directions, Phee spoke to no one in particular. "And I'll stay here and look after Fawn and Granddad."

"Who?" Phee's grandpa asked. "Who're you looking after?"

"You, Granddad. And Fawn. Your littlest granddaughter."

"Well, okay, then. You're doing a mighty fine job, girlie." He dug in his pocket and pulled out a lint-covered mint. "A sweetie for my sweetie?"

"Thanks, Granddad." Her grandfather beamed at her as she reluctantly took the mint. Sometimes his dementia was just a matter of fact. But right now, in the midst of everything, she felt terribly, terribly sad about it. She didn't have the heart to pretend, and he was watching her with such an earnestly pleased smile, so she popped the sticky old mint into her mouth and grinned back at him. "Thanks."

THEY WERE HOME in time for dinner, and no one—certainly not Phee's grandfather—minded that the celebration was more about Gryph's good fortune than an old man's birthday. The twins hung off Gryph like a couple of ardent fans, though they were far too young to admire him for anything other than being the cherished older cousin, and Fawn had one of her customary before-dinner tantrums. This sent Phee's grandma and aunt off on a lecture about Fawn's getting away with bad behaviour, which put Eva on the defensive and gave Oscar the platform to preach about gentle discipline. By the time the cake was brought out with a candle lit for each of Granddad's seven decades, Phee was done. Done with the long day, done with wondering what was going on with Gryph, done with Saul's secret, done with it all.

As her grandfather protested that it wasn't his birthday at all and he certainly wasn't seventy, Phee joined in with the rest of them singing "Happy Birthday." When he refused to blow out the candles, Fawn was happy to do it for him. As she did, Phee made her own silent wish. To have everything go back to the way it was before.

AFTER DINNER Phoenix retreated to the porch swing for some peace and quiet while the rest of them played charades in the living room. She'd been out there a little while, long enough to get a chill, when Gryph appeared and asked if he could join her. He'd brought her a blanket and set it over her lap now as he sat gingerly beside her, careful not to strain his wound. Phee waited for him to explain what was going on. With what happened earlier, with his relationship with Chrysalis, with the story behind his attacker. So she was unprepared when he started talking about her.

"I want you to know something about when you died," he said, as if plucking the subject out of midair. "The second time. When you were six."

Phee shifted to look at him. "What?" She tried to keep her excitement at bay. Gryph rarely talked about that day at the church picnic, and never unprovoked.

"I did it."

Phee waited for more, not understanding.

Gryph noted her confusion. "I pushed you in," he explained. "It was my fault that you died."

Now Phee was dumbstruck. "You ... you *what?*"

"I wanted to see what would happen, with the recon. I was curious." Gryph held her gaze as he talked. "Mom and Dad don't know."

"Why are you telling me this now?" Even as she spoke, Phee was rewriting the story as she knew it, trying to place her brother in this new role, shoving her into the fast-moving waters.

"I want you to know the truth."

"In general? Or just about this?"

"About this."

Phee gritted her teeth. She wanted a *real* memory. She didn't want to take his word for it or her parents' word for it. She wanted her own recollection of events.

"You're mad."

"Of course I'm mad! You killed me!"

"I was just a kid—"

"So was I!"

"Just like Fawn," Gryph said. "You know? Curious. I'd just begun to understand about recons. I didn't make the connection to the fact that you'd already had one and what that would mean. And I had no idea that some people lost their memory. I'm sorry, Phee."

"You're sorry? Is that why you're telling me? So you can apologize and feel better about the fact that you drowned your own little sister? And now I only have one recon left! Thanks to you, my dear brother."

"I understand that you're angry—"

"Oh, shut up!" Phee stood and faced her brother, fists on her hips. "Don't talk to me like you're Dad talking to one of his parishioners."

"I just wanted to explain before I ... I just ..." Gryph seemed to be arguing silently with himself. "Look, Phee, I just know how badly you want to know the truth about what happened."

"I want to *know* from my own memory!"

"If I'd known that you'd lose your memory ..." Gryph's words trailed off. Just as quickly as her anger had swelled, it abated, and

Phee could easily imagine her brother, just eight years old and full of curiosity. Just testing. Just wondering. Just experimenting, the way Fawn did so often. Both Fawn and Gryph were the types of people who needed to experience things in order to understand them. It didn't matter how many times she'd told the toddler Fawn that the stove was hot, it was only after Fawn had burned herself that she'd understood. Phee could imagine Gryph's anticipation, the wanting to know. She could imagine the push, and then how horrible he would've felt, watching her float away, face down, lifeless after just a few minutes of struggling.

"Why didn't you jump in after me?" Phee asked, her voice softer. "Why didn't you try to pull me out?"

"The river was so fast. I got scared. I couldn't swim that well yet. I knew I had to go for help. If I'd jumped in, we both would've died."

"At least that way you might have had an idea of what it's like to be me."

"True."

"Well"—Phee sighed—"I won't tell Mom and Dad, if that's what you're worried about."

"It's totally within your rights to tell them," he said. "They wouldn't tell Chrysalis."

"Of course they wouldn't tell Chrysalis. Don't be ridiculous."

A long silence passed between them, until Gryph finally broke it. "Are you sorry that I told you?"

"No. Maybe." Phee tossed aside the blanket. "I don't know what I think." With that, she left Gryph there and went back into the house and upstairs to bed without so much as a goodbye to her visiting relatives. She climbed under the covers, fully dressed, her mind churning so vigorously that she felt faint, even lying down. The room practically spun. She hated having all these secrets. She hated not knowing the real truth, *her* truth. And she hated Gryph for killing her when she was six. Or she told herself she should hate him.

But she didn't.

She didn't hate him. She wished she did, because it seemed appropriate, and maybe she'd feel better if she did. But she didn't hate him. Why not, she couldn't understand.

She kept coming back to the same thing. He'd only been little. Just a kid himself.

No matter how determined she was to hold it against him, she just couldn't.

She felt sorry for him, carrying that lonely version of events by himself for so many years. If his version of events was true. Just as she felt sorry for Saul and his burden of truth. She surrendered to her exhaustion before she could drive herself crazy with all the pondering, and fell soundly asleep.

THE NEWS

She might not have hated him, but for good measure Phee didn't talk to Gryph for over a week. And he, thank goodness, didn't try to make her. She had no idea what she could possibly say to him, what with her brain all in a bother and her heart tied up in knots. They skirted each other on the few occasions they were both home at the same time, and other than that she steered clear of him altogether. As for Saul, he was earnestly avoiding her too, so she had no idea what to tell Nadia when she phoned Thursday morning, before school.

"Saul's mom just called, looking for him." Phee could hear the panic in Nadia's voice. "She says he didn't come home last night. After he left here."

"I'm sure there's nothing to worry about." Phee held her phone to her ear as she padded down the hall to ask Gryph if he knew where Saul was.

"If he's going off with the guys he always tells me."

"Is Neko home?"

"Oh, my God, I didn't think to check!"

Phee could hear Nadia hurrying down the hall at her house as she knocked on Gryph's door. There was no reply.

"Neko's door is locked."

"Knock harder."

Nadia pounded on the door. Finally, she could hear Neko greeting Nadia with a groggy yawn. "Hang on," Nadia said as she put her phone on speaker. "Do you know where Saul is?"

Nothing. Phee assumed the fourteen-year-old had shrugged.

"Neko! Come on, this isn't funny."

Then Neko's small voice. "I'm not laughing, am I?"

"Well, don't be cheeky, either."

Phee listened but was distracted by footsteps coming up the stairs behind her. She turned, and there was Gryph, dressed in exactly what she'd last seen him wearing the night before.

"Gryph just got in," she reported to Nadia.

"No I haven't." He pushed past Phee and opened his bedroom door. "I just went to take a piss. I've been here all night. Everyone knows that. Right?" He gave her a sly grin before disappearing inside and closing the door behind him.

"You haven't! I can tell!" Phee lowered her voice as she heard her parents stirring in their own room. "Gryph! I've got Nadia, worried sick, on the phone, wanting to know where Saul is."

"Home in bed, I imagine."

"Open up, Gryphon." Phee rapped on the door. "Or Mom and Dad will hear."

Gryph appeared again, shirtless, the bandage from the stabbing a neat rectangle on his abdomen, the bags under his eyes more evidence to support her suspicion. "What?"

"Look, I know you go out without Mom and Dad knowing, and I don't care. Well, I do, but that's beside the point. Just tell me where Saul is and if he's okay."

"He's fine. He'll be home soon." Another smirk. "Does this mean you're talking to me again?"

"No." Phee stalked off to her own room. She hated how indifferent Gryph could be when everyone else was in a flap. He took after Oscar that way. Nothing fazed either of them. Or at least, that was what it looked like.

SURE ENOUGH, a couple of minutes after she got off the phone with Nadia, she texted Phee. "He's home. Safe & sound. Commencing scolding-wench routine. Xoxo."

Phee wanted to march right back to Gryphon's room and demand to know what the hell was going on. With the guys' clandestine nighttime ramblings, what Gryph knew about Saul and his situation, the stunt Gryph pulled in the mall, and—if she had the guts to bring it up—why he was blowing his win record to smithereens and ruining his career with Chrysalis.

The fact was, she didn't have the guts to confront him on any of it.

She was still stuck on exactly how she was supposed to react to the news that her brother had cost her a recon. It wasn't something that happened. At least not to anyone Phee knew. She'd heard a horrible story of a man who'd backed out of his driveway and run over his toddler, but that was the only circumstance she knew of that even came close to resembling her bizarre situation. She might have to tell Nadia, if only not to be so alone with such a big part of her history.

PHEE AND NADIA helped out at the church's strawberry tea, working in the kitchen. By the time it was winding down, they both had stains on their clothes. Phee had picked a sundress to wear that morning, in the hope of seeing Tariq later, and now it had a streak of chocolate sauce down the front. Nadia had noticed the dress right away and had given her a hard time about it. Now she was far more concerned about her own soiled shirt.

"It's ruined." Nadia pointed at the strawberry-juice splotch. "This was not cheap, you know."

"I told you not to wear anything fancy."

"So then again I ask, why did you wear a dress?"

"It's just a sundress." Phee looked away so Nadia wouldn't see her face. No matter how hard she tried to conceal her feelings, Nadia could always read her like a book. "So again I tell you, I picked it up off the floor this morning."

"I know exactly where you got it from. Your closet, left-hand side, behind the frou-frou dress your grandma made you for Christmas. Floor, my ass."

"For your information, I did get it off the floor." Phee got up. She reached for Nadia's hand and helped her up too. "And anyway, it doesn't matter. I promised my mom I'd take Fawn out this afternoon. I can change when we pick her up."

"We?"

"You're coming with me."

"Only for an hour. Saul's taking me to that sushi place for dinner."

"Then come on, so we can go swimming. And you can eat a hot dog or something before he picks you up, because I know for a fact you never eat when you go out with him."

"Uh-huh. Just like I know you didn't get that dress off the floor."

BECAUSE IT WAS the first day of summer vacation, the beach at the Shores was dotted with teenagers spread out on towels, playing volleyball in the hot sun, or strolling along the sand, all of them aiming for an air of nonchalance but failing. The whole beach simmered with summer potential. Phee could practically hear the desperate hopes for the next two school-free months as she and Nadia, with Fawn swinging between them, searched for a spot to lay out their blanket. Right away, Fawn spotted a group of her friends building sandcastles under the watchful eye of a couple of mothers settled in for the day with their books and baskets of snacks.

"Thank God." Nadia unfurled her beach towel and arranged herself on it as if she were in a magazine ad for bronzer. "We are blissfully Fawn-free." With her darker skin, she needed only five minutes in the sun to look even more exotic and sultry than she normally did.

"Don't pick on her." Phee spread out her towel beside Nadia's and started slathering on the sunblock.

"I love Fawn. But sometimes she can be a pain in the ass."

"Then you two have a lot in common."

"Ha, ha." Nadia sneered at her. "Guess what Saul and I did last night?"

"Do I have to?"

"Get your mind out of the gutter, girl. We picked out baby names."

"*What?* You're not—"

"No!"

"Thank God." Phee let out a sigh of relief.

"I don't know," Nadia said with a shrug. "It'd be kind of neat having a baby around, wouldn't it?"

"You just finished saying that Fawn was a pain in the ass and she's not even a baby. And you hated looking after her when she was a baby."

"I was just saying."

"Well, you can just keep saying all you want, just keep being safe while you do."

"We decided that if we have a boy, his middle name will be Gryphon, and if we have a girl, her middle name will be Phoenix. We can't decide on first names, though. We have a list that's forty names long. But we both agreed on the middle names right away."

Phee grinned. "That's sweet. But you mean *if*, like way in the future *if*, right? Because I think you should probably finish high school and get your degree before you get into babies." Phee spread a glob of sunblock down her calf. "Just saying." She winked at Nadia.

"That stuff *blocks* the sun, Phee, honey." Nadia pulled down her sunglasses and fixed Phoenix with a bored look. "If you want to tan, you have to let the sun do its thing unfettered. Just saying."

"*Unfettered.*" Phee grinned as she spread the white muck along her pasty legs. "That's a pretty chunky word for such a little girl."

With a smirk, Nadia chucked a fistful of sand at her. It stuck to the sunblock like glitter to glue, so Phee headed down to the water to rinse it off while Nadia laughed at her.

THE SUN ARCED OVERHEAD, Nadia napped, Phee swam, first alone, and then, when Fawn's little friends left, with Fawn too. It was late afternoon when Phee dragged Fawn out of the water for the last time and headed back to the towels just as Nadia was waking up.

"I just had an awful dream." Nadia glowered at Phee. "And now I hate you."

Fawn peered up at Phoenix, surprised.

"She doesn't mean it, Fawn." To Nadia, she said, "And what terrible, horrible, no-good rotten thing did I do to you in your dream?"

Nadia's lips thinned into a prissy straight line. "It had to do with Saul."

Phee laughed. "As if."

"You know ..." Nadia ducked her chin so she could peer at Nadia over her shades. "I bet I'm way more intuitive than you give me credit for. I don't think I was so way off. You guys have been acting weird lately—"

"Weird how?"

"Weird in general. I don't know," Nadia said with a shrug. "Like, one day I'll see you two whispering and then you avoid each other for days. That 'weird' kind of 'weird.'"

"It's always about you."

"When you avoid him? That's about me too?" Nadia took her sunglasses off altogether now. Phee braced herself as her best friend carefully folded the frames and tucked them in the case. Whenever Nadia got all deliberate and calculating like this, it was always just before she was about to blow.

"This is a stupid conversation."

"So now you're calling me stupid?"

Fawn tugged Phee's arm. She glanced down at her sister, her thin arms covered in goose bumps. "Here." She picked up a towel and folded her into it, rubbing her dry.

"Are you?"

"This is so ridiculous," Phee said as she towelled Fawn's hair. "You had a dream. It's not real."

"Your dad says God can speak to us through dreams."

"My dad says God can speak to us through pretty much anything."

"Well, maybe God was telling me to watch my back." Nadia gathered her book and lotion and water bottle and hat all in a jumble in her arms and sprang up. "Maybe God was telling me to mind who my friends really are."

"Oh, please." Phee rolled her eyes. "Give it up, drama queen."

"Don't fight!" Fawn yelped from under the towel.

Nadia leaned in and whispered harshly. "And don't try to tell me you're planning my birthday because that's *months* away. And you know that I hate surprises. Hate them." She shoved her things into her bag and stalked off across the sand, her flip-flops clutched in one hand, the bag in the other. Phee was just about to run after her, but then she spotted Tariq running across the road, coming from the train station. He was alone. Nadia slowed, confused. Phee dropped the towel, sensing at once that something was wrong.

"There's Tariq!" Fawn took off in his direction, but he ran right past her. Phee thought he was coming to see her. Later she would remember feeling a tremendous sense of relief that she'd switched the soiled sundress for a clean one. Later she would look back on that easy sense of relief as being the last easy thing for a very long time.

Tariq stopped when he reached Nadia. He grabbed her shoulders as though he was about to shake her. In those few seconds, Phee knew it was bad. She thought of Saul, of course. No recon. His precarious web of lies. Maybe the guys found him out? Maybe he'd been seized? Relocated to where he was supposed to belong. Tariq said only a few words before Nadia crumpled to the sand. It was Saul! Something terrible had happened! Phee broke into a run, but no matter how she willed her legs to go faster, she felt as if the distance between her and Nadia stretched out forever, as if she'd never get to her friend's side when so clearly she needed her the most.

"What's wrong?" Fawn fell into step beside her.

"I think it's Saul." Phee kept running, the sand slowing her down. At last she was at Nadia's side. She fell to her knees beside her and folded Nadia into a tight embrace. "What is it?" She looked up at Tariq. His mirrored sunglasses prevented her from reading his eyes. She saw that his hands were clenched into fists, that he was holding himself apart from whatever had happened. "What happened?" Phee could hear the panic in her voice. "It's Saul, isn't it? He's hurt? What *happened*?"

"Oh, honey ..." Nadia shifted to face Phee. Now it was Nadia hugging *her*. "Everything will be okay. He'll be as good as new. Better, even."

"What?" Phee's heart crumpled, taking her breath with her. "What are you talking about?"

Tariq opened his mouth, but the words didn't come at first. "Phoenix ... I came ... there's been ..." With a deep breath, he tried again. "It's your brother. Gryph is dead."

ACCIDENT, MAYBE

Phoenix had no recollection of how she got home. One moment she was gasping for breath, feeling as if Tariq had punched her hard in the gut, and then the next thing she knew she was stumbling up the back steps, desperate to be with her parents.

"Mom?" She flung open the door. No answer. "Dad?"

"You have to slow your breathing down, Phee. You're going to pass out." Nadia gripped her hand. "Maybe they're down at Chrysalis already."

Tariq came in last, carrying Fawn, who clung to him, bawling. She looked even smaller in her polka-dotted bathing suit, her head resting on his shoulder, as if she were just a toddler. Phoenix lifted her from him and held her. She sat on a kitchen chair with her little sister in her lap, not sure what to do. Fawn whimpered, snot running down her face. Nadia found a napkin and wiped her cheeks dry.

"They wouldn't leave without me."

"Check your phone. And the lync." When Phee was clearly not able to move from where she sat, Nadia nodded at Tariq. "You do it."

Tariq crossed the kitchen to the little desk where Eva kept the household organized. Under the glass surface of the desk the lync screen swam with the dim clouds of its standby mode. Tariq ran a finger across it to wake it up. "They're at your grandparents'," he said after reading the message Eva had left. "They'll be back—"

The front door slammed open. "Phoenix? Fawn!"

Eva ran into the room and drew her two daughters into her arms with a sob. Oscar came in behind her, his face drawn with worry. Phoenix raised her eyes to greet her father and knew immediately that things were far worse than they should have been. Her unshakable father looked deeply, deeply shaken.

"What's going on?" Phoenix set Fawn down and stood. Fawn clung to Eva's leg. Eva sank into the chair. They should already be down at Chrysalis, collecting his things, sending him to the recon lab with a kiss and a prayer.

"They say he jumped."

Tariq hadn't told her anything yet. Phoenix had no idea what her mother was talking about. She looked from Oscar to Eva to Tariq and back again. "What?"

When Oscar finally spoke, it was with his minister's voice. Calm, steady, and careful. "He was hit by a train. At the Steveston Pier."

BY THE TIME her parents had to leave to meet with Chrysalis, Fawn had fallen asleep, exhausted from all her crying and an afternoon in the sun at the beach. Tariq carried her upstairs, Phoenix trailing behind him, to tuck her into bed. She folded down the quilt and sheet, the cheerful pink rabbits on the linens at odds with her heavy heart. Tariq set Fawn on the bed and drew the sheet up to her shoulders. He reached for the quilt, but Phoenix stopped him.

"It's too hot."

Tariq nodded and then reached for her hand. He pulled her out of Fawn's room and steered her to hers. He sat her on the bed and then retreated to the doorway, not sure what to do with himself.

"Tell me what really happened." Phoenix glanced up, eyes rimmed red from all the crying. "Please?"

He'd told her parents before he'd come to the beach. And her parents had told her. Oscar had described what had happened as if he were ministering to one of his parish families. In plain language. No euphemisms or platitudes. As he'd spoken, Phoenix's shock and confusion had lifted briefly to let in a tiny slice of anger at her father. But almost as quickly as it had occurred to her, it vanished, and she was only thankful for her father's steadfastness. His calm amid such uncertainty. She wanted the story from Tariq now, though. She wanted to hear it from someone who'd been there. From someone who'd *seen*.

"We were on the way to the arcade—" Tariq started.

"From where?"

"Me and Huy and Neko had been at my place. We were meeting Saul and Gryph."

"Where?"

"At Steveston. They'd been in the Industrial Sector."

"Why?"

"They ... I don't know. It doesn't matter." Tariq took a step into the room and leaned against the wall, just inside the door. "I told your parents that he tripped."

But it did matter! Phoenix wanted to know everything. She wanted to hear Tariq's version, and then the other boys' too, in their own words. And she wanted to see the security footage too. Any pictures bystanders might have captured. People were always taking pictures of Gryph. Why should this have been any different? A sudden thought catapulted her off the bed. She brought up her own lync screen at her desk and drew her finger to the News icon.

"I told your parents that he tripped—" Tariq insisted, watching her.

The screen darkened momentarily and then lit up mid-newscast.

"*World-famous Chrysalis-sponsored athlete Gryphon Nicholson-Lalonde was struck and killed by a train earlier today.*" As the newscaster spoke, the screen shifted to play footage of the train station up in one corner. Yellow tape was strung from wall to rail, and a knot of Crimcor agents were down on the tracks, on their knees, combing the ground. *"An official statement is expected later today from the Chrysalis-Crimcor joint task force."*

Phoenix narrowed her eyes at Tariq. "What does Crimcor have to do with it?"

Tariq reached over her shoulder and paused the image. On one side of the screen the lips of the carefully coiffed newscaster were frozen open, her eyebrows furrowed in appropriate sobriety and concern. The little side box showing the agents searching was frozen too, the camera in mid-swing toward a massive pool of blood on the far side of the tracks. The side nearest the wall. Where no one had cause to be. Ever. No doors opened on that side at that station, and the rail was normally electrified. It would've been shut down only after the incident so that the Crimcor agents could investigate. So that Gryph's body could be collected. Phee looked hard. She didn't know that station well, had only been to it that one time the night of the rave, and on a Saturday it wouldn't have been busy. Businesses in that district were Monday to Friday. So Gryph couldn't have lost his footing in a pushing crowd.

"He didn't trip, though. Did he?"

"No." Tariq's reply was almost a whisper. "He didn't trip."

"Of course he didn't! He has the balance of a superhero!" Phoenix kept her eyes on the screen as she spoke. "I don't believe for one moment that he tripped. And my parents won't either." She stabbed at the screen, breaking it from its pause.

"There has been no word from Chrysalis, but they are expected to launch the investigation into this tragic incident as soon as this afternoon. Again"— here the woman paused for effect—*"we are saddened to be bringing you the news that much-loved athlete and world-class champion Gryphon Nicholson-Lalonde is dead for the first time at the age of eighteen."*

A file photo filled the screen. Gryphon and his lopsided grin, the bright blue of his eyes catching the sun at the surfing competition. His hair was slicked back, damp, and the gold medal around his neck caught the hot glint of the sun.

"Why is she talking like that?" Phee's heart sank. "Why hasn't she mentioned his recon? What really happened, Tariq?"

Tariq stood very still. "I didn't see anything until it had already happened."

"Phee?" Nadia stood in the door, hugging herself. "You okay?"

"No!" Phoenix shut the screen. She pointed an accusatory finger at Tariq. "He says he didn't see anything. I know he's lying."

Nadia drew Phoenix back to the bed and sat beside her, her arm slung across her shoulders. "Everything will be okay."

"It might not be, Nadia."

"He'll be as good as new. Better, even. I bet they'll put titanium kneecaps in, seeing as he's cracked both. And a new whatever cuff."

"Rotator cuff."

"Yeah. And maybe they'll clear up his acne problem too."

"He has perfect skin." Phee smiled sadly at Nadia's attempt at humour. "And you know it." A horrible thought occurred to her. Gryph had been destroyed. He hadn't quietly died as she had the first time, her skin duskier until her lungs finally gave up. And he didn't die intact, as she had the second time when she'd drowned. He'd died violently. With pain and blood and terror. She opened her mouth, a mute protest against the images playing in her mind. The train, the screeching brakes, the thump, the fall, the blood. The screams. She felt a meltdown cresting inside, but then Nadia spoke and broke the swell.

"Everything *is* going to be fine"—Nadia squeezed her in a hug— "and you know it." Any remnants of the girls' earlier spat had entirely vanished, and Nadia smiled at her now with eyes filled with equal parts fear and support. "Honest."

Awkwardness filled the space between the girls and Tariq. They looked up at him, waiting for him to chime in and agree that everything would be fine, but he just fixed his eyes on the floor, his hands shoved resolutely into his pockets.

"Tariq!" Phee shouted. "Say something!"

But Tariq turned in to the hall. He took the stairs so quietly that Phee wasn't sure if he was just lurking in the hall or had left. When she stepped into the hall to see, he was gone. "He left."

"He didn't." Nadia's eyes widened in surprise. "That prick!" She ran out of the room and stomped down the stairs and out the front door. Phee hurried down the hall to Fawn's room and looked out the front window. Fawn was fast asleep, her cheeks still flushed from crying, arms buried under her pillow. Nadia had caught up to Tariq at the corner. Phee quietly pushed the window all the way open and leaned out, but she couldn't hear them. She could only see Nadia scolding him. And he stood there, taking it, shoulders curved in defeat. And then Nadia's voice rose into a yell and Phee could hear her clearly.

"You get back in there now and *talk* to her!" she yelled at him, her fists planted on her hips. "Now!"

As Tariq backed away, he pulled his hands from his pockets and raised them in submission as he shook his head, refusing.

"Don't you walk away from me, Tariq!" Nadia was the way she'd been any number of the times when she yelled at Saul during an argument. And Saul always stayed, always gave as good as he got. But this time it was Tariq, the boy of few words. He kept walking. At the end of the block he broke from his slow pace and headed for the station at a dead run.

NADIA GLANCED BACK at the house and saw Phoenix at the window. She shrugged in bewildered apology. Phee waved for her to come back and then went downstairs to meet her at the door.

Nadia started talking when she was halfway up the path. "I told him he had to tell us and that we deserved to hear it from him. I told him we know something is fishy." Nadia was at the door now. She looked at Phoenix with sad eyes. "We do know something is fishy, right? This is not happening like it should."

"You're right. It's not. The news is talking like he's never coming back."

The girls retreated to the kitchen, where Nadia poured them each a glass of iced tea from the pitcher in the fridge. Phee stared at the amber liquid. Had it only been that morning when her mother made it? Had it only been that morning when she and Nadia were arranging date squares on china platters and cutting crusts off cucumber sandwiches? Had it only been—and now she glanced at the clock above the stove—not even an hour since Nadia had stalked off in a huff, convinced Phee and Saul were up to something?

Saul. And the others. "What about Neko? He was there."

"He won't talk," Nadia said. "Not if Tariq told him not to."

"We can make him talk. He's your brother. Call him."

Nadia brought her phone to her ear. "No answer."

"Try Saul."

"I did." Nadia set the phone on the table. "When you were upstairs. No answer."

"Text him, then. And Huy. Copy them all on it. Tell them I want to talk to them!"

"I already texted Saul a hundred million times." With a wary eye on Phee she picked up the phone again and started a new text. "I'll try again, but they're not answering. I'm telling you, Phee. They're in some kind of brotherly lockdown. Neko too."

"Then get your parents to call Neko and order him to come home." Phee stood. She paced the kitchen, cutting through the same slice of sunlight, back and forth, back and forth. The chime at the front door sounded and her grandparents shuffled in, neither of them looking all that concerned.

Her grandmother sat her back at the table and made her and Nadia bologna sandwiches with fixings she'd brought from her house. White bread and cheap bologna, a bag of ripple chips. Three things Phee's parents never let them eat. Phee almost cried at her grandma's small comforting gestures.

"Now don't you pay any attention to the news," her grand-mother said as she set a pickle and a pile of chips alongside each sandwich. "There's just been some kind of misunderstanding. That's all. It'll get sorted out."

Her grandfather sat at the head of the table in his gardening clothes, dirt under his nails, his filthy sunhat misshapen and faded atop his bald head. "Misunderstanding," he echoed. "That's all." Phee's grandma wetted a towel and went about scrubbing her husband's hands clean from his morning puttering around in the garden.

"That's right." Phee's grandma patted her shoulder as she passed on her way back to the sink. "This will all work out just fine. Look at you, dear. You're the perfect example to us all. You reconned beautifully. Twice."

Except that Phee didn't remember a thing from before she was six. That was not a beautiful recon. And if she died again, that was it. Some perfect example.

"Reconned beautifully," her grandfather mumbled through a mouthful of sandwich.

"You just wait and see. Six weeks, and he'll be in the news again for another one of his competitions. Getting another blue ribbon or what have you. All this fuss is over nothing. We're blessed to be three-pers for a reason. Your job, Phoenix, dear, is to stay calm and help keep your mother calm."

"Calm," her grandfather echoed.

"I'll try, Grandma."

But her grandmother was wrong. If there was an investigation, it meant only one thing. Someone at Chrysalis or Crimcor had reason to believe that Gryph's death was no accident.

What if he'd jumped?

Phee felt the colour drain from her cheeks.

Chrysalis did not recon suicides. Ever.

And it was widely known that no champion athlete could ever have been reconned, due to the likelihood and opportunity for performance-enhancing adjustments. What if he had jumped?

To get out of his contract once and for all?

What if he'd staged his own death?

No, no, no. No. Phee shook her head, arguing with herself. Gryph would not have killed himself. No way.

And she'd never believe that he'd fallen.

Which meant that he had to have been pushed.

And if they thought he was pushed, then who pushed him? If they caught whoever did it, they'd be decommed. Decommissioned. Chrysalis's tidy term for the death penalty.

No matter how this went, it was not going to go easily.

Phee glanced up at her grandmother, who smiled at her. Phee knew her grandma was going for a reassuring smile, but to Phee it looked like poorly disguised panic.

"Everything will be okay." Still with the smile. "You'll see, dear."

Her grandmother was a smart woman. She was hiding behind this homely nurturer act only because she was scared. Well, they all were! And should be! Phee wanted to grab her grandmother by her collar and march her out of the house. She didn't want to be placated. She didn't want to be soothed. She wanted answers! Her grandma turned to the sink, and Phee glowered at her grandma's back.

"Don't you—" Her grandfather's tone was angry. Phee realized he'd seen her glare at his wife and didn't like it. She couldn't tell when he was as good as oblivious or when he caught on to something with fleeting lucidity.

"Sorry, Granddad."

"Calm." He patted her hand, still frowning. "Okay?"

"Yes, Granddad." Phee couldn't stand to sit still for one moment longer. "Grandma? You'll stay here and look after Fawn?"

Her grandma smiled at her. "Of course, dear."

"Come on." She grabbed Nadia's hand.

Nadia went along with her until they were out of the house. "We should stay here. Your parents will be back soon."

"With what?" Phee felt frantic. "Not with answers! Not real answers, anyway! We have to go find the boys." She pulled Nadia across the green, heading for the train station. Nadia followed reluctantly.

"We shouldn't—"

"Hurry!" At the top of the stairs Phee could hear the whine of a train coming to a stop. She took them two at a time until she reached the platform. The five-car train stretched the length of the station like a polished serpent. Heavy. Predatory. Nadia caught up to her and stood at her side while the warning bell sounded and the automated voice announced the train's departure.

A terrible screech. A crash. Blood. So much blood.

Phee couldn't move. She closed her eyes, willing away the images. The expression on Gryph's face when he realized he couldn't get out of the way. He would've tried. He would've scrambled up from where he'd fallen and tried to get a leg up. But there hadn't been the time. Or so the boys claimed.

INVESTIGATION

Phee wanted to sit them all down and grill them until they told the truth, but the boys were nowhere to be found. Phee and Nadia checked the Balmoral, the arcade, and even went as far as to make their way to the Steveston Pier, but Crimcor had the entire train station taped off. The train slowed well before the station, switched tracks, and took a detour. The girls had to get off at the next station to turn around. As they were waiting for the train Phee glanced up at the layout of the station, at the security cameras in particular. All the stations were the same, right down to doorways and staircases. There were ten cameras in total, three at the far end, where it had happened.

According to the news reports, the cameras on that end of the station platform had been destroyed moments before the collision, and the ones elsewhere on the platform wouldn't have caught anything relevant. The boys were not talking, even to Crimcor. There were few bystanders, and all of them had been at the other end of the platform, and claimed that they hadn't seen anything or noticed anything was wrong until the train screeched to a stop and the boys screamed for help.

"You can appreciate the situation." This from the Chrysalis recon rep, sitting in the Nicholson-Lalonde living room not even twenty-four hours after Gryph's death. Oscar and Eva stared hollowly at the man. He was wearing a suit jacket, despite the heat, but he wasn't sweating. He'd rung the doorbell not ten minutes earlier, and now here he was telling Oscar and Eva that they were investigating the possibility of suicide. "Of course," he carried on while the grief-numbed parents kept staring at him, "we'll go ahead with the recon process until we can accurately determine the events of yesterday afternoon."

"Thank God," Oscar said with an enormous sigh. "Thank God for that."

"And when will we know?" Eva fiddled with the locket at her throat. It was a tiny triptych, each section with a photo of one of her children as newborns.

"I can't say at this point." The Chrysalis rep tried for a sympathetic smile and failed. It was more condescending than anything, or that's what Phee thought. She sat across from her parents, listening intently, holding the one hand that wanted to wipe off his smile with her other hand. "Soon, we all hope. We love Gryphon as much as you do—"

"What a retarded thing to say," Phee blurted. Oscar caught her with a warning look. "Well, it is! Gryph is just a cash cow to them. He's not a part of their family—"

"Actually—"

"Don't you dare say he's part of the Chrysalis *family*."

"I was going to say that." The man straightened, indignant. "And I still will. He *is* a part of the Chrysalis family."

Scoffing, Phee looked away, disgusted. This man clearly hadn't talked to Lex lately. She bit her lower lip, willing herself to shut up before she could make things worse.

Eva caught Phee's glance and gave her tiny, appreciative smile before turning her attention back to the man. "What measures are you taking to determine what exactly happened?" Eva sounded

exhausted because she was. No one had slept well the night before—
except perhaps Fawn—but no one had a worse night than Eva, who
hadn't slept at all. After Phee and Nadia couldn't find the boys,
they'd stayed up most of the night, poring over the news podcasts
and online frenzy surrounding her brother's death. Her mother had
spent the night in the kitchen doing the same. Phee had finally
fallen asleep sometime around three, but according to Oscar, Eva
hadn't been to bed at all. That morning her eyes were puffy, with
shadows rubbed underneath, and there was a tired huskiness in her
voice. She clutched a handkerchief in her fist and leaned forward.
"How can there be any doubt? He was *hungry* for life."

The rep straightened his papers, readying to leave. "I can't say
anything more on the matter at this point."

"Where's Lex?" Eva reached out for the man and caught his
pants as he stood. She held a crease tight in her fist and implored
with a catch in her throat. "Why can't we see him? He's been his
agent for years. He can tell you about Gryph. He can tell you
Gryph would never do such a thing. He's a Chrysalis agent, and he
knows Gryph the way we do. You would trust Lex, wouldn't you?"

Phee raised an eyebrow at her mother. Had she forgotten Lex's
recent suspicions? The scene in the hospital? She shouldn't include
Lex in the picture at all.

"Mother ..." Phee tried to infuse the one word with as much
warning as she could.

"Dr. Nicholson-Lalonde, please." The rep, clearly mortified by
Eva's desperate display, stood stock-still, unsure of what to do.

"Dear." Oscar put his hand over his wife's and gently loosened
her grip.

"Lex will not be involved in this process." The man backed away
with a start. "Until further notice, any and all communications
with Chrysalis go through me. Not Lex." He smoothed his pant leg
as he backed toward the door.

Phoenix's eyes blurred across the pamphlet in her lap. He'd
handed them out to her and her parents on his arrival. "When a

loved one dies ... what you should know about the recon process."
There was a picture of a woman on the front, smiling down at a
framed photo of a man, handsome in a soap-opera-star way.

The rep was still droning on. "We'll send updates to your lync,
coded only for you and your wife to read." This made Phee glance
up. She wanted to read them too, of course. Oscar winked at her.
He'd let her read them. "Our aim is to have a conclusion by the end
of the week."

Eva nodded. "In time for the DNA test."

The man ignored her demonstration of inside knowledge. The
DNA test needed to happen within ten days of the patient's death.
Within hours of the death, the stem-cell sample that had been
taken from his umbilical cord blood at birth would've been
retrieved from the cryopreservation tanks, kept two storeys under-
ground in an earthquake-proof lab. The sample was allowed to
thaw slowly so that the cryoprotectant fluid could gradually be
replaced by the accelerator. After ten days, if the cells had multi-
plied accordingly, the recon could proceed. If not, the process was
started with another stem-cell batch from the same cord blood. It
had never occurred to Phee before just how many steps there were
to the recon process. Just how many things could go wrong. She'd
always had this rather magical idea of it. One day you're dead. The
next you're walking out the front doors of Chrysalis into the arms
of your loving family, returned to life like a fairy-tale princess who's
been kissed by the prince.

Or in Gryph's case, the prince himself.

Phee's phone vibrated in her pocket, breaking her macabre
thoughts. She slipped it out and read the message from Nadia.
"Neko's home!"

He'd stayed out all night, much to his parents' concern and
anger. None of the boys had gone home after questioning at
Crimcor headquarters. They hadn't answered any calls or
texts—except Saul did send one text to Nadia. All it said was
"We're okay." What was that supposed to mean? And what had

they been up to all night? Getting drunk? Sitting on the bluff and staring out at the ocean, not talking? Dodging further questioning from Crimcor? Phee had no idea what they'd been up to. Now was her chance to talk to one of them. Even if it was only Neko.

HE WASN'T OPENING his door. Nadia banged on it again.

"Open this door or we will break it down!"

No response.

"Come on, Neko." Phee leaned her forehead against the death metal posters and KEEP OUT signs. At home, Neko seemed even younger than when he hung out with Gryph and the guys. Nadia said Phee used to change his diaper when he was little, but Phee didn't remember. "Let us in."

Still nothing. The two girls slid to the floor and sat cross-legged, blocking the way. "He can go out the window," Nadia mentioned after they'd been sitting there for a while. "He always sneaks out that way."

"I know. But do you think he would?"

"Maybe." Nadia nodded. "He stayed out all night. His friend is dead. He's upset. Just because he's grounded doesn't mean he's going to stay put. Look who he hangs around with."

"Neko!" Phee reached up behind her and pounded on the door. "If you don't open this door I'll get an axe and chop it into little bits."

Another moment passed, and then they heard him. "We don't own an axe." His voice sounded so small and scared that Nadia immediately started crying.

"Oh, Neko, come on, honey," she begged through the thin wood. "Open the door!"

They heard footsteps and then the lock releasing. The girls scrambled to their feet. Neko opened the door a crack. He was pale, his eyes bloodshot. He stared at the girls.

"Neko—"

"I'm not talking." His head was bowed, his black hair falling across his face. "None of us are. So don't even bother."

Nadia was immediately indignant. "You owe Phee some answers."

He kept silent, but Phee could see his reserve shaking. He'd been in with Gryph and his friends only since the New Year, after chasing Gryph's shadow his whole life. "Sorry, Phee." His voice was even smaller. "I'm sorry."

"What happened?" she asked as gently as she could, setting aside her impatience and trying for kindness instead. "You can tell us. We won't tell the guys that you said anything."

"He tripped."

Phee stared at him, her arms crossed. "He did not."

Neko tried to shut the door. "Oh, no you don't." Nadia stuck her foot in. "Tell us what happened."

"I can't."

"You can!" Nadia tried to shove her way into his room, but he resisted, barring the door with his shoulder. "You can tell us, Neko. We promise we won't tell."

"I just can't."

Phee reached for one of Neko's hands, and he let her take it. She held it in both of hers and looked him straight in the eye. "My brother ... my brother is dead, Neko. He's dead, and I need to know what happened. I *need* to know."

With a glance at each of the girls, Neko relaxed his grip on the door.

"Now, talk." With a graceless heave, Nadia pushed the door open, overpowering her little brother. Phee followed her into the room. The shades were drawn, and it stank of dirty clothes. Empty plates scattered the floor, and the desk was heaped with junk. There was nowhere to sit but the bed, but the sheets reeked of teenage boy, and she didn't want to sit.

Phee glanced at her watch. "Neko, we don't have much time."

He plopped onto the bed. He was only wearing pyjama bottoms, and his skinny torso just added to how little he looked. He was hardly more than a kid, yet he thought he was as mature as his older friends. "I told you. He tripped."

"Tariq told you to say that, didn't he?"

He shrugged.

"You were going to tell us something and you changed your mind." Phee glared at him. "Didn't you?"

"No." It was a tiny word, but he'd managed to pack it full of remorse.

"What really happened?" Phee knelt amid the mess beside the bed, all the better to plead with him. "You have to tell us so that we can help, Neko. If we don't convince Chrysalis that it was an accident, he won't be reconned. He'll be dead forever. No more Gryph. You'd do that to my family?"

With an anguished groan, Neko turned to the wall. But he talked. "We were just standing around, goofing off, and then the train was coming, and he just tripped. Is that so hard to believe? That he tripped? That the perfect Gryphon Nicholson-Lalonde actually tripped?"

"The cameras were broken. Who did that, I wonder?"

His answer took a beat too long. "There was a drug deal. Okay?"

Nadia grabbed for her brother's bony shoulder. "Drugs?"

"Yeah." He looked up at her and then at the wall again. "That's why we busted the cameras."

"So"—Phee looked at the ceiling, tired of Neko's lies—"that's your story and you're sticking to it?"

Neko shrugged. "Yeah."

"A drug deal. What kind of drugs?"

"Some performance-enhancing shit ... you know. Roids or whatever."

"Gryph gets tested all the time, Neko." Phee glared at him. "*All the time*. He doesn't do steroids, or anything else, for that matter. You have to come up with something better than that."

"Look, I don't know what it was about, okay?"

"You're full of shit, Neko."

"So what if I am?" Neko sat up and glared at them. "Apparently you're not going to believe me no matter what I say!"

"Neko ..." Nadia grabbed her brother's earlobe and twisted it hard. "If I find out you're messing around with that crap I will kill you three times in quick succession so that you will really and truly be dead, once and for all."

"Like Gryph will be." Phee heard herself say the words, but still they shocked her. "Like your friend and my brother and my parents' son will be if you guys don't start telling the truth."

BUT WHAT IF the truth did them no good? Phee wandered home alone; Nadia's parents had asked her to stay home with her brother. Phee waited for the train on the platform, but when she heard it coming in the distance, she was gripped by a sudden, horrible panic that sent her running down the stairs and into the courtyard under the station. There was no other way home, but she didn't want to get on that train. If she had any money she could hire a private shuttle, but she hadn't even thought to bring her wallet with her.

It had been easier on the way here, when she was distracted by the thought of interrogating Neko. But now, after a fruitless visit with him—he was clearly in shock from the events of the day before—Phee could only obsess about the train. She spun around slowly, glancing at each safety feature. The cameras, the yellow painted line at the edge of the platform that set off an alarm when you stepped over it, the sensors on the track that shut off the current when there was an impact.

Impact.

He would've been in so much pain. Her stomach knotted sympathetically, and she had to double over to keep from passing out. He would've been afraid. Even Gryph. He hadn't meant to die. She knew this to be true. Now she only had to convince Chrysalis.

WHAT WILLIS KNOWS

Phee got off at the last stop before the Shores and walked the rest of the way. She wanted to collect her thoughts, and she knew home wouldn't let her do that. Not with her parents dripping with sadness, and confused little Fawn with all her questions and all the friends and neighbours with their casseroles and plates of cookies and good intentions.

The sky was clear and blue, and the air off the ocean smelled salty and clean. Phee wanted nothing more than to run into the waves and float on her back with the pelicans bobbing alongside her, none of them with a care in the world. She walked on an old road that had been made into a pedestrian boulevard that linked Pacific Heights with the Shores. It wasn't used much, so she had the wide stretch of concrete to herself. Until she cleared the last turn and caught sight of the gated entrance to the Shores. A knot of private shuttles and people blocked her view of the little hut that housed the security guard and their bank of closed-circuit televisions. More media. She could see the station logos and the robot-like antennas that reached up from the shuttle roofs, twisting in constant search of a better satellite connection. Phee had two choices. Walk all the way back to Pacific

Heights and get the train, or carry on. The sun was high, and she was hot, and she had no water and she was tired. So really, she had only one wise choice. She kept walking, all the while trying to see who was on shift in the little hut. And then someone in the throng spotted her.

"It's his sister!" A man with a spray-on tan jogged up to her, his whitened teeth gleaming in the sunlight. Out of breath, he shoved a tiny microphone at her. "Tom Archer, KLTV News. What do you have to say about yesterday's tragic events?" His cameraman caught up to them, one eye squeezed shut as he zoomed in on her startled expression. And then, within moments and before she could think of anything to say, she was swarmed on all sides.

"What's the word from Chrysalis?"

"Recon, or no recon?"

Phee felt the chill of panic race up her spine. "I don't—"

"We understand there were several witnesses, and that they've all been questioned by Crimcor ... is this correct?"

Where was the security guard? Phee strained to get a look beyond the designer-clad shoulders and carefully coiffed, TV-ready hairdos. The door to the hut was open.

"Did your brother express any hints that he might've been suicidal? Was the pressure getting to him?"

"No comment," Phee whispered, with a catch in her throat. These people were the same media hounds who had nothing but praise and smiles and congratulations for her brother before yesterday. The very same people had been invited into his dressing room and to countless podium presentations, and now they were no better than vultures. Phee felt the panic melt into rage.

"Get out of my way," she growled.

She could see the security guard Willis running toward her now, his utility belt bouncing against his bulk. At last! But still the reporters pushed in on her, tightening their scrum.

"Will your parents appeal Chrysalis's decision if they rule Gryph's death a suicide?"

Phee sensed something inside her snap, as if she'd cracked a bone. "Get out of my way!"

"Just a couple of questions—"

"How is your family coping amid—"

Phee elbowed the woman who blocked her way. She recognized her shimmering copper hair and plump lips from her prime-time podcast. "Leave us alone! All of you!" The woman stumbled back, but was kept from falling by the horde pressing up behind her. "He'll be reconned—"

The woman had hardly missed a beat. She shoved her microphone in Phee's face. "But reports leaked by Chrysalis state that—"

"Everyone back away!" Willis's bellow cut the flurry of questions. He pushed into the crowd and grabbed Phee with his enormous hands and dragged her out of the chaos. Phee let herself be led away by him, his beefy arm shielding her the way she sometimes did for Fawn. How she wished she were Fawn right now … too little to understand. Too little to be compelled to make it right.

"Where were you?" Phee cried, as Willis hustled her into his air-conditioned hut.

"Helping Rawlins at the other gate." Willis steered her to a chair before taking his own seat, panting, a sheen of sweat on his brow. "We thought all the jerkoffs were at his gate, and then I get the call that they're over here too." He swivelled to pour Phee and himself each a glass of water. "Now, you tell me. Why didn't you take the train all the way home? What were you doing walking on your own?"

"There's no law against it."

"No," Willis replied, "but plenty would say it's not the brightest idea, especially now. All things considered. What your family's going through."

"What my family's going through?" Phee almost laughed. "What *is* my family going through?"

Willis wisely let the question float between them, unanswered.

"I just wanted some fresh air," Phee said. "Okay, I admit it. It was stupid. I should've taken the train."

"That's good to hear." He reached over and rapped gently on her skull. "Nice to know that you still have your brains in there."

"My brother doesn't." Phee heard herself say the words and couldn't stop the rest. They were as unstoppable as the train would've been. "His brains are all over the tracks at the Steveston Pier station."

Willis sucked in a breath as he wiped his face with a handkerchief. "And once this is all worked out and he's reconned, his brains will be exactly where they're supposed to be. New and improved." He heaved himself onto his feet with a groan and offered her a kind smile. "Now, come on. Let's get you home."

"You're not worried, are you?" Phee didn't budge. "Why aren't you worried?"

"I know your brother well enough to know that he didn't jump. So once the controversy is sorted out, all will be well."

"What else do you know about him?"

"What do you mean?" Willis asked brightly, his expression betraying his attempts at appearing carefree.

"You let him come and go, don't you?"

Willis stared at her, his lips parted, mid-thought.

"Well, you do, right? How else would he get in and out?"

He crossed his arms. "And if I did?"

"Tell me what you know. Like, where he went—"

"Don't know."

"Who he went with?"

Willis paused. "His friends, of course. All good boys. All of them."

"And what did they get up to?"

"You'd have to ask them that, kiddo." Another pause, during which Phee watched his eyes shift away from her, fix nervously on a spot on the floor for a long moment before returning to meet her inquisitive gaze. "That would be a good place to start."

"Start what?" Phee was really alert now, and anxious.

"Proving that this whole idea of him killing himself is ridiculous and unfounded." Willis fiddled with the keys to his golf cart. "Let me take you home. Okay?"

As Willis drove her home, Phee was full of questions she knew better than to voice. She eyed Willis out of the corner of her vision, curious about him for the first time. Normally she didn't give him a second thought. He was just the kind, constant presence at the south gate, but now she knew he was much more than that. He knew something. And he wasn't telling her.

She was grateful to see him leave after he dropped her off. She was ready for a break from the mystery. Her father ran down from the porch to meet her, worry creasing his already tired face.

"I was going to come get you, but Fawn—"

"I'm okay, Dad." Phee hopped out of the cart and let her dad fold her into his arms. "It's just the media. I can handle them."

"You shouldn't have to." Oscar thanked Willis and then walked Phee up the steps and sat her on the porch swing. "I'm keeping an eye on your grandfather. Fawn too. She's upstairs with Lana, playing. Your mother and grandma are down at Chrysalis. We managed to get them to agree to start things in motion for your brother's recon."

"Fawn's *playing*? With the neighbour kid? Like everything is *normal*?"

"She doesn't understand." Oscar tightened his arm around her shoulders. "She figures he'll be back soon as good as new."

"And he will, right?"

Oscar was silent. He focused his gaze on the green, where a group of boys a little younger than Gryphon were tossing a football back and forth with the laziness that tends to accompany hot summer afternoons. Phee wished she was somewhere else. Far away. With Nadia and the boys. Back at the rave, when Tariq came to dance with her. Back when everything was normal and her crush on Tariq was her biggest concern.

"Dad?" Her father's silence unnerved her more than she could describe. It meant his hope was fading. "Daddy?"

Finally, he spoke. "God's will be done, on earth as it is in heaven."

Phee felt herself tense up. "What are you saying?"

Oscar took her chin in his hand and lifted her eyes to his. "You know what I'm saying."

"You're right. I do." Phee stood up abruptly, sending the porch swing shimmying backwards. "And you better not talk to Mom like that or you'll be all alone in this house, and she and Fawn and I will be camped out at Grandma and Grandpa's again."

As if he'd been listening in, Phee's grandfather pushed the front door open and stepped out onto the porch. "Oscar? Phee?" he asked, as if trying out the names for the first time. "Where's the kettle?"

"It's too hot to boil water, Granddad." With a warning glance at her father, Phee took her grandfather's arm. "I'll make you some lemonade instead, okay?"

"What a nice idea." Her grandfather twisted away, though, and went down the steps, minding each one carefully. "I'll go tell Gryphon to come in. He'll know where the kettle is." He headed off in the direction of the green, focused on the little boys kicking a soccer ball at the far end.

"I'll go get him." Oscar gave Phee a sad smile. "You go make us that lemonade."

AS PHEE JUICED THE LEMONS, her phone beeped with a text message. From Saul. "Need 2 talk. Meet me @ arcade. Now." She texted him that she'd be there in half an hour. She made up a story for Oscar about the ever-needy Nadia, and took off at a sprint for the train station. She was so eager to hear what Saul had to tell her that she didn't think of Gryph being hit by the train, not even once while she was racing on one herself, heading for the shopping district. She pushed her way out of the train at her stop and took off running again, this time across the promenade to the arcade.

The steady soundtrack of electronic gun blasts and squealing tires was almost soothing to her. This place was so normal in the midst of all the recent strangeness. Teens crowded each machine, watching friends fire on terrorists or race rally cars. The smell of popcorn met her as she made her way to the back, where the little concession stand was, surrounded by a few tables and chairs. She expected to find Saul here, but didn't. She made another circuit of the arcade, searching intently through the shadows and colourful bursts of light cast by the games. He wasn't there. She stopped to reread the text message in case she'd gotten it wrong. "Need 2 talk. Meet me @ arcade." She retraced her steps back to the concession to talk to the pimply-faced girl who worked there.

"Have you seen Gryph or his friends today?"

"Why you asking?" The name tag pinned to the girl's orange polyester uniform said Shirley, but Phee knew her name was actually Melissa, and she was one of the one-pers who were transported in every day to do service jobs like this.

"I'm looking for Saul. He's the beefy one."

"I know who he is." Melissa narrowed her eyes. "And I know who you are. You're Gryphon's sister."

Phee nodded. "And Gryphon is the reason I'm looking for Saul. Look, it's important. Was he here or not?"

"They say your brother isn't going to be reconned—"

Phee felt herself taking on the shape her mother took just before she was about to get into it with someone. "I am not having this conversation with you. Tell me if you saw Saul or not or I'll get you fired."

"I couldn't care less, princess." Melissa helped herself to a gumball from the display and popped it into her mouth. She chewed it noisily between pops of a couple of obnoxiously large bubbles. "There's always another scummy job for someone like me to slave away at for you scummy people."

Phee spun on her heel and stalked off before she could do something to "Shirley" that she'd get in real trouble for. She stopped at the deer hunter game and asked the group of boys there if they'd seen Saul.

"Yeah." A pudgy kid dressed all in black with matching makeup around his eyes answered without taking his gaze from the screen. "He just left."

"He did?"

The kid looked at her now. "Oh. You're Gryphon's sister." He paled. "I ... he ..."

Phee didn't want to hear more, so she took off into the mall, texting Saul as she walked hurriedly. "Where are you? I'm @ arcade."

The message sent. Which meant his phone was turned on. She called Nadia.

"Where are you?" Nadia asked over the din of the mall coming from Phee's end of the call. Phee told her, and then told her why.

"That's so strange," Nadia said. "He just texted me, like a couple of minutes ago."

"What did he say?"

"That's just it. Hang on—I'll read you it exactly." A moment later, Nadia was back. "It says, 'Whatever happens, know that I love you and always will, xoxo.'"

A chill washed over Phee. That sounded like a very thinly cloaked goodbye.

"Phee?"

Phee took a steadying breath. "I'm here."

"It's weird, right?" Nadia's voice was small and scared.

"Yeah."

"You think he and the boys are up to something about Gryph? Neko's still here."

"They're always up to something."

"But now, even with the investigation and everything? Can't you talk to Saul and get him to be realistic?"

"If I could find him, I'd try." Phee kept walking as she talked with Nadia. She scanned the crowd, not spotting Saul or anyone else she knew. "Look, you keep trying to get hold of him. I'm going to have a look around here. He has to be close."

"Maybe he went to the bathroom? The ones by the food fair?"

Phee almost cried at the naivety in her best friend's voice. Always the optimist to Phee's pessimism. Always willing to give herself over to denial, whereas Phee was all too aware of how bad things were. Saul's text to Nadia was ominous. Foreboding. Right now, Phee feared for the worst but didn't want to share that gut-churning unease with Nadia. She said goodbye to Nadia and then sent a message to Tariq and Huy. It didn't bounce back this time.

She glanced in each store as she quickly made the rounds of the ground floor. Halfway through her circuit of the second floor she got a text from Tariq. "Go home & be with your family. You're crazy to try to figure this out on your own."

His words made her so mad that she growled out loud as she deleted them and replied, "Don't you dare tell me what to do." She kept texting. "I want to know what's going on! Where's Saul?" She sent the message and kept on looking for him. On the third floor she stopped at the security kiosk. The two men were duelling on some handheld gaming thing and hardly looked up when she approached.

"I need to page someone."

"Hang on." The one glanced up and then, recognizing her, set his game down and gave her his full attention. "Hey. Hi. You're—"

"Gryphon's sister."

"We're so sorry about your brother's ... death." He cast a look at the other guard to include him in his condolences. "It's all over the news that they're trying to find out what really happened. Any development?"

"The page?" She knew she sounded cold, but she was far more worried about Saul than Gryphon right now. Gryph was being kept in stasis at Chrysalis. And as for Saul and his big fat, dangerous secret ...

"Sure, sure." The guard fished a pen out of his pocket. "Who're you looking for?"

"Saul Morrisey." Phee kept her eyes on the crowd coming up the escalator. Still no sign of him. "Get him to meet me here."

"You got it." He smiled at her, a watery sympathetic smile that raised her ire.

"I'm going to keep looking for him," she said, turning to leave. "I'll come back in a little while."

Not even a few steps away and the page sounded. *"Saul Morrisey, please meet your party at the third-floor information kiosk. Saul Morrisey, to the information kiosk on the third floor."* Phee glanced back and gave the guard a thumbs-up. He was wise not to mention her name in the page. Countless people were bound to be curious enough to ask her about Gryphon.

By the time she'd had a look on the fourth floor, she was sure she wasn't going to find him. And worse, she was increasingly sure that something bad had happened. She had no idea what, but it was entirely unlike Saul not to get in touch. And that cryptic message to Nadia. Phoenix made her way back down to the information kiosk and was met with a wave by the guard who'd helped her earlier.

"He hasn't showed."

That was obvious, and Phee was already interested in something else. On the counter behind the guards was a cellphone that she recognized. Army cammo sleeve.

"Whose phone is that?"

He glanced over his shoulder. "Lost and found."

"It's mine."

He raised an eyebrow and stepped a little to the left, blocking her view. "Describe it."

This was Saul's replacement phone, the one he got when he'd dropped his other one that day that Gryph pulled the stunt on the train. Phee and Nadia had been with the boys when Saul picked it out. In this very mall, in fact. As soon as he'd purchased it, Nadia had grabbed it and carved a tiny heart on the back, into the plastic. Phee described it now.

"Wouldn't peg you for a cammo kind of girl." The guard handed her Saul's phone, his eyebrows raised in doubt.

"Where'd you find it?"

He checked his logbook. "Cleaners found it outside the Granville Street entrance on the ground floor."

"Thanks." Phee rushed off, Saul's phone clutched in her hand.

When she was out of sight she stopped, her back against the wall, and examined the phone. It was still powered on, and the screen reported that Saul had eleven new messages. That would've been between when he'd texted her and she'd collected the phone. Phee did a quick count. She'd left him five, Nadia a few more. Without another thought, she retrieved the text messages, skipping the ones from Nadia.

Along with hers, there was one each from Tariq and Huy, wondering where he was.

There were a couple of voice messages too. Phee listened to the first one.

"We're out of time. Get back here. It's happening now. We can't wait for you." She didn't recognize the voice. Female. Older? She checked. It had been sent from a blocked number.

The next one was also from a blocked number. There was noise in the background, an industrial sort of grinding, a metallic creak. Her voice more urgent. "Code blue! I repeat, code blue!"

Phee played the message again, and then a third time, trying to discern what was in the background. She couldn't concentrate, though, unnerved as she was by the woman's message. She'd sounded terrified, panicked. The same way Phee felt now.

There was one more voice message. This one from Neko. Sent from his home number. Twenty minutes ago.

"Saul? I just wanted to tell you ... I just ... I'm just really, really sorry about everything."

Neko's voice was thick, as if he'd been crying. He was just a kid, really, despite how hard he tried to appear older around the guys. He'd convinced more than a couple of girls that he was older than his years, but his message now made him sound about ten. Phee grinned at the memory of him with his ears sticking out and his gangly limbs growing so fast that a month after he'd get new clothes they'd be too small for him.

Enough about Saul for today. Clearly, Phee wasn't going to find him here. And by the sound of it, both Nadia and Neko could use a friend. She slipped the phone into her pocket and headed for the exit, every cell of her being vibrating with worry. She took the Granville Street exit, glancing around, not expecting to find anything to do with Saul, but hoping nonetheless. The fresh air was a godsend, clearing her head enough for her to shake just the tiniest bit of the unease weighing her down. What had happened to Saul? And what had happened to her brother? What was happening to them all?

The whoosh of the trains speeding by overhead only served to pin her focus on Gryph's death, and the shape of Saul's phone in her pocket on his sudden disappearance. Phoenix tucked her earphones into place and scrolled the index on her phone for what she was looking for. Within seconds, the pulse of music was taking her away. She'd downloaded everything she could find from that DJ who'd been at the rave. She closed her eyes and let the rumble of drum and bass lift her out of her life and into an easier place. When she opened them, the music was still with her as she climbed the stairs to the station, and even though the stairs were steep and stretched up farther than she could see, the music made the trek up all that much easier.

STRANGER

Saul was gone. His ominous message to Nadia was the last anyone heard from him. After Phee gave up looking for him at the mall, she went to Nadia's house, only to find that Neko had forced his way past his sister and had taken off. The two girls had sat with each other, silent with anxiety, waiting. For something. Anything. Any small piece of news to move the wretched day forward, out of the quagmire of disquiet. It never came. Hours passed, and no one heard from Saul. Nadia's parents came home from work and Neko still hadn't returned, so Nadia had to admit that he was gone. Nadia's parents had told Phee to go home, so she did, leaving Nadia behind to get lectured and likely grounded for not being able to keep her little brother home.

That night, no word came from Chrysalis. No word came from Saul. Neko showed up in the wee hours, silent and unrepentant. The next day, still no word about Saul. When her parents left for another meeting with Chrysalis, Phee took the chance to go to Saul's house and talk to his parents. It was odd that they hadn't called to see if Phee knew where he was, but maybe they didn't want to impose with their seemingly trivial worries compared with Oscar and Eva's worry about not getting Gryph back.

Saul lived in the Lions, which was a suburb on the other side of the city centre. The houses there were bold and angular, all designed by the same avant-garde architect, Geneva Simard. Even the green space was artfully situated, forming a graphic puzzle from an aerial view. Put together, the shapes of lawn and garden formed a pair of lions, although the suburb itself was named after the mountain to the north, which featured two peaks commonly referred to as the lions. A certain kind of three-per lived in the Lions. People who were newly three-per after having grown up in lesser families, artists whose acclaim had won them honorary three-per status, musicians whose fame demanded their upward bump, professors and politicians of the left-leaning sort. Oscar and Eva had put an offer in on a house there just after Fawn was born, but it hadn't worked out. They did want to live there, but with Eva's father's dementia progressing as it was, they didn't want to leave him with only his aging wife to deal with him.

On the train to the Lions, Phoenix had been listening to her pod, hoping the music would distract her from her reality, which at the moment was fairly unbearable. It hadn't worked, though, no matter how many playlists she'd scrolled through. She'd even tried playing *The Princess Bride*, the old movie that usually worked to calm her. Her apprehension was consuming, and as the train neared the Lions, Phee gave up and tucked her earphones and pod into her pack.

It was a weekday, but because the Lions was populated by an eclectic group of people who didn't necessarily work Monday to Friday, nine to five, it was more bustling than other neighbour-hoods. People were out on bicycles, others were walking their dogs, and parents and kids played in the park. The laughs and splashes from the water playground were harsh to Phoenix's ears.

She pulled Saul's address up on her pod screen and then opened her map program to see where his house was situated in the Lions. According to the little red star, it was two blocks to the west from her gold star on the map. Phee started walking, checking on the map screen to make sure that the gold and red stars were getting closer. Sure enough, when the two stars joined into one pulsing green one, she was there.

The house was tall and skinny, like several others on the block, all of them painted in cheerful colours. Saul's house was lime green on the bottom half and purple on the top. Nadia had described it as odd, but Phee was surprised nonetheless. Nadia wasn't very good at description, or all that observant, really, being more of a "living in the moment" kind of girl compared with Phoenix and her painfully keen sense of past and future and here and now.

The yard was neatly trimmed, likely by the same crew she could see working several doors down, mowing and weeding and pruning in their coveralls and goggles and ear protectors. Phee pushed open the gate and started up the walk, unnerved by the trepidation coursing through her body, filling each footstep with dread. She glanced up at the house. Broad daylight, yet every shade and curtain was drawn, as if the house were squeezing its eyes shut against the sunshine. Phee glanced at the houses nearby. All of them had their blinds raised and curtains opened. Such a small thing, but it made Phee's heart lurch with worry. This house might look as cheerful and content as the others, but Phee—and perhaps only Phee—knew that the family living inside was living a complicated lie.

Pots of flowers stood sentinel on each step to the front door, where Phee reached for the knocker. She knocked twice and then waited. Silence. No footsteps, nothing. She tried again, this time rapping the heavy knocker several times before pausing. Still nothing. With a surreptitious glance to make sure no one was watching, including the labourers down the street, Phee tried the door. It was locked. She put her face to the window and tried to peek through the slit in the curtain, but there were no lights on inside, so she saw only the dim outline of a sofa, and beyond it, the curve of a banister stretching up.

She went around to the backyard, trying to walk purposefully, to appear as if she was supposed to be there. She marched up the back steps and grabbed the doorknob. It turned and the door opened, so Phee went with it, swinging the door wide open and calling out "Hello? Anyone home?"

Inside, she pulled the door closed behind her. "Saul?" She was in a little room off the kitchen. "Mr. and Mrs. Morrisey?"

The kitchen was a mess. Or, not really a mess ... more in suspension, as if Saul and his family had all gotten up and left in the middle of a meal. Lunch, by the looks of it. Sliced roast beef waiting in a fold of butcher's paper, a loaf of bread on the counter, a half-sliced tomato on the cutting board and an open jar of mayonnaise. A bowl of fruit salad was turning bad in middle of the small kitchen table, flies buzzing over it. A mug filled with coffee was cold to the touch, and a quick pinch of the bread told her it was stale. On the other counter, a bowl of raisin-oatmeal cookie dough was attracting its own legion of flies, the baking sheet beside it half full of carefully portioned dollops waiting to go in the oven.

"Hello?" Phee left the kitchen and made her way through the more formal dining room and down a dim hall. She instinctively reached for the light switch, but then changed her mind and carried on to the front room in the dark. Unlike the scene in the kitchen, everything in the living room, and the den off it, looked to be in order.

She stood for a moment in the middle of the living room, looking at the couches where Saul and his parents spent their time, all the while imagining. How had they come to be here? And where were they now? Clearly, they'd left in a hurry. Phee ran her hand over her phone, wondering what she should do. Phone Nadia? No ... that would only make her friend freak out and wouldn't accomplish anything. Phone Crimcor? Definitely not. Saul's family didn't need them looking into things, not if it meant the risk of uncovering their secret status. Her own parents? No. They were still down at Chrysalis, pleading for Gryph's life to be restored to him. Tariq. That's who.

"Hey, Phee." His voice sounded odd, but then everything nowadays was odd.

"I'm in Saul's house and he's not here and it looks like his family up and left in a hurry," she said in a breathless flurry.

Tariq didn't reply.

"Tariq!" Phee shouted. "You have to start talking to me!"

"Get out of there."

"I'm going to have a look upstairs first." Phee headed up them as she talked. "What's going on—"

"Get out of there now!" There was a grim firmness to his demand that made Phee stop, mid-step, one hand on the railing, the other holding her phone to her ear.

"Why?"

"You're trespassing, that's why."

"No one saw me."

"Just get out of there. Now, Phee!"

"Don't tell me what to do, Tariq. I won't leave unless you tell me what the hell is going on!"

"I can't—"

"You can't? Or you won't?"

"Just get out of there."

Phee sank to the stairs and sat. "I'm going to hang up on you unless you start talking to me. For real, Tariq."

"Phoenix, listen to me. You need to get out of there now."

"Talk."

"I'll tell you everything, but you have to get out of there!"

"Tell me now."

"No!" Tariq shouted down the phone, panic in his voice. "Listen to me, Phee—"

"Maybe you should listen to me!"

"Just go! Don't be such a stubborn bitch! Get out of there!"

"You just called me a bitch ..." Phee's voice caught in her throat. She was confused and hurt and wanted so badly to understand what was going on. All of this was so complicated. And now Tariq was being cruel, on top of everything.

"Phoenix, I'm sorry, I am, but I need you to hear me. Really hear me, okay?" He waited for her answer, but Phee was still muddling through her thoughts. "Phee?"

"Okay," Phee finally replied in a whisper. "I'm going. I'll call you when I'm on the train."

She hung up on him. Even before she had time to slip the phone into her pocket, it rang. Tariq. As she brought the phone back to her ear, prepared to argue with him, she heard sirens, not that far off in the distance.

"Tariq? There are sirens."

"Don't panic, Phoenix." Now he sounded sure, careful. "Go upstairs." Phee climbed the stairs, her legs trembling as she did. "To the end of the hall, into the room on your right." The sirens were getting louder. Tariq could hear them now too. "Quick!"

"I'm in the room." With a glance she realized that it was Saul's room. Pictures of Nadia in frames on his nightstand. His leather jacket tossed on the chair beside the desk. A poster of the football team from last year's homecoming game tacked above his bed. The quilt thrown back, the sheets rumpled.

"Pull his dresser away from the wall."

Phee prepared to heave it aside but found it surprisingly light. "Okay ..."

The sirens were right outside, shutting down into an awful silence, one by one.

"Feel along the wall—"

"What am I looking for?" Phee ran her hand along the wainscotting. "There's nothing!" Just as she was about to give up and meet Crimcor as if they'd come for supper, she felt a slight give. She went with it, and a section of the wall folded inward, exposing a tiny wedge of space between the wall and the outside of the house. Phee dived into it at the first sounds of the Crimcor men pounding on the front door.

"I'm in!" Phee reported, noticing the cutouts in the back of the dresser. She pulled it toward her until it was flush with the wall and she was cloaked in darkness. She scooted out of the way of the secret door, and pushed it shut.

"Jesus, Phoenix." Tariq was breathless on his end of the call.

"Crimcor! We have a warrant to search the residence. Open up!"

More pounding, harder, and then she could hear the front door being broken open and then footsteps and shouting.

"Living room clear!"

"Tariq?" Phee dared whisper.

"I'm going to hang up. Text me if you can. Just be sure to silence your phone." With that, he was gone. And Phoenix was alone as the Crimcor men trooped up the stairs, banging open doors, searching.

"Kitchen clear!"

More footsteps. Closer. In the room.

"This is the kid's room," someone said. "I want everything and anything you think might be important."

"Yes, sir."

"Box up his computer."

"Right away, sir."

A noisy search, the closet doors yanked open, stuff being pulled down from shelves, things kicked across the floor ... and then the heart-stopping sound of the drawers in the dresser being pulled out and emptied onto the floor. Phee pulled her knees tighter to her chest and hugged herself hard, willing herself to stay calm, breathe in and out. In and out.

"How many pairs of socks and underwear can one kid have?" The nearest voice.

"Never too many, I say." Another voice, farther off.

"But a teenager?"

"Probably wears the same ones over and over, which is why he's got a dresser full of clean, folded ones."

A drawer made a scraping noise as it was ripped from the dresser and dumped onto the floor.

"Was that necessary?"

"Is this?" This time a crash. And then another one that sounded like the lamp being knocked onto the floor. Phee prayed they didn't topple over the dresser.

There was some laughter, and then silence for a while as the interlopers rummaged through Saul's things and Phee listened to the crash of her heart as it laboured through her terror. She was dizzy in the tiny, airless space. She explored around herself with curious, cautious touches. She could hardly imagine Saul fitting in here in the first place, as tall and broad as he was. But he must've, at some point, because she felt the flutter of pages, a comic book maybe, and the soft, reassuring feel of a small square pillow that she dared not try to wedge behind her back, where her spine was pressing rudely against something sharp. In small increments, she brought the pillow up to her face and tried to examine it in the dark. It felt like corduroy, and smelled like Saul. Or the cologne he wore, more aptly. Phee nudged the pillow between her head and a rafter and closed her eyes as the shuffling and rummaging carried on so close to her hiding spot.

PHOENIX CAME TO with a start, knocking her head against the rafter. She sucked in her breath, remembering at once where she was. She'd fallen asleep, and had woken to her phone buzzing. A text from Tariq. "What's happening?" he wanted to know.

"I don't know," she texted back. And then, "I fell asleep!"

"Crimcor still there?"

Carefully, Phee pressed her ear to the false door. She listened intently, but could hear nothing except the whine of a lawn mower outside, and a dog barking somewhere in the distance.

"I don't think so."

"Then get out of there! Carefully!"

Phee thought for a moment and then replied, "Meet me at the arcade in one hour?"

Tariq's answer came immediately. "I'll be there."

PHEE MADE HER WAY OUT into Saul's room as quietly as she could, having to remind herself to breathe on occasion, so caught up in being stealthy that she was neglecting to breathe normally. Her head spinning, she pushed the dresser away from the wall just enough to have a clear line of sight to the door. She watched it for a while, listening for anything that might suggest that Crimcor was still in the house, looking for whatever it was they wanted. When she was as sure as she could be, she squeezed out of the hiding spot, and stood, shaky on her feet after hours folded up in the hole in the wall.

Daylight was flattening into dusk as she crept down the stairs, worried that a Crimcor agent might've been left behind to keep an eye on things. But the house appeared to be as deserted as it was when she'd arrived. That was the only similarity, though. Whereas it had been fairly neat before, every room had been ripped apart, the minutiae of Saul's family life tossed about as if a giant had lifted the house up and shaken it like a snow globe, unsettling everything into a chaotic storm. Phee tried not to panic, the worry for Saul rising in her throat like a scream. Out the back door, and to the gate that opened onto the lane behind the house she went, waiting until she was certain that the coast was clear before letting herself out of the yard.

Finally safe and sound, Phee doubled over and clutched her knees, gasping for breath, willing her nerves not to fail her as she teetered from a sudden wave of nausea.

Even though she wanted to phone Nadia and tell her about her ordeal and that Saul was gone, she phoned Tariq instead. Nadia wasn't ready to hear any of this. Not yet. "I made it!" she reported to Tariq. "I'm outside. No one saw me."

"Good."

Phee waited. "That's it? That's all you've got to say after—"

"I'll meet you at the arcade." He hung up.

Phee started to dial him again but then thought better of it. Clearly, he didn't want to talk. On the phone, anyway. She'd save her million questions for when she saw him face to face.

HE WAS ALREADY THERE when she arrived. He was sitting at one of the tables at the back, by the concession stand. Melissa, the girl at the counter, scowled at Phee when she noticed her. Tariq stood as she approached, ever the gentleman. Overcome with blistering relief, Phee threw herself at him, forcing a hug from the boy who could barely make eye contact at the best of times.

"Hey, it's okay," he said, pushing her away. But Phee wasn't ready to let go. She clung to him, not caring who was watching, not caring how uncomfortable she was making Tariq feel. She'd been trapped in a hole in the wall in a strange house with Crimcor just a breath away, and Gryph was dead and who knew if he'd be reconned, and Saul was missing, and everything was upside down and screwed up.

"Phoenix, you're okay. You're fine." Tariq pried himself out of her grasp and steered her into a chair. "You made it."

Phee sat, dazed with relief, stunned by confusion. "Tariq, you *have* to tell me what's going on. How did you even know about that cubbyhole?"

"We used to play in there when we were little."

"Really?" She looked at him, challenging him to admit whether he knew the truth about Saul.

"Prisoner of war," Tariq said. "That was the jail." He slid a mug toward her. Hot milky tea. And then a chocolate-chip-banana muffin on a small plate. Two of her favourite things.

"How did you know ...?"

"You order it all the time. Go ahead. Eat."

Phee stared at the food.

"Phee, you must be hungry."

Phee nodded, but couldn't imagine eating the food. Her tummy was awash with anxiety, and even just looking at the sandwich made her gut churn uneasily. She pushed the plate away and took the mug in her hands, holding it tight. She concentrated on the heat against her fingers ... anything to pull herself away from the edge of nausea. She took a sip and felt the liquid travel down her parched throat. He'd even put in the perfect amount of sugar.

"I can't tell you anything right now," Tariq started. He leaned forward, prepared for the look of protest Phee gave him. He put a hand on her arm, his oak-coloured skin dark against her pale and freckled arm. "Trust me."

"Trust you?" Phee didn't even know where to start, but was sure she didn't want the entire arcade to hear what she had to say. "How can you say that? After everything! You guys *know* what happened to Gryph and you won't say and now he might not be reconned! You *know* he didn't kill himself ... and what about Saul? Where is he?"

"I don't know where he is."

"You do!"

"No. I don't. Honestly." Tariq's gaze was calm, steady. "But I can tell you that it'll all work out, Phoenix."

"I don't believe you for one second," Phee snapped. "Gryphon is gone, Saul is gone. What about you and Huy and Neko? Are you next? Is this some kind of weird suicide pact or something?"

With a small smile, Tariq replied, "No."

"Would you tell me if it was?"

"No," he murmured. "I wouldn't."

Phee sat back, giving up on that line of questioning. She cocked an eyebrow at him. "I know that you know what really happened to Gryph. Please, Tariq. Why won't you tell me?"

Tariq's expression, flat and unresponsive to her coy gesture, didn't particularly unnerve her. Tariq held his emotions and thoughts close, never letting on when he was rattled. If he ever got rattled, that is. Phee couldn't think of a time he'd ever seemed ruffled, even when Gryph or the guys pushed too far and found themselves in sticky situations. Like that day when he and Saul got caught in the train doors. He was always the voice of calm reason. Now was no different. He would not tell her anything he didn't want to. Once again, he was playing his hand the way he wanted to.

"Come on, Tariq. Give me something. Please."

He set his hands on the table, fingers splayed, and leaned slightly toward her. Phee caught the scent of his aftershave, a smoky, seductive whiff that sent her back to that night at the rave when he had danced with her. She blinked the memory away, struggling to stay in the moment even though she would have given anything to go back to that night.

"I'm going to ask you to do something very difficult—"

"Harder than dealing with Gryph dying? Harder than not knowing where Saul is? Harder than hiding in a secret hidey-spot with Crimcor agents just feet away?"

Again, he didn't rise to her words. "I want you to trust me. Give me a week, and if things haven't been sorted out by then, I'll tell you what I know."

"Gryph hasn't got a week."

"He'll get the extension." He was referring to the Chrysalis policy of permitting the stasis period to be extended for up to ten days.

"You don't know that."

"I do. He's Chrysalis's poster boy. They're not going to let him die. Not for real."

"What if they want to make an example of him?" Phee voiced one of the bigger worries that had kept her awake over the past few nights. "What if they want to prove to people that there's no special treatment for celebrities?"

Instead of answering her, Tariq rose from his seat. "I have to go."

"Where?" Phee leaped up too and reached for him. She caught his wrist as he turned. "I want to come with you."

"No." He pulled away easily. "I'll call you. In the meantime, Phoenix, you have to trust me." For the first time since meeting him that afternoon, she saw his expression shift, letting in the smallest hint of concern as he stared hard at her. "Do you? Trust me?"

In the moment, Phee wished she could deny him. But the truth was that out of all of Gryph's friends, she probably trusted Tariq the most.

"I do." Phee nodded. "Trust you."

She was so tired that her head felt like a bowling ball on her shoulders, too heavy. That one nod took the last bit of energy out of her. Her day had been so bizarre, and so scary. And everything was so unsettled, and she didn't know anything at all for sure. And her worry for Gryphon—and now Saul too—gnawed at her constantly. She wasn't sure she could carry on. She let her chin drop to her chest and stared at the smooth tabletop. She was so tired that she just wanted to curl up on it, go to sleep, and wake up later to find everything as it should be.

RULING

While Phee was overwhelmed with the complexity of it all, Nadia was finding her own sort of comfort within her own world of denial. Phee wished she could exchange her curiosity and need to know with Nadia's complacent denial. Phee had worried about what Nadia would think about Saul's disappearance, but as it turned out she didn't need to explain a thing. Nadia made her own assumptions about Saul and his family's disappearance. As hard as it was to watch her friend suffer, Phee forced herself to keep her discoveries to herself. There was no mention of the raid on his house in the media, no mention of the family's sudden, unexplained disappearance. After a couple of days of not hearing from him, Nadia had three ideas she was batting back and forth.

"If he wanted to break up with me, he could've just said!" Another swell of tears as she threw herself on Phoenix's bed. Phee sat cross-legged beside her and patted her back, not daring to comment. The flaw in this version according to Nadia was that his entire family was gone. Another few minutes passed, and Nadia had flipped to her second idea. "Or if this is how he deals with death, he's got a thing or two to learn." And then the final alternative. She sat up and gripped Phee's hands in hers. "It's something his father did, I'm sure of it. Fraud. Tax evasion. They're in hiding. He'll contact me. I know it!"

And the cycle would start again as she vacillated between the scenarios she'd fixed on. Nadia tried her hardest not to let her own crisis overshadow Phee's family's ongoing battle with Chrysalis, but often her despair overwhelmed her and she had a small fit every once in a while. Like this one, which was almost over.

"Phee, I'm sorry." Nadia pulled Phoenix to her and gave her a tight hug. "I'm awful. Tell me the latest."

The latest was not good. "Chrysalis is leaning toward ruling it a suicide—"

"But they won't." Nadia smiled sympathetically. "Not when it comes right down to it."

Phee shrugged. "I don't know, Nadia."

"He's their pride and joy!"

"Not lately."

"That won't affect their ruling though, right?"

"I don't know, Nadia." Phee wrung her hands in her lap. "I'm going with my parents later. To Chrysalis. And Grandma too. And Auntie Trish, even. They told us to bring as many family members as we could today. Grandpa and Fawn will stay here with Uncle Liam and the twins."

"What for?" Nadia paled. This was not lost on her. "There's one more day, right?"

"Not if they've made the decision already."

"Your mom and dad can demand the extension."

"Maybe."

"Is your lawyer coming?"

Phee nodded. "Four lawyers. My mom thinks they're going to rule against him."

"Oh, my God." Nadia dropped her hands into her lap. "This can't be happening."

"It is, though."

"Oh, Phee ... this is the worst summer in the history of terrible things."

"It is."

"Do you want me to come too?"

"I wish, but it's family and legal team only. Thanks, though."

Both girls looked up at the sound of Fawn yelling up from the bottom of the stairs. Nadia hurriedly wiped her teary eyes as Fawn's graceless steps grew closer. Something sounded clunky in her gait, so Phee wasn't surprised when she burst into Phee's bedroom, each foot perched atop the bottom of a large, empty tomato can strung through with twine, which she held tight in her fists, lifting each tin as she stepped in theatrically.

"Look!" Fawn stomped in a little circle. "Grandma made them. They're kilts."

"Stilts," Phoenix corrected her. "You mean stilts."

"Yeah. Grandma says she and her friends used to make these when they were kids. Can you imagine Grandma as a kid? I can't. Not at all. She showed me how to use them and I was laughing because she looked so silly in her old lady shoes and big bum and legs with all those purply veins running up and down like worms."

Phee was as ever amazed at her little sister's capacity to set aside the worry about Gryph and carry on, business as usual. She was exhausted just looking at her, and could hardly think of one thing to say other than to scream that their brother was dead and how could she be playing at a time like this.

"That's something," Phee finally managed. "Bizarre for sure. Grandma as a little girl."

"With purply leg veins." Fawn galloped past the girls on the bed. "I bet you can't walk on these."

"I can so. Grandma made them for me too." Then again, Phee wasn't sure that she could, come to think of it. There was a picture of her on ones their grandma had made for her, shortly before her second death. But, of course, Phee had no memory. Really, she just wanted one less thing to deal with. Fawn. "Can you leave us alone, Fawn, hon? Please?"

"Why?"

"We're talking grown-up stuff."

"You're not grown-ups."

"We are more than you are," Phee said. She got up and pushed Fawn toward the door. Fawn stumbled off the cans and landed on her knees. She jumped up, rearranged herself on the stilts and fixed Phee with one of her spectacular scowls.

"You made me fall!"

"I didn't. You tripped."

"You did! You made me fall."

"Fine. I'm sorry."

"No you're not!" Fawn yelled. "I hate you! You're no fun! Gryphon would've played with me. He would've tried my kilts out and been goofy and fun and you're just boring! I wish you'd died and not him!"

"Fawn!" Nadia gasped. "You little shit—" In one movement Nadia was off the bed and lunging for Fawn. Fawn jumped off her stilts and dodged her. She dragged her cans with her as she backed into the hall.

"Fawn Nicholson-Lalonde," Nadia hollered, "you get back here and apologize to your sister!"

"No! And you're both boring old meanies, that's what!" With that, Fawn stomped down the hall into her own room, slamming the door behind her.

"She's horrid!" Nadia draped an arm across her best friend's shoulders. "She didn't mean it."

"She probably did." Phee shrugged. "But that's okay. I'm kind of relieved, actually. I was honestly beginning to think Gryph's death had no impact on her whatsoever. That little tantrum proved me wrong. In a good way. Proves the little monster is, in fact, at least partially human."

"I'll go make her apologize."

"No. It's okay. She doesn't understand. It's not her fault."

"She can at least say she's sorry for being such a little toad about it, though."

"Nah." Phee retreated to the bed and flopped backwards. When all of this was over, no matter how it played out, she would pay more attention to Fawn. Right now, though, she was too worried about the meeting that afternoon with Chrysalis to even go down the hall and try to explain things to her scared and angry little sister.

THE CHRYSALIS HEADQUARTERS took up four square blocks in the section of the city designated for science and technology. The SciTech District was a lesson in building with steel and glass, the towers and warehouses alike gleaming with a sterile brightness that gave Phoenix a chill as they made their way to Chrysalis in one of their private shuttles, the logo on the side as good as advertising their grief. The mood in the shuttle was sombre, with the lawyers seated along one wall, silent and stiff, and Phee's family along the other, trembling with worry, patting knees and whispering empty assurances to one another.

"Don't you worry, dear." Phee's grandma handed her yet another hard candy, which Phee tucked away in her pocket, along with the others her well-intentioned and undeniably nervous grandma had foisted on her during the trip. "Everything will be just fine."

Phee tried to smile back, but knew her face had contorted into the opposite expression, producing a pained sort of frown. She caught one of the lawyers watching her, so she gave the man her full attention, daring him to keep on with his prying curiosity. He blushed and turned his eyes down, fixing them on the briefcase carefully balancing on his lap.

The shuttle dock was built into the expansive glass foyer of Chrysalis itself. Phoenix did not recall ever being here, although she had been in this very building for the duration of her recons. When she stepped out of the shuttle, her eyes went straight to a lush wall of green. One whole end of the foyer was an enormous wall crawling with cascading ivy and thick ferns and waterfalls of periwinkle dotted with nasturtiums. Instead of being surprised at such an incongruous sight, she smiled, happy to see it again. Then she caught herself, marvelling. She did remember the living wall, as it was called, the vertical garden that knitted itself all the way up to the ceiling. She remembered it from leaving, waiting for the provided shuttle after her last recon when she was six. She went up to the wall while the others behind her signed in and passed around the visitor tags. Phee ran her hand over a spray of feathery fern and breathed in the earthy perfume. A surge of optimism cheered her, and when she rejoined the others, she took her grand-mother's hand and whispered, "You're right. It will be okay." There was no way that they would refuse to recon Gryphon. No way.

Her father took her other hand, and with her mother and auntie holding hands in front of them, they were led like so many wary tourists down an echoing hall lined with windows on either side, the sunlight pouring in despite the group's sombre mood. At the end of the hall was a lounge, and this is where they were left, with the lawyers, to wait for the Chrysalis executive who'd arranged the meeting. There was a table of snacks to one side of the door, a spread of fresh fruit and expensive cheeses, pâté, and croissants alongside silver carafes of tea and coffee and a pitcher of orange juice with slices of orange floating on top.

"It's like the continental breakfast at Hôtel l'Atelier," Eva muttered none too kindly. "As if any of us could eat."

The family maybe not, but the lawyers were convening around the buffet, stacking muffins and fruit atop dainty china plates and talking quietly among themselves, casting glances back at Phoenix and her relatives every once in a while.

"Hôtel l'Atelier?" Auntie Trish said, to fill the gaping silence.

"Oscar and I and the children stayed there, in Paris."

"Ah." Auntie Trish nodded. "That time you went to the medical conference."

The sisters fell into silence with the others while the lawyers eagerly grazed.

Suddenly, the door swept open and in stalked a pair of Chrysalis executives, a matching set, both women wearing pointy black high-heeled shoes and smart pantsuits, without the jackets, as if to convey a casual friendliness, approachability. Behind them by a royal couple of steps came Lex, and with him the rep who'd been to the house almost a week earlier, and bringing up the grim parade was Lex's assistant, Aggie. She was the only one of the party to look each family member in the eye, offering them a small, conciliatory smile.

"Mr. and Mrs. Nicholson-Lalonde," the first woman said, arm extended. "You've been offered tea? Coffee? How have you been managing since we last met?"

Phee narrowed her eyes at the woman. So this was who her parents had been meeting with since Gryph's death. And her colleague, who was giving orders to Aggie discreetly, their heads together. Aggie scurried off, catching Phee's eye as she did. Phee tried to read her look, but couldn't, and wasn't sure Aggie was trying to send her a message anyway. She did seem relieved to be sent away on whatever errand it was.

Phoenix and her family had been huddled together on two loveseats, ignoring the expanse of furniture available to them in the room. With a glance, the second woman asked Lex to bring chairs for them, and soon they were sitting across from the family, with only the sleek coffee table as a buffer between them. The lawyers positioned themselves in a lounge chair each, two on either side of the family. They remained silent and official-looking, waiting for Eva or Oscar to bring them into the discussion, their laptops open and ready on low tables beside them.

"Thank you for coming down today." The first woman was clearly the communicator, the other woman the overseer. While the first woman talked, she leaned over and whispered something to Lex, and he got up and quickly returned with two boxes of tissue, which he slid onto the coffee table. "Let's get started."

"As some of you may know, I am Nora Hueson, executive director of recon services. And my colleague"—here she gestured to the second woman—"is Tamara Shapiro, executive director of client relations. Lionel Campbell, your client liaison officer. You know Lex, of course."

Eva nodded for everyone, while Oscar offered Lex a more familiar smile.

Hueson leaned forward, hands clasped, trying—Phee assumed—for an intimacy she was not going to get in return from the family. "We've asked you to come down today so we can discuss, in person, recent developments with the decedent's file."

"Gryphon," Phee blurted without thinking. "His name is Gryphon Nigel Nicholson-Lalonde."

Shapiro blinked kindly at Phee while Hueson carried on. "We have some reports to share with you."

Lex handed a stack of pods to the family, including Phee's grandmother, who hadn't ever figured out how to use them. "You can follow along with me as I go over it on the screen."

Eva and her sister shared a grim look. Oscar clutched his wife's hand, not touching the pod set in front of him. Phee tapped the screen of hers, and the swirling Chrysalis logo, a helix that rebuilt itself over and over, brightened the little screen. The lights in the room dimmed, and the same image appeared on the wall opposite the couches. The lawyers shuffled their positions for a better view. Phee's heart sank. This wasn't going in any direction that could be called good.

"Starting with the data transfer from the decedent's logger," Hueson said, referring to the tiny microchip imbedded into all citizens shortly after birth that recorded vital signs in a ten-minute loop, and also notified Chrysalis immediately upon death. She aimed a laser pointer at a column of numbers to one side of the image. "These are the epinephrine and norepinephrine levels produced by the adrenergic nerve terminals in the autonomic nervous system in the moments leading up to the time of death.

You'll notice the elevated levels were consistent over a period of nine minutes and forty seconds before the incident."

"Accident," Phee said, adding as much heft to the one word as she could.

Another placating smile from the Shapiro woman.

"These findings are in line with research that indicates people experiencing heightened sensations not typically consistent with a genuine 'accident'—"

PHEE BLANKED OUT the woman's voice. With Hueson droning on about this number and that level of whatever chemical indicator, Phee took a moment to consider exactly what was happening. By now she was sure they were here for bad news, and that any moment Hueson and Shapiro would announce that Chrysalis would not be reconning her brother.

And then what? Phee could feel her pulse quicken at the thought, and tried to calm herself. And then ... then the lawyers would make themselves useful and demand an extension. They'd take Gryphon's case to arbitration. It would only mean he'd be gone a little longer. He'd miss the X Games, but maybe Saul would be back by the time he was. Phee smiled to herself. It was easy, in a way, to imagine Saul and Gryph off on some big adventure. Except, she reminded herself, that wasn't the case at all. Gryph was being kept in stasis somewhere in the labyrinth of this facility, and Saul was God knows where.

"—oxygen in the blood was also indicative of a wilful action in the moments before the incident."

"Spare us, please." Phee's mom broke in. "I'm sure I speak not only for myself but for all of us sitting here listening to you blathering on with your 'findings.'" Hueson sat back a little in her chair, knowing full well that she was about to receive the ire of a grieving mother. Clearly she'd been to this very place before, if not often.

"Perhaps we should take a little break?" Hueson offered.

"Or perhaps," Eva snapped back, "you could just tell us Chrysalis's decision so that we can arrange ourselves accordingly."

"Excuse me. One moment ..." Hueson held up a finger and then tapped her phone bud tucked in her ear beside a gleaming diamond earring. "Hueson ... Yes, thank you," she said to whoever was on the other end of the call.

Within seconds there were footsteps out in the corridor, and then the door opened and Fawn fled across the room to Eva, flinging herself into her mother's lap.

"What's going on?" Eva said, thoroughly confused.

"Liam?" Oscar met his brother-in-law's entrance with the twins in tow with a perplexed look. Trailing behind them was Phee's granddad, shuffling along, unperturbed. He greeted his wife with a broad grin and kissed each of his daughters on the top of her head as if they were little girls. He cast a suspicious look at the Chrysalis people.

"You go on, get outta here."

Phee reached for his hand. "They work here, Granddad."

"Oh yes!" He smiled at her suddenly and handed her a quarter. "Off you go and ride the carousel with your sister, Eva."

Phee and her mother shared a look, and then Eva started again with the questions.

"Why have you brought them here? We made the decision—as a family—about who would stay home and who would come today."

Hueson smiled, the lines at the corners of her mouth stretching as if in an odd exercise. "We felt it was appropriate for you all to be together."

"What patronizing drivel!" Eva leaped to her feet, sending Fawn scrambling. Eva balled her fists at her sides and glared at the Chrysalis executive. "We are not your pawns, nor are we your responsibility. Get to the point, and get to it fast, or I will sic each and every one of these lawyers on you so fast you'll be out of a job before you can get out of this room!"

"Your son will not be reconned." Hueson took a breath. "The decision is final. I am sorry."

Oscar gasped. "Dear Lord ..."

Eva pulled Fawn to her instinctively, protectively. "That's impossible." As she spoke, she reached blindly for Phee too, her eyes locked on Hueson, imploring her to say more, say differently. Phee moved into her mother's embrace, as the twins found the toy corner and their stunned father went to keep an eye on them.

Phee's grandma took her husband's hand and held on tight, her eyes tearing. Phee's auntie Trish stood alone, not sure what to do. Fawn blinked up at her mother, aware that she should cry but not understanding exactly why.

"Are we getting Gryph back today?"

"Yes," Eva said firmly, eyes still on Hueson. "We are."

The lawyers huddled, voices meshing into a cacophony as they planned their strategy.

"You can't do this!" Eva's voice was shaky, and growing louder. "You *cannot* do this! He didn't kill himself! He didn't! I don't know why you're making an example of him, because he's done nothing but earn you money and prestige ... *nothing!* You're ... you're ... you people are making a terrible mistake!"

"We are confident of our findings." Hueson slipped her laser pointer into her pocket. "The decision is final. I am sorry."

"You're not sorry! You're punishing him because he's come in second a couple of times!"

"His recent athletic performance has nothing to do with this."

"You knew he wanted out of his contract!" Eva broke away from her daughters and lunged at the woman, grabbing her around her throat and squeezing. "You're punishing him for that?"

"Let go of me!" Hueson croaked.

Shapiro leaped to her feet and pressed an intercom button on the wall. "Security! Annex Room, immediately!" Lex rushed forward and pried Eva off.

"You bitch! You horrible, horrible bitch!" Eva crumpled to the floor as the lawyers rushed forward to calm Hueson, who patted her throat as if she'd merely lost a necklace. Eva stayed on her knees, sobbing. Oscar knelt beside her, leaning his forehead against hers, murmuring to her, trying to calm her down.

Phee was stunned.

Not so much by her mother's outburst, but by her very vocal admission to knowing that Gryph wanted out of his contract. Phee had thought she was the only one who'd been thinking that.

"And if he's reconned, he can't compete for you anymore," Phee murmured in agreement. "He's not worth anything to you now."

"Not true," Hueson said, having heart. "As I have already said, his performance is an entirely separate issue. It is no secret that we have had concerns about his recent commitment—or lack thereof—to his contract. But we are more than capable of separating our sponsorship relationship with him from our larger role— and responsibility—of organizing recons."

Security came and stayed, and the other Chrysalis executive took over representing the organization while the lawyers went off with Nora Hueson to discuss the options, if there were any at all.

The one called Shapiro addressed the family, speaking clearly.

"The reason we've gathered everyone is so that you can have a last visit with Gryph as he is now."

Horror washed over Phoenix. She did not want to see him dead.

Beside her, Oscar blanched. He lowered his voice to a whisper. "Please, Ms. Shapiro, could my family have a moment alone?"

"Of course." Shapiro retreated into the hallway, taking the security guards with her. She left the family in a bewildered state, hovering close to each other like skittish wild horses, except the twins, who frolicked with the expensive toys provided by Chrysalis, and Phee's granddad, who wasn't sure what was going on. Even Fawn understood the gravity of the situation, and kept herself small and folded up, pressing against Phee for comfort.

Without protest from anyone—even Phee's uncle, who was an ardent atheist—Oscar prayed on behalf of everyone in the room. When he was done, he asked each one of them if they wanted to see Gryphon. Eva did, of course. She would take any opportunity to see him, spend time with him, no matter what. And Phee, despite her fears, wanted to as well. Her grandmother wanted to at first, but then changed her mind. Fawn refused from the outset. Her auntie Trish and uncle Liam would pay their respects too, after Phee and her parents went first.

PHEE AND HER PARENTS were led to a viewing room, where a glass pane with curtains drawn closed on the other side filled one whole wall. In front of it stretched a low, cushioned bench, with discreet boxes of tissue set atop low tables positioned at either end. They were alone in the room once the heavy door sighed shut behind them. After what seemed like a very long wait, the curtains were drawn, exposing another, smaller room. That room was bare, except for soft lighting and a track that ran along the floor.

Phee stepped up to the glass as a set of heavy doors swung open at one end, and a sleek metal capsule slid along the track, stopping in front of her.

"He's in there," Eva said, her voice thick. She sat on the bench, her back to the window. "I don't want to see him like this." A sob caught in her throat. "I can't!"

A buzzer sounded, and the capsule locked into place. A moment later, it opened like a clamshell, revealing another smooth, clear capsule within.

And there was Gryph.

He rested suspended in a milky fluid, lit from below so that his new skin practically glowed. His eyes were closed. They'd halted the recon after reknitting his bones and repairing the external damage, right down to the gryphon tattoo on his arm, so he looked as if he were just asleep in a very small, quiet ocean.

Phee placed her hands on the window and leaned closer. How could they stop now when they'd already gone so far? He looked perfect. She had to remind herself that sometimes Chrysalis only ever went this far, after third deaths, so that the body was presentable for the funeral, so that family could say goodbye without having to behold their beloved's mangled corpse. This wasn't unusual. They might've planned on only going this far all along. It didn't mean anything to them that he was so lifelike that Phee half expected him to help himself out of the capsule and come home with them, back to his life.

"He's beautiful, Eva." Oscar put his hands to the glass too, trying to get closer. "Our son." He closed his eyes. Phee hoped he was cashing in every favour he could with his God, begging him to change Chrysalis's decision. Begging him to give Gryph back to them.

It couldn't end like this. Phee stared hard at her brother, his hair floating like a dark halo around his smooth forehead. She'd been in the same state, twice, and she was fine now. So he would be too. She had to believe, because if she thought for one moment that this was truly the end of her brother, she would lose it. And for her mother's sake, for Fawn's and Oscar's too, someone had to hold on to what little hope was left. Someone had to have faith, other than Oscar and his acceptance of what he could rationalize as God's will.

"The lawyers will figure something out." Phee turned away at last and sat beside Eva. "This isn't the end, so you don't have to say goodbye, Mom. This is not goodbye."

Oscar winced at her optimism. Him, of all people! "Phee, perhaps this is a goodbye. We can't be sure. Not at this point."

"It's not, Dad. I know it."

Oscar turned back to the window. "I pray that you're right."

Eva squeezed her daughter's hand. "Go get your auntie Trish and uncle Liam."

Phee left the viewing room, her knees shaking, her head spinning. She told her aunt and uncle that they could go see Gryph now, and then she took a seat near the twins as they played on, cheerfully oblivious. Fawn climbed onto her lap with her bunny and took Phee's cheeks in her cool, small hands.

"Did you tell him that he has to come back because we were in

the middle of a game of snakes and ladders? Did you tell him I kept
the board just like it was and everything?"

Fawn had asked her to do this before Phee had left the room
with her parents. Now Fawn looked up at Phee with such trust and
faith that Phee couldn't bear to tell her that she'd forgotten. It had
been so unsettling, seeing Gryph like that, that it hadn't occurred
to her to indulge Fawn's simple request.

But she nodded anyway. "I did."

"What'd he say?"

"Fawn, he can't talk right now."

"Oh."

"And he can't walk and he can't think and he can't come home
yet. It's like he's sleeping."

"Stasis." Fawn tried on the word Oscar had explained to her
earlier.

"That's right. Stasis."

In his seat across from her, her grandfather was tugging off his
shoes and socks. Fawn pointed, grinning. "Look at Granddad."

Phee shared a wink with her little sister before calling across the
room. "What're you doing, Granddad?"

"I'm going to the beach." He balled up socks and stuffed them in
his pocket. "To feel the sand between my toes."

"True, Granddad." Phee slid Fawn off her lap and crouched at
her grandfather's feet. "But we're not going until after dinner."
Another white lie slid easily off her tongue as she found his socks
in his pocket and fitted them back onto his callused, hairy feet.
"Right now, we have to wait."

"For Gryphon." Her grandfather nodded sombrely. "We must
wait for your brother or he will be fit to be tied."

"Right, Granddad." The tears that Phee had been diligently
holding at bay rushed forward, soaking her cheeks in seconds.
"That's right."

MARLIN

The team of lawyers assured Phee's parents that it wasn't over yet. When they emerged from their meeting with Hueson, they were subdued but hopeful, or at least that's what the lawyers told Oscar and Eva. They'd managed to get an agreement in writing, stipulating that Chrysalis would not to do anything to Gryph while he was in stasis that might harm any future recon. So he was, and would be for who knew how long, quite literally in an indefinite state of suspended animation. Part of Phee wished she hadn't seen him like that, but mostly she was glad for it, preferring his renewed skin and rebuilt bones to the images of him broken and bleeding on the tracks.

The family took two Chrysalis shuttles home, the first one filled with Oscar, Eva, and Fawn, Eva's mother and sister, and Phoenix. Her uncle Liam accompanied the rowdier group that included the twins and her grandfather, who'd put his shoes and socks back on, but rolled up his pants, still sure he was going to the beach. At first, Fawn had wanted to go with her cousins, perhaps lured by their rosy-cheeked cluelessness, but just before the doors closed, she'd changed her mind, yelping for her mother to wait for her and Bunny.

She sat on Eva's lap and cuddled her stuffed rabbit as if she wasn't much older than the twins, and Phoenix envied her that. She felt she had to be strong. Not for herself—she'd hole up in her room and weep for weeks if she thought she could—but for her parents. Eva tried to be the strong one, but she was as much a victim of her grief as Oscar was, who at least readily admitted it and prayed for the heavenly fortitude to carry on. Eva's weakness was chilled with a rage only a mother could experience, having her child denied life. Oscar, on the other hand, had a quiet grace to his sadness.

And Phee? What did she think? She stared out the window as the tidy buildings and manicured lawns passed below in a blur. She didn't know. She didn't know what she thought. Only that nothing felt right. Everything felt amiss, as if the world had made a wrong turn and now couldn't find its way home.

The shuttle sped toward the Shores with a low hum that drowned out the quiet, sad murmurings of her family. She wished they could keep going until they came full circle around and arrived at Chrysalis again to collect Gryph, fully and impeccably reconned. She wished she'd been with the boys that fateful day so that she'd seen what the boys had seen. And so that she'd know why they weren't talking.

Under her fear and sadness burned a blaze of determination. They had three days until the appeal would be ruled on. Phee wouldn't spend one waking moment of that wallowing in hopelessness. She would find out the truth. With Saul gone, Tariq was the key. Neko was just a little kid. And Huy, too devastated about Gryph's death to string a solid sentence together, was of no use to her right now. Maybe when—or if—he ever calmed down.

She shut her eyes and imagined telling Tariq what had happened at Chrysalis that day, how close her family was to losing Gryph forever. She would describe the way he looked, strung like a thread between life and death. Tariq had to understand. He'd have to tell her what he knew, the secrets he kept.

UNCLE LIAM took the twins and his father-in-law across the green to Phoenix's grandparents' house so that the others could have a quiet supper. Hardly anyone touched the food, each of them picking disheartenedly at the platter of sandwiches that a neighbour had brought over for them. Oscar poured everyone except Fawn a glass of wine, and for once Fawn didn't protest at being left out. Phoenix sipped hers, the fruity heft of the alcohol rushing to her head. Eva and Trish spoke softly to each other, going over the events of the day, trying to make a plan. Phoenix reached for the carafe and refilled her glass as she strained to listen. No one noticed. She could hear only bits, but it sounded as though her auntie Trish wanted to have a backup strategy if Chrysalis ruled not to recon Gryph. And it sounded as though she didn't trust the lawyers. Right now, Phoenix could not bear the thought that they might fail.

"Excuse me, please?" She set her empty wineglass down and pushed herself away from the table. Oscar looked up, eyes filled with worry.

"You've hardly eaten, honey."

"None of us have." Phoenix shrugged. "I'm just not hungry. May I be excused?"

"Of course." Her dad put a hand on Fawn, seated beside him, a plate of cheese and pickles untouched in front of her, a carefully stacked pillar of crackers on her napkin. Fawn glanced up.

"Can I come with you?"

She meant right now, of course. But for a second, Phoenix wondered how her little sister knew she was going to go out later, to meet Tariq and Huy and Neko, the three guys left.

"Sure, brat." She offered Fawn a hand and she eagerly took it, after tucking the crackers in her pockets. The sisters climbed the stairs in silence, and once at the top Phoenix went to drop Fawn's hand, but Fawn held tight, tugging her into her room with her.

For a little kid, Fawn kept her room in surprisingly good order, especially when she was stressed. The bed was made as neatly as if their grandmother had done it, and the floor was bare, every toy in its spot, all her stuffed animals lined up along the end of her bed, facing the door.

"They're waiting for Gryph to come home," Fawn explained as she handed out the crackers among them, one each. Phoenix didn't have the heart to lecture her about crumbs in her bed. "He said he'd read a story to them."

Phoenix's throat swelled, catching her words. "How about I read it to them?"

"No," Fawn replied. "I don't think so."

Phoenix's eyes welled. "Just until he comes back?"

"Well ..." Fawn dropped Phoenix's hand and clasped her own together, thinking hard. "I guess maybe just one."

"Okay, then. You pick."

"The stuffies pick," Fawn said matter-of-factly. She surveyed her troop of plush teddies and sad-eyed dogs, spending a little more time in front of her cherished stuffed rabbit. Then she went to her bookshelf, searching.

Even before Fawn had pulled it down, Phoenix knew which one it would be. *The Velveteen Rabbit*. Phee's heart did a flip in her chest.

"How about a different one?" She didn't know if she could bear the story of the toy rabbit being brought to life. Before, it had always resonated with her because of her own two deaths and subsequent recons. But now the story held so much more weight, what with Gryphon being in stasis at Chrysalis.

"This is the one Bunny picked." Fawn held out the book, the cover worn, the corners of the pages softened with age. Inside the front cover, Fawn had written her name under their grandmother's and Eva's and Phoenix's. Phoenix didn't remember writing her name there because she'd done so only a couple of weeks before she'd died the second time. Gryph had never written his name in it. He'd preferred stories about ogres and knights and sports adventures. He had never liked *The Velveteen Rabbit*. As Phee turned the pages to the first illustration, she wondered if he would appreciate the story as much as she did, when he came home. *If*, she reminded herself. If he came home.

Without being asked, Fawn changed into her nightgown and crawled into bed, although it was still light out and not even eight o'clock. She gathered Bunny in her arms and waited for Phoenix to start reading. With a steadying breath, Phoenix started the story. When she got to the part where Horse tells Rabbit about being made real, Phoenix had to pause to will back the tears that threatened once again.

"Keep going," Fawn said as she stifled a yawn.

"'Does it hurt?' asked the Rabbit.

"'Sometimes,' said the Skin Horse, for he was always truthful. 'When you are Real you don't mind being hurt.'" Phoenix sighed. Chrysalis claimed it didn't hurt, being reconned. But it had to, didn't it? Despite their intravenous drips and sedation? As your bones knitted together? As your new skin stretched over muscles and tendons? So accelerated? Did Gryph feel anything right now? Had she? The two times she'd been where he was now?

"Read." Fawn's eyes were closed now.

"'Does it happen all at once, like being wound up,' he asked, 'or bit by bit?'

"'It doesn't happen all at once,' said the Skin Horse. 'You become.'

"I can't—" Phoenix's voice was thick. "I just can't read this one tonight, Fawny."

But Fawn was now, thankfully, asleep. Phoenix closed the book and set it gently on the bedside table, and then she just sat there on the edge of her little sister's bed as the dusk grew, and slowly the tiny pinhole lights set into Fawn's ceiling reacted to the dark and brightened into constellations. Exhausted, Phoenix stretched out beside Fawn, who breathed heavily with deep sleep. But Phoenix couldn't sleep. Instead, she lay staring at the starlit ceiling, waiting for the household to creak into slumber. The sound of her aunt and grandma leaving, old Riley being let out for one last pee, then Eva and Oscar climbing up the stairs to bed.

Phoenix feigned sleep when she heard her parents' footsteps near. Oscar and Eva stood together in the doorway, watching their daughters sleep, before shuffling down the hall to their own room. When she heard their door shut, Phoenix crept out of Fawn's room and sat on the top stair until her parents were in bed and the lights turned out. Then she made her way down the stairs, avoiding the same creaks that Gryph had mastered on his many illicit midnight field trips. She collected a jacket and her backpack and let herself out the back door so stealthily that not even Riley stirred in his bed just steps away.

PHOENIX RAPPED on the little window on Willis's hut by the gate. He'd fallen asleep sitting up and came to with a guilty start. He didn't ask why she wanted to be let out, and she was thankful for it. He just buzzed her through, as he probably had done the same for Gryphon many a time.

"Hang on just a minute there, kiddo," he said when she was on the other side. He passed her a slip of paper with a phone number. "That's mine. You call me if you get in trouble."

"Thanks, Willis." She tucked the number into her pocket, doubtful he'd be of help where she was going.

As if reading her mind, he nodded sagely and said, "I know people."

"Okay." She thanked him again and headed off toward the nearest train station outside the Shores, which was a good half-hour walk. She couldn't take the train right out of the Shores, because the station had constant surveillance. She'd never walked this way alone after dark, and she was dismayed to discover that she was frightened of the eerie night silence and the fact that she was the only person— not that she'd necessarily want to meet anyone out here.

The station was well lit, and she was glad to see it as she came around the last corner. It shone like a beacon, and she practically ran the last block. She rushed up the stairs and onto the platform, then pulled out Saul's phone and composed a text to Tariq, copying Huy and Neko as well. "Meet me at the Balmoral in one hour."

Tariq was the first to reply. "Saul? Is that you?"

So he was suspicious. Or surprised to hear from him, at least.

Huy and Neko's replies came while she was boarding the train, and both texts consisted of just one word. "Okay."

PHOENIX PUSHED HER FEAR ASIDE as forcefully as she could manage as she made her way to the diner they'd gathered at after the rave. She was the first one of the group to arrive, so she chose a booth at the back and ordered a cup of coffee and a muffin, just to get the waitress to stop hovering.

Tariq pushed through the doors not five minutes after she got there. He looked around frantically, but when he spotted her, his expression swiftly changed to disappointment. This stung, but she had tricked him, after all. He slid into the booth across the table from her and nodded when the waitress gestured at him with the coffee pot. He didn't say hello, and she didn't either, so the two of them sat there like silent lovers after a quarrel, he stirring cream into his mug with angry clinks of the spoon and she sitting as still as she could, not touching her coffee at all, her muffin tilted on the plate in front of her, the pat of butter melting beside it in the humid heat of the diner.

"Air conditioning's busted," the waitress said by way of apology when she eyed the yellow slick on Phoenix's plate. To Tariq, "You want your usual, honey?"

She knew him, of course. Gryph and the guys came here often enough.

"Thanks, Penny, but not right now. Maybe later."

Penny left, placing the coffee pot back onto the burner at the server station. Tariq waited until she was well out of earshot before sliding the muffin out of the way and leaning across the table.

"What are you doing?" His tone was angry, to match the dark glare of his eyes.

"You better start telling me what's going on, Tariq." Phee's voice shook. She was more nervous than she'd thought. "I'm serious."

Tariq sat back, his arms folded. "What is 'serious'"—he put quotes around the word with his fingers—"is that you came here alone. By yourself. To a dangerous part of the city. Gryph would be furious."

She cocked an eyebrow at him. "Well, he's not here to comment ... is he?"

"I'm working on it, Phoenix." Tariq's look was so intense, so earnest, that she had a sudden wash of regret for her midnight stunt. But before she could apologize for tricking him to meet her, in came Huy—impeccably dressed as usual, despite the hour—and Neko, following close behind, his hoodie pulled over his head in defiance of the heat, the cuffs of his baggy pants dragging on the ground. He looked as though he'd rolled out of a deep sleep and straight in through the café's front door. She'd probably woken them all up. Well, good. God forbid that anyone should get a good night's sleep while Gryph's future hung in the balance.

"Have a seat," she said, already angry with them all.

"She's got Saul's phone," Tariq announced to the others by way of explanation. At first, Phoenix wondered at how quickly he'd pieced together her little puzzle, but then she saw that she'd left the phone sitting out on the table. As she reached for it, Tariq did too, snatching it before she could and tucking it in his pocket.

"Tariq! That's mine!"

Huy shook his head. "It's Saul's, Phoenix."

"But I found it."

"Where?" Neko asked.

"Do you know where he is?" Huy added.

They were certainly acting as if they didn't know what had happened to him either. But it could be just that. An act. With no leverage left, she told them about looking for Saul in the mall, after he'd summoned her there with a cryptic message.

"So," she said when she was finished with her story, "where is he?"

"We don't know," Huy said.

Phee looked at Neko. "Do you know?"

He barely looked up. "Nope."

"Tariq?"

He shook his head.

"Does this have to do with what happened to Gryph?"

The three boys shared a look. Tariq spoke for the three of them. "I don't think so."

"That's it?" Phee slammed a fist on the table. "That's the best you've got? 'I don't think so'?"

The waitress, startled, looked up from her seat at the counter, where she was nursing a cup of tea and chatting with the short order cook. The cook and waitress glared at Phee, but soon went back to their conversation. Phee lowered her voice.

"You have secrets. All of you. About Gryph. And Saul too, I bet—"

"Hang on," Neko said, interrupting her. "What makes you think you know anything about any of us?"

"Let her talk," Tariq said.

Neko ducked his head again and jammed his hands into his pockets with a scowl.

"Neko Balkashan, of all of you boys I know you the most. I've known you since you were *born*, so don't tell me that I don't know you."

With a nonchalant shrug, Neko muttered something under his breath.

"What did you say?"

Neko glanced up from under his cowl. "Nothing."

Tariq gave Neko a shove. "Show some respect, kid!"

"Sorry." Neko had fixed his sight on the cutlery in front of him. "But ..."

"But what?"

"But ..." His shoulders still hunched, he lifted his eyes. "You really don't know me, Phee. I'm not two, or five, or ten anymore and you have to stop treating me like Nadia's kid brother because I'm more than that. More than you'll ever know."

Phoenix was taken aback. Neko had never talked to her like that. And she had to admit that he had a point. Before she had to come up with something to say, Tariq broke in.

"I think we should all go home." He pulled out his wallet and laid enough money on the table for the whole bill. "It's late."

Phoenix felt her cheeks flush with frustration once again. "And my brother is still dead!"

Huy looked away, his face suddenly pale and drawn, betraying his bravado act. Neko didn't look up from his angry slump at all. Of the three boys, only Tariq met her pleading eyes.

"Phoenix—"

"No!" She could hear the lies already. "I want the truth. You guys know what happened! You could fix this mess."

Tariq cast a quick glance at each of the other boys before answering for them all. "What if you don't want to know the truth?"

Phoenix sat back as if she'd been slapped. "That's ridiculous."

Tariq held her gaze.

"Tell me," she practically whispered. "Tell me anyway."

"Don't," Neko said.

"Don't," Huy echoed. "Not yet."

"Tariq. Tell me." Phee waited. But Tariq said nothing.

"Fine." Furious, she grabbed her backpack and shoved her way out of the booth. "All three of you can thank yourselves for keeping Gryph dead."

"Wait." Tariq ran after her. "I'll go with you."

"No!" Before she could think better of it, she shoved him so hard that he fell back, crashing against the counter, upsetting the tip jar. It fell to the floor and shattered, spilling coins and glass across the linoleum. The waitress half stood, but then paused when she caught Phoenix's angry glare, meant for Tariq. "Don't patronize me! Don't *see me home safely*, don't *spare me the truth*, don't even *talk* to me until you're ready to be real! I'm sick of your lies! All of you!" She slammed open the door to the street, the hot humid stench of rotting fish hitting her hard as she sucked in a deep breath, trying to slow her shallow, panicky gulps for air.

She ran for the station, not out of fear but because she wanted to feel something other than the terror and sadness that sat heavily across her shoulders. She welcomed the ache in her lungs and the hot stretch of her muscles as she took the stairs two at a time up to the platform. Exhausted, she sat directly in the line of sight of the security camera. It was safer, and while she'd told Tariq that she didn't want him to see her home safely, the truth remained that it was dangerous down there, and she was nervous.

WHICH IS WHY she leaped up, ready to flee when she saw a boy approaching, his eyes fixed on her.

"Hey!" She waved both arms at the camera. "Security!"

"Phoenix!" the boy shouted. Still waving, Phoenix squinted to get a better look at him. Tall and lean. Dark hair, curly. Long nose. Glasses. No one she'd ever seen before. "Wait!"

Behind her on the nearest wall, the intercom crackled. *"Security. State your emergency."*

But the boy was talking, and within seconds he had her full attention.

"Phoenix Elaine Nicholson-Lalonde." He wasn't yelling. He was speaking calmly, hands out in front of him in a gesture of goodwill. "You live at the Shores, 26 Abalone Drive. Your mother is Eva, your father is Oscar. She's a doctor. He's a minister, and he's always praying." The boy smiled, and it was for real. Not fake. Not forced. "Like that time the media got pictures of us in one of his pray-ins."

Us? "Who are you?" Phee stared at him, trying to place him. But she'd never seen him before, she'd swear to it.

"I have something to tell you. In private."

The voice sounded again, tinny and bored. *"Security. State your emergency."*

With her eyes locked on this stranger, Phee answered the security guard on the other end of the intercom. "It's okay. False alarm."

"It is a violation of the Transportation Safety Act to activate an emergency resource without due cause," the voice reported as if reading it from a card. *"Be advised that your identity has been recorded and this infraction will be added to your file."*

While Phoenix was being lectured by some faceless, half-asleep security guy, the stranger hung back in the shadows, quiet.

The train came, and Phoenix got on, trailed closely by the boy. He sat opposite her and stared at her, unnerving her to the point that she quickly regretting getting on the car with him.

"I'm called Marlin," he finally said.

Phoenix thought it was odd he'd say it that way, as if he were from another country and the idioms didn't quite translate.

"Okay then, the one called Marlin," she said, "what do you want with me?" Maybe he was a fan of Gryph's? Someone who followed him in the media?

"Remember when Nadia broke her arm?"

That had certainly never been in the media.

"Who *are* you?" And why was he speaking so casually about people he didn't know? About things he couldn't—shouldn't—know about?

"It was at Deer Lake. We were camping—"

"You weren't there." Phee knew this as a fact.

"And she jumped into the lake, only not exactly the same way everyone else had. She whacked her arm on a rock underwater and bust it almost in half."

That's exactly how it had happened.

Phoenix's skin crawled. Everything about him was at once creepy and compelling. "Who are you?" she asked again.

He leaned forward. He was wearing a button-up shirt, checked, open over a black undershirt. Baggy jeans and a studded belt. Skater shoes. Arms muscled and tanned. Eyes green behind the chunky frames. No one she'd ever met, not that she could remember anyway.

"Do you go to my school?"

"Sort of."

"Sort of? What kind of answer is that?"

He ducked his head out of view of the security cameras and lowered his voice. "I'm Saul, Phee." He held her confused gaze. "It's me. Saul."

"Liar!" Phee gasped, her voice catching in her throat and refusing to budge. "I don't know who you are or what kind of freak you are, but you're sick."

He reached for her knee and she scooted into the next seat.

"Get away from me!"

"Okay, okay." Arms up, he sat back, the aisle between them an inadequate moat. "Take your time, Phee. Think about it."

Phee leaped to her feet and pressed the button for the train to stop at the next station. "Get the hell away from me, you asshole."

"Ask me anything." The boy crossed his arms. "About anything you want." Casting a wary glance to the cameras, he added, "For obvious reasons, I'd rather not get into it here. Not in detail, anyway."

The train was slowing, and Phee was getting off. Whether or not she would call security would be based on his answer.

"Fawn's favourite book?"

"*The Velveteen Rabbit.* At the moment anyway." Not even a hesitation. And then, "I read it to her at that downhill race at Winter Park, in Gryph's change room. Nadia was wearing that jacket with the fur trim. And a pink thong." He grinned.

The train stopped, and Phee backed onto the platform, dazed and frightened, but mostly curious. Marlin followed her, and when the train pulled away again and they were alone on the platform, Phee gestured for him to follow her down to the street level and away from the cameras.

THEY SAT on opposite benches that lined a walkway through a little park outside a subdivision Phee wasn't familiar with. It looked a lot like hers, and she could see the orange glow from the lights of the security hut at the gate. She took comfort knowing someone was there, and within sprinting distance if she needed to get away. First she had to figure out who this person was, and how he knew what he did.

"You're a smart girl, Phoenix," Marlin said. "Think about it. Saul disappears. This guy shows up, claims to be Saul. Strange, but not impossible. You've heard about illegal recons. Everyone has."

It was true. She had heard about them. But the same way she'd heard about terrorist attacks in faraway lands, or clandestine drug labs exploding out in the desert. It wasn't a part of her life, and she could hardly imagine it any better than she could a fairy tale brought to life. Marlin noted the skepticism on her face and continued.

"Like I said. Ask me anything."

"What's my dog's name?"

"Riley. He's fourteen, and can hardly make it up the stairs anymore. Your dad picks up his rear end and walks him up them like a wheelbarrow. Or Gryph carries him up."

Phee's mind slowly opened to the possibility, but the mental shift was painful, as if it were her rib cage being sawed open instead. "Tell me about my granddad."

"Alzheimer's. He's losing his marbles, but your grandma won't put him into a home, even though your auntie Trish thinks she should. Your mother doesn't. She wants him at home as long as possible."

Phee's head spun. She gripped the edge of the bench and leaned forward, putting her head between her knees. "You could find all this out somehow. On lync. Anyone could." She said it, but she didn't really believe it.

"But why?"

"I don't know." Phee shrugged. "I don't know anything anymore." To her horror, she was about to cry. She kept her head down, not wanting this boy to see how he'd completely unhinged her.

"I can tell you something that no one could know. No one."

"Okay." Phee's voice sounded small. Defeated. She dared a teary peak at him. "Give it your best shot."

"Your brother pushed you into the river."

Phee sucked in her breath as if she'd been punched.

"He only told you"—Marlin counted back on his fingers— "eleven days ago. And I know that because he called me afterwards and told me that he felt like shit about telling you. He wondered if he made a mistake."

"Did you know before?"

Marlin nodded.

"And you never told me?"

"I swore I wouldn't tell a soul," Marlin said. "So long as he wouldn't tell anyone my secret."

"So he knew. About your status."

Again, he nodded.

"So you lied to me when you said I was the only one who knew."

"True."

How could they be sitting on this ordinary bench talking about such crazy things? Such unbelievably unordinary things? How could Phee's life be so crazy, yet this bench was still just a plain old bench? She gripped the edge in her fingers and watched them turn white. She closed her eyes and willed the world to return itself to its upright position, but when she opened her eyes nothing had changed, and there was Marlin, standing in front of her, a stranger who knew her so well.

REVEAL

She was full of questions, and Marlin—or Saul—had an answer for every single one. Marlin, as he instructed her to call him, joined her on her bench. Phee couldn't see him as Saul anyway, even if he was. Saul was blond and tanned and every bit the star football player with the physique to match. This guy looked like a badass four-eyed skater boy who rarely ate. And besides, no one was ever supposed to be reconstructed into a different identity. That had been made law decades ago, after a string of criminals had done just that, looking to evade capture based on their appearance. That's when the technology became classified, and the various labs combined into one master lab, Chrysalis. But the illegal recon aside, Phoenix had much more simple questions.

"How did you find me tonight?"

"I was following Neko." Marlin's eyes reddened. "And keeping an eye on Nadia."

Nadia! What about Nadia! "She knows?"

"Of course not. She'd never believe me, and she'd probably be the first one to turn me in. You know her."

"But she loves Saul. I mean, you."

"Not me. Not anymore. She'd be scared. Confused. I don't want to put her through that. I don't want her to have to lie. Not when the consequences are so high."

"Do you think you'll ever be able to tell her?"

"I can't see how I could ever get her to understand," Marlin said sadly. "Do you?"

Phoenix had a flash of what it would look like if Marlin tried to convince Nadia that he was really Saul. There'd be screaming and hysterics, and yes, Nadia would be on the phone to Crimcor so fast that he'd hardly have time to beg her not to. The punishment for illegal reconning was decommissioning. Death, in less polished words. Phoenix pushed that awful thought far away.

"Where have you been all this time?"

"I can show you. But not now."

And the most important question of all. "What do you know about Gryphon's death?"

He paused before locking eyes with her. "Everything."

"But?" Everything about the way he said that one word told her that he wasn't going to tell her.

"But I can't tell you. Not yet."

"Was it suicide?" That's all that mattered. If she could just prove that much.

Marlin glanced up at her. "What do you think?"

"When Gryph gets curious about something, he needs to experience it for himself before he'll let it go and move on."

"You think he was obsessed with death?"

"Not obsessed necessarily, but fascinated, sure."

"Especially after he found out about me."

"Let me guess, about a year ago."

"Yeah. You noticed?"

"I noticed how reckless he'd become. How often he blew his wins."

"Sometimes he said he wished he could be reconned so he'd know what it was like. What you and I went through. I wondered if maybe he was trying to punish himself for pushing you into the river."

"Not like this. I can't see him killing himself."

Marlin paused before answering with a voice thick with misery. "There's your answer, then."

"You have to help me prove it," Phee implored.

"Does Chrysalis honestly think he'd kill himself?"

"They're investigating it as a possibility."

"Maybe"—Marlin thought as he spoke—"maybe they think it's his way of getting out of his contract."

"Why would he want to do that? Why has he been screwing it up so bad lately?"

"It'll all make sense. Soon." Marlin glanced at her. "Before the final ruling. I promise. Gryph will come home."

"It was almost over today, you know." Phee told him about the meeting at Chrysalis, about seeing Gryph in stasis. When she finished describing her brother as he was now, she was surprised to see Marlin's eyes welling with tears, until she reminded herself that he was Saul underneath the disguise.

"But it's not over. We'll fix it. We'll bring him home."

The sun was starting to crest over the pitched roofs nearby. Phee had to get home. No matter how badly she wanted to lock herself and this apparent stranger in a room until she knew everything, she had to be home before her parents noticed she was gone. If she got caught, she'd never be able to sneak out again.

"Who's we?" Phee asked. "The guys? They know about you?"

"Only Gryph."

"I'm supposed to believe you?"

"I only told you and Gryph. And Gryph doesn't know about this." He gestured at his new body.

"Only because he was dead when you"—Phee didn't have a word for what Saul had done by getting a new identity—"when you became Marlin?"

He nodded. "And the others don't know about any of it. It's too risky. For everyone involved." Marlin put a hand on her shoulder but quickly took it off when she flinched. "Look, Phee. I know you have to get home. And I promise I'll meet you again, whenever you want. But I can't explain everything now, okay?"

"No. Not okay." Phee shrugged her backpack onto her shoulders. "But if you are Saul, for real, then I know you're only going to tell me when it suits you. So. Fine. Whatever. Okay."

He grinned at her, pausing a long time before replying. "It's good to see you, Phee. Really good. I've been watching Nadia and she's been so sad. You're a really good friend to her. And me. And a good sister to Gryph, even after he admitted pushing you in that river."

It was bizarre to hear him talking to her so familiarly when he looked like a complete and utter stranger. But still, she sensed something more from him—Saul's inner self shining brightly enough that she was warmed by it, even at this odd distance. He was in there. Saul was. In that stranger's body. And who was Marlin? Or his cells and DNA and bones, rather? Where did Saul get the illegal recon? Was it safe? Had his family been reconned in the same manner? And why? The questions that lurked in all the shadows.

Phee reeled from the overwhelming hugeness of it all. She wished she could stay and interrogate him. But she had to go home. The sun was above them now, and the day was warming up.

"I have to go. How can I get hold of you?"

"You can't," he said. "I'll be in touch."

She had so many questions, but no time at all. She had to get back. She said goodbye to Marlin ... or Saul ... or whoever he was, and sprinted back to the station.

WHEN SHE GOT TO THE SHORES, Willis was frantic.

"There's only five minutes left on my shift!" He ushered her through the gate. "What would you have told the day guy, huh? You're only lucky he's not here yet."

"I'm sorry, Willis. It won't happen again."

"That's right!" he replied to her back as she sprinted across the green. "Because I won't let you out in the first place!"

Thank God, everyone was still asleep. Riley wagged his tail but didn't bother to get up as she crept through the kitchen. As she passed the fridge, she realized how hungry she was. She opened the door and was just reaching for an apple when her mother appeared in the doorway, bleary-eyed, her robe hanging loose on her drooping shoulders. Phee froze, apple in hand. What if Eva had gotten up in the middle of the night and found her gone? What if she'd been waiting for her all this time? But no, her mother smiled weakly at her, then took the apple from her.

"Let me make you a proper breakfast." Eva stopped in front of the sink and set the apple on the counter, where it promptly rolled onto the floor. Eva glanced down at it, as if it were an enormous distance and that's how far she'd have to trek to retrieve it. "Oh dear."

Phee hurried to pick up the apple. "How about I make you something?" With gentle hands, she steered her mom into a chair at the table and went about putting on a pot of coffee; grinding the beans, pouring the water. Normal things that did not feel in the least bit normal anymore.

EVA SAT AT THE TABLE while Phee mixed up the batter for waffles. Her father came down as the waffle iron was heating up, and then Fawn too, bounding down the stairs and into the kitchen with an armload of stuffed animals.

"Bunny said Gryphon is coming home today," she announced as she sat the stuffed rabbit in his usual spot, only the tips of his ears appearing over the tabletop. "So he and the other stuffies want to be waiting for him. Like at a surprise party. I'm going to line them up on the front steps."

"Fawn, honey," Eva began. "I don't think ..."

"Actually," Fawn shifted her armload and plucked Bunny out of his seat. "I better do it now. In case he comes home in time for waffles." With that, Fawn flounced out of the room with her plush entourage.

"Oscar?" Eva raised bewildered eyes to her husband. He nodded and got up to follow Fawn.

He kissed Eva's forehead as he passed. "I'll take care of it."

BUT FAWN would not be swayed. She set up her stuffed animals on the steps and all along the front walk. She strung the banner from her recent birthday party along the porch railing, and arranged her tea set on the little table beside the swing. At some point, after waffles and before Fawn was finished her preparations, Eva retreated to her bedroom, defeated by Fawn's enthusiastic determination and refusal to accept the truth about her brother.

Oscar had to go to the church to take care of some neglected work, so it was up to Phoenix to try to dissuade Fawn from insisting on her ill-timed and inappropriate party.

Phoenix joined her little sister on the porch swing, where Fawn was taking a little break from her party preparations.

"Hey." Phoenix offered Fawn a glass of iced tea.

"Can you make some iced tea for the party? And maybe a cake? The chocolate one he likes with the cherry goop in the middle? You know, what he had for his birthday?"

"Look, Fawn—"

"Or cupcakes," Fawn said with a shrug. "That'd be okay too."

"Gryph isn't coming home today." Phoenix took Fawn's hand, knowing full well Fawn's mind was already ten steps ahead and out of the door of this conversation. She had to make Fawn understand before she drove Eva crazy with her childish optimism. "He's not coming home today, and he might not be coming home ever. Do you understand?"

"Grandma will make a cake. Want to go over with me and ask her?"

"Fawn!" Phoenix gave her a stern shake. "Listen to me!"

"I am!"

"No you're not."

"I am." Blatantly, and with a cheeky grin to boot, Fawn tipped her glass of iced tea into Phoenix's lap. "And I think you're stupid. So there."

Phoenix resisted the urge to grab her little sister by the arms and hurl her off the porch in one furious move. "Get me a towel," she growled. Fawn stood up, arms folded defiantly.

"I don't want to. I'm busy."

"Get me a towel!" Phoenix tried to account for Fawn's absurd behaviour. She was only little. She didn't understand. She was as upset as the rest of them but couldn't communicate her feelings the way they could. And all the while, the cold wet splotch on her lap widened, seeping between her legs as if she'd pissed herself. "Now!"

"No!" Fawn stamped her foot. "And you should shut up and stop talking about Gryphon like that!" With that, Fawn took off. Down the steps, out the gate, and across the green at breakneck speed toward their grandparents' house. Phee let her go. She got up to go back inside but left the stuffies where they were.

WHEN EVA finally dragged Fawn home that night, she still refused to bring in her stuffed animals. Only Bunny was taken in, because she slept with him. The others stood vigil in their designated spots on the steps, and were still there when Phoenix left after dinner for Nadia's. She told her parents that she was sleeping over, but she'd told Nadia she had to come home, to be there in time to go to church with Oscar the next morning.

Truth was that Saul—Marlin—had texted her after Fawn had taken off, instructing her to meet him at the benches at eleven that night. She would hang out with Nadia until it was time to meet him.

NADIA, AS USUAL since Saul disappeared, was in her pyjamas when she answered the door. She and Phee settled in the kitchen, perched cross-legged on the island counter, a tub of double-fudge ice cream between them.

"Where are your parents?"

"They took Neko to a psychiatrist in Brampton." Nadia dug her spoon into the carton, aiming for the ripple of fudge.

"On a Saturday?"

"No." Nadia talked through a mouthful. "His appointment is Monday morning. But they're worried he'll stay out all night again or do something crazy, so they took him early." She swallowed. "They promised him a day at the go-cart track. Like he's six."

"A psychiatrist?"

"You know my parents." Nadia nudged the carton toward Phee. "They don't give a crap unless we slit our wrists or lock ourselves in our room and starve to death. They think Neko is screwed up because of Gryph's death being ..." Nadia let her words trail into silence.

Phee said it for her. "Permanent."

"Yeah." Nadia nodded. "And Saul disappearing."

"But they think you're okay? Even though he's your boyfriend?" Phee clutched her spoon tightly in her fist, giving over to the pain of it digging into her palm instead of giving in to the urge to tell Nadia about Saul. Part of her argued that if the tables were turned, she'd want Nadia to tell her the truth. But the larger, more convincing part of her reminded her that she was not Nadia, and that Nadia was a very different person. Someone for whom denial truly worked wonders. Someone for whom truth was not as valuable or all that questioned in the first place. Nadia was not like Phee. Not in the least. She didn't need answers and explanations nearly as badly as Phee did.

"Oh no, they think I'm totally screwed up too," Nadia went on. "But in their funny math, him seeing a friend die is worse than my missing boyfriend, so he goes first. Even though Gryph was my friend too." She glanced at Phee. "Sorry—I mean, Gryph *is* my friend too."

"It's okay," Phee said. "I know what you mean."

"Anyway," Nadia said with a sad sigh, "I have to go on Tuesday, but I convinced them I wouldn't do anything rash in the meantime. Plus, they said I can go on my own. You can come, if you want."

"Maybe."

"You're lucky your parents aren't freaks like mine."

"They're freaks in their own way, trust me."

"But like, only teaming up to charge one of us off to a specialist. Like, would it kill them to just sit us all down together and *talk?* Like you guys do."

Phee nodded. She was thankful for her parents. She'd never envied Nadia hers, with their cool exchanges and schedules carefully designed to avoid each other and their kids wherever possible. Except times like this, when they were more than willing to put on a show and make it look as if they were attentive and involved. When they weren't. Not really.

THEY TALKED MOSTLY about Saul and Gryph, of course, with Phee editing herself so much that she finally gave up and let Nadia do most of the talking. She worried that her best friend would be able to read it on her face, or in her body language. That she could tell something was up and that Phoenix was lying. But Nadia was awash in sadness, and couldn't see past her own misery to inquire much about Phee's. Normally this would bother Phee, but not tonight. Tonight she was thankful that she didn't have to lie any more than she already was. They put a movie on, but mostly for an excuse for a couple of hours of silence, and then it was time for Phee to go.

She hugged Nadia hard before leaving. Nadia stood at the door, waving, which made Phee so sad that she almost cried. Nadia had no idea what was going on around her, how her friends were sinking in the quicksand of secrets and deception. Phee prayed she could fix it before it all crumbled and everyone was made to pay for the sins, great and small. Nadia too, for if she wasn't so narrow-minded about things, Phee could include her in some of the mystery, and there might've been some hope that she and Saul could be reunited, if only in his new form. But then Phee couldn't blame her. She wasn't even sure she knew what she thought about it all. Except that it was illegal. And dangerous. And ultimately fascinating.

LATER

Marlin was waiting for her on the same bench near the station. Phee couldn't believe that it had been only hours earlier that she'd said goodbye; it felt as though days had passed since then. She sat beside him, and neither of them said anything for a while. Then he spoke, his face shadowed in the glow cast from the street lamp. He looked worried.

"Where'd they take Neko?"

He'd obviously seen Nadia and Neko's parents leave with him. "To see some shrink."

"When's he coming back?"

"I don't know. Tomorrow, I guess."

"Tomorrow or not? Don't you know?"

"No! Let it go, already."

"Why do they think he needs a shrink?" He emphasized the word *they* as if he had his own idea about why Neko would need a psychiatrist.

"Why do you think?" Phee gawked at him. "One of his friends is dead, another one has disappeared, and he's keeping some big fat secrets that are eating him alive."

"And Nadia and Neko's parents only know how to shuffle their kids off to some quack."

"Exactly."

"Has he talked to you?"

"A little."

"What did he say?"

"Nothing. Like the rest of you guys."

"And Nadia?" Marlin asked. "How's she holding up?"

"She's next for the shrink. Her appointment is Tuesday."

"God, Nadia. I miss her." Marlin dropped his head in his hands with a heavy sigh. "I miss her so much."

"Then tell her the truth."

"She'd never understand."

"She might not. But she might come around."

"I can't force her to make that kind of decision. What if she decided to tell on me? And even if she didn't tell, I can't put her at that kind of risk. And what would be the point? I can't hang around forever, Phee. I'd have been long gone by now if it weren't for having to sort out this mess with Gryph."

"How *are* you going to sort it out?" Phee asked. "If none of the guys know about you?"

"I have a plan," he said. "But I don't want to use it. I'm hoping the guys come up with something on their own. Something better."

"Better than what?"

Marlin stared at her.

"Never mind," Phee said. "You're not going to tell me, are you?"

"Not yet."

Phee changed the subject instead of beating the dead horse a little more. "Where will you go? When it's over?"

"To be with my parents."

"They're changed too? Like you?" She thought back to the message she'd listened to on his phone. The woman's voice. *"It's happening now. We can't wait for you."*

"That was my mom," Marlin explained when Phee told him about the message.

"That's why you couldn't meet me. You had to go be ... what? What do you call it?"

Marlin shrugged. "Reconned, I guess."

"But you didn't die."

"No."

"Do you have the same DNA?"

Marlin shook his head.

"But how not?"

"You don't need to know that. Not right now anyway." Marlin stood. "Come on. Let's go."

"Where are we going?" Phee followed him as he strode toward the station.

"I'm going to show you something Gryph wanted you to see."

"Then why didn't he show me himself?"

"He didn't get a chance."

"Or he didn't want to."

"He wanted you to know about it." Marlin stopped in his tracks. "You especially. In case."

"In case of what?"

"In case anything happened to you."

"What are you going to show me?" Anxious excitement rode up her spine, making her shiver. But Marlin didn't answer, so she just followed him, hoping she could handle whatever was coming next.

THEY GOT OFF the train one station before the stop for the Balmoral. This too was still part of the fish-packing district, but the far edge of it. Beyond the last street lay the abandoned freeway, and beyond that reclaimed parkland, and beyond that, the two-per settlement nearest to the city. It was common knowledge that the area between this edge of the city and the two-per settlement was rife with criminal activity. Phee hesitated.

"I'm not going in there." She pointed at the vast darkness that stretched out beyond the chain-link fence topped with barbed wire.

Marlin gave her a friendly shove toward the fence. "Oh come on, you're chicken all of a sudden?"

"You *are* Saul, aren't you?" Phee muttered.

"I told you not to use that name, Phee." His tone sharpened. "I meant it. You keep doing that and I can't see you again. Understood?"

Phee nodded. "Got it."

"Good." Marlin slowed down to let her catch up after gawking nervously at the thick brush on the other side of the fence. "And just so you know, we're not going over the fence. Not tonight, anyway."

"Fine," Phee said. "And just so you know, I'm not chicken."

HE LED HER, in what seemed a very circuitous route, on a good half-hour trek between squat warehouses and rambling factories, all reeking of rotting fish. He paused only once, to toss something into a garbage can on a dark corner, where the street light had burned out or broken. Finally, he stopped in front of yet another long, sprawling warehouse. Standing derelict on the roof was a large billboard once meant for drivers on the freeway to see as they passed: CAPTAIN MURPHY'S FAMOUS FISH STICKS, starring a cartoon fisherman—Captain Murphy, presumably—with an anchor tattoo and a net slung over his shoulder greeting the commuters of days gone by with a corny grin.

"What is this place?"

"Home, sort of. For now, anyway." Marlin rapped on the door. It opened a crack, and then wider. A woman peered out, eyes squinting with suspicion. Classical music wafted from a room illuminated at the end of the dark corridor behind her. Mozart—Phee recognized the melody. Oscar's favourite.

"Who's she?"

"The one I told you about."

"Of course, of course." She smiled and opened the door wide. "Come in, come in. I'm Polly. You're Phoenix, right? Gryphon's little sister?"

Before Phee could ask her how she knew Gryph, Marlin broke in with "I haven't explained things yet."

"Hi." Phee let the woman shake her hand before turning eyes full of questions to Marlin. "And will you?"

"I will." Marlin put a comforting hand on her shoulder and steered her down the hall after the woman. "After Polly makes us a cup of tea. She won't let us do anything before that."

Phee lowered her voice. "Is she your mom? Reconned?"

"No, no." Marlin laughed. "Polly is just Polly."

The warehouse was a labyrinth of hallways and rooms. It quickly became apparent that it was a laboratory of sorts, although it was damp and smelled vaguely fishy. She caught a glimpse into one of the rooms that opened off the hall. Inside were several capsules like the stasis ones at Chrysalis. She could see only the one nearest her well enough to recognize that it *was* a Chrysalis capsule. It had the logo on the side, and a number stamped into the metal, like the one Gryph was being kept in.

"This is an illegal recon lab, isn't it?"

"Bingo," Marlin said lightly.

"Be serious," Phee said. "How'd you get the capsules?"

"Chrysalis was finished with them," he said with a shrug. "Funny thing happened on the way to the scrap metal factory."

"I *said* be serious!"

"Why?" Marlin gestured around him. "Isn't this all serious enough for you as it is?"

"I shouldn't be here. I shouldn't even know this place exists." She turned angry eyes to Marlin. "Why did you bring me here? What if I have to do a lie detector test for Chrysalis?"

"Why would you?" Marlin asked. "You weren't there."

"But what if I have to take one anyway?"

"Look, you wanted to know what's been going on. Well, this is what's been going on."

Confused, Phee asked, "What do you mean?"

"This is where Gryph was coming to when he left the Shores at night. And when he spent the night at my place."

"Here?" Phee had imagined all kinds of things: the skate parks all to themselves, stupid double-dog dares, general boy mischief, even long dull hours of bottomless coffee at the diner. But not this.

Marlin nodded. "When I told him about my recon, he wanted to see this place."

"He didn't freak out?"

"Not at all," Marlin said.

"Not even for a second?"

"No. He said he was raised right. That Oscar and Eva brought up kids who knew better than to judge."

All of a sudden Phee felt tremendously guilty for ever having thought less of Saul—Marlin—because of his status. And the day at the no-per zone, how she'd judged all those people for who they were.

"He wanted to show you this place. He wanted you to know that you had an option, if you ever needed it."

"I still have one recon."

"And after that?"

"I don't know," Phee replied. "Hopefully there won't be an 'after that.'"

"Well, if there ever is, you know that it doesn't have to be final."

"It is for Gryph. It is for anyone who ends up at Chrysalis. You can't help him. And you wouldn't be able to help me."

"Well, not if you died suddenly, maybe. But if you knew you were going to die, like from cancer or something. If you knew enough in advance."

"To come here?" Phee asked, amazed. "To let some under-ground, filthy lab recon me? Of my own volition?"

"We do good work at these labs," Marlin said evenly. "Gryph thought you would understand."

"I'm trying to," Phee said. "But you have to admit it's all a lot to take in all at once."

"Well, Gryph trusts you. And I can tell you that he wanted you to know about this place. Especially because it's his fault that you only have one recon left."

"When were you guys going to tell me?"

"I don't know."

"You told Gryph over a year ago."

"Yes. Not long after the X Games, I guess."

"But not me."

"I'm telling you now."

"Only because Gryph is dead."

"And because I have to go away."

"Where?"

"Better if you don't know."

"Why can't you tell me?" Phee felt a sudden panic. Saul, in this new form, felt like the last tenuous connection to Gryph. If he went away, she'd be that much more alone.

"It's just better if you don't know, Phee."

"And so he won't tell you." Polly was back with the tea fixings. "Right, Marlin?"

"Right," Marlin said.

"But you can trust me, Saul—"

Polly and Marlin frowned at her.

"Marlin. Sorry." Phee wasn't sure if they could trust her, but hoped they could. She hoped that she would make the right decisions too, and not reveal this place to anyone, even under the pressure of a Chrysalis lie detector test. "You can trust me."

MARLIN EXPLAINED that he'd finally decided to tell Gryphon the truth about his family and where he'd really gone when he'd left for a couple of weeks in Grade 8. He'd died in fact, at home, from meningitis, the same strain that had sent three of the boys' class-mates to the hospital. He couldn't go, though, as his DNA was not on record with Chrysalis. So he'd died, where the others had not, and then he'd come here, or to its incarnation at the time, which had been an old mill out by the delta.

"We keep moving the lab," he said. "Every few months or so."

"How did they recon you?"

"We have my cord blood," he replied. "My parents were fugitives long before I was born. They've been recon activists since they were in college."

"But how is it a secret?" Phee wanted to know. "How come you can be identified along with the rest of us, like at the train station and on school registration day?"

"All that's facial recognition and fingerprints, retina scans. No one except Chrysalis actually checks DNA. We can hack everything else into the various systems."

Phee hadn't known that. She'd always assumed that the identity technology was all-encompassing, right down to DNA.

"So there are lots of illegally reconned people out there?"

"A significant number," Polly broke in. "Yes."

"And what about now?" Phee aimed her question at Marlin. "Whose DNA do you have now?" She imagined them harvesting DNA from dead people they couldn't save, or worse.

"My own, still." Marlin touched his hands to his face. "This is all surface reconning, along with things like fake glasses. Coloured contacts. Practically starving myself," he added with a laugh. "Lifts in my shoes. And hair dye."

"Hair dye?" Phee could hardly believe that something you could get at the drugstore was part of such an elaborate disguise.

"We do the least number of medical interventions as possible," Polly said.

"I see," Phee said, although she didn't. But she'd had enough details for the moment, so she changed the subject. "What did Gryph say when you told him the truth?"

"I'd double-dog-dared him not to tell anyone," Marlin said with a smile. "He never breaks a double-dog dare. He got it. And more important, he got why he had to keep it a secret. Even from Tariq and Huy."

"Why'd you tell Gryph in the first place?"

"I didn't want to be alone with the secret anymore." He fixed his eyes on Phee now. "And because he'd told me about you."

"That he pushed me?"

Marlin nodded. "It was eating him up. He wanted to tell you the truth but wasn't sure if he should."

"A secret for a secret?"

He nodded again. "A doozy given deserves a doozy in return."

The two of them smiled, Marlin for his own reasons, and Phee because she could just imagine the two boys swapping deep secrets as if trading hunting knives.

After a long pause, Marlin continued. "At first, he was going to tell your parents. He thought they could help. But I persuaded him not to."

"But they *could* help. My mom anyway. I'm not sure about my dad. He's on the Congress."

"We were going to try to get your mom on board. We only have two doctors right now, so we'd really be able to use her."

"But?"

Marlin cocked an eyebrow. "But then Gryph died. He's taking a break from his regularly scheduled programming."

"It's not funny."

"I know, I know."

It all made sense now, how Gryph had changed. She had to smile at herself, for all those times she'd thought he was using drugs. She'd been so wrong. So very wrong.

"What about Chrysalis?" she asked, coming back to the present.

"He was trying to get out of his contract," Marlin said. "In the meantime, we were super careful not to give them any reason to be suspicious."

"But they are," Phee said. "They know he's up to something."

"They'd never guess *this*." Marlin gestured around them. "They'd never guess that their top athlete was slumming with a bunch of rogue reconners."

"And he was okay with all of this?" Phee thought back to the fated trip to the no-per zone. How Gryph had seemed open to it all in a way that Phee wasn't.

"Not at first. He was as confused as you are." Phee didn't deny it, so Polly carried on. "But then he really started to make up his own mind about the way things are. How they should be. And what he could do about it. Like the rest of us here, he came to believe that everyone should have the same access to the same number of recons in a lifetime."

Marlin nodded. "Equal rights, equal recons."

"What was he doing about it?" Phee asked. "What was he doing here?"

"Making a difference."

"But how?" Phee imagined him in a lab coat, handling stem cells and test tubes of accelerator. That was ridiculous, though. He was just a teenager, not a scientist at all. So she wasn't surprised when Marlin set her straight.

"Nothing glamorous," he said. "Bringing food from your garden, cleaning up. He helped move the lab to this location. Brought clothes for people to leave in. Biggest help was physiotherapy, or sort of. He'd help the patients get back onto their feet, get healthy before they left. He taught them stretches, exercises."

"He even played basketball with them." Polly smiled, remembering. "He brought one of those nets, you know? The ones you fill at the base with sand so it doesn't topple over. He tried to get me to play, of all things."

Phee listened, her cup of tea balanced on one knee cooling as she rolled this new information about her brother around in her head, trying to make it fit with her idea of who her brother was. *Is*.

"That explains why he was acting different about Chrysalis," Phee said. "They used to be so important to him."

"True." Marlin nodded. "And he was trying to break free from Chrysalis."

"Maybe he should've started genuinely losing every once in a while." Phee laughed. "But he wouldn't do that, would he? He might be able to give up first place, but not second."

Marlin grinned. "He was victim to his ego—that never changed."

"Just his ideas about right and wrong when it comes to reconning."

"Right and wrong on a much bigger scale, Phoenix."

"Indeed." Polly took Phee's empty teacup. "Your brother has strong convictions. He is a born activist. He's willing to take risks where others won't. He does valuable work here. And he will again, when he comes back."

"*If* he comes back."

"He will." Polly put a reassuring hand on Phee's arm. "He will come back."

Phee raised her eyes to fix Marlin with a dark look. "Tell me how he died."

"Not yet, Phee."

"But you will?" Phee was too tired to protest. "You promise you will?"

Marlin nodded. He reached out a hand. She took it and he helped her up. "I'll give you a tour and then make sure you get home without falling asleep in the middle of the street, okay?"

HE SHOWED HER the door that led to the wing of small rooms housing the newly reconned, giving them time to get their heads around their new appearance, and to settle in to the logistics of a new identity.

"Everyone's sleeping," he said, leading her away. "And I wouldn't introduce you to anyone anyway, for obvious reasons."

He pushed open a heavy door that separated the actual lab from the rest of the building. The lights came on, casting a harsh, surgical light onto the gleaming stainless-steel surfaces and the polished tile floor. Everything glinted with cleanliness, much to Phee's relief. The same sort of track that she'd seen at Chrysalis crossed the room on the far wall. Marlin saw her notice it.

"We use the same equipment. You saw the capsules. We use the same vitrification fluids, the same molecular compounds."

"Aren't you the scientist," Phee joked, although she felt nothing but unease at this clandestine set-up.

"Not at all," Marlin replied. "But I can sound smart. We have insiders working for us. Chrysalis agents who siphon from the main tanks. Just a few ounces at a time. Shipping agents who fudge the inventory. It's a big movement, Phee."

"Apparently." Phoenix spun on her heel so she was face to face with Marlin. "And will this *big movement* be able to do anything to bring Gryph back?"

"Maybe."

"How?"

"If the appeal fails, and we can get into Chrysalis and retrieve his stasis pod—"

"*Steal* him?" Phee laughed again—the notion was so absurd. "Have you ever even been to Chrysalis? You couldn't steal a ballpoint pen from there, let alone the body of one of their celebrities!"

"You weren't listening. We steal stuff from them all the time."

"But people? Have you ever actually stolen a whole, entire person?"

"Obviously, we're hoping we won't have to consider it." Marlin's eyes darkened. "But if it comes down to it, I'll try. He's my best friend, Phee. And I've got nothing left to lose. My parents are in hiding on the other side of the continent because my father's role in this lab was about to be exposed—we had to relocate the entire operation because of him, or else the whole operation would've been compromised—and I'm as good as dead to everyone else."

"Not to Nadia."

His eyes brimmed immediately. "I don't want to talk about her."

"She's desperate to know what happened to you. She doesn't know what to think. That you're hurt, or ran away, or are in trouble. Or just plain left her."

He turned away, hiding real tears. "I said I don't want to talk about it."

Phee let it go for now. She couldn't imagine what Nadia would think about all of this. Nadia, like Phee until recently, had never had reason to adjust her ideas about reconning. But Nadia—unlike Phee—was someone who rarely shifted her thoughts on anything. Nadia liked being a three-per and what it meant in relation to people with fewer recons. She liked her status just as much as she liked jackets with real rabbit trim, and tubes of mascara that cost more than most one-pers made in a week. Phee understood that, but whereas she was willing to rethink things, she couldn't imagine Nadia doing the same. Maybe, if Phee could explain everything, just maybe Nadia would come around. Phee doubted it, though, and by the look on Marlin's face, so did he.

CONSEQUENCE

If none of the guys would talk, there was only one other person Phee could think of who might be able to shed some light on how Gryph died.

After church, Phoenix arranged to meet Clea at Seaside Park, where she worked as a lifeguard at the water park built at the ocean's edge. Phee took Fawn with her, feeling guilty for not hanging out with her more, and wanting to give the rest of her family a break from the six-year-old's relentless energy.

"The water park!" Fawn skipped ahead of her as she exited the train at the stop nearest the park's pool. "Gryph brought me here. You can swim in the real ocean, but the water park is way funner."

"I know, Fawn. We've been here before together, remember?"

"It's really cool." Fawn wasn't listening. "There's a waterslide and a tube river and everything. Gryph bought me two ice-cream cones last time. He's a better brother than you are."

"I'm your sister."

"You know what I mean," Fawn said with a sneer. "He's nicer to me than you are."

"Shows how much you know ..." Phee couldn't resist a jab in response to Fawn's hurtful words. "He only brought you here because he wanted to see Clea, and girls love boys who act all nicey-nice to their little sisters, so he was only bringing you as an accessory."

Fawn blinked. "Huh?"

It had all sailed right over her head thankfully, because Phee was already sorry she'd said it. She didn't mean to hurt Fawn. Phee was just tired and sad and frustrated. And entirely overwhelmed by recent events. "I said I'd buy you as many ice creams as you want, but if you throw up you're on your own."

The sunshine made her feel a little better. She adjusted her sunglasses and bullied Fawn into putting on her sun hat before finding them a place to set out their blanket. There was a grassy knoll behind the big slide, which suited Phee just fine. She could see Clea perched atop her lifeguard stand, looking tanned and beautiful, and not at all grief-stricken.

That was from afar, though, because as she and Fawn approached, and Clea took off her shades and climbed down to give Fawn a big hug, Phee noticed dark circles under her eyes and an uncharacteristic sloppiness to her ponytail. And she wasn't wearing so much as a smidgeon of makeup. Phee reeled in her assumptions, deciding she'd better clear the slate for once.

"Hey, Clea."

"Phoenix. Hi."

Clea held Fawn to her for another long moment before letting her go with an affectionate shove. "And you, little miss mischief, you stay where I can see you."

"I will."

"And where you can see us, okay?"

"Promise." With that, Fawn headed for the shallow end of the pool. "So"—she turned her attention to Phee—"I wondered if I'd ever hear from you."

Phoenix considered telling Clea that she'd thought about calling her, seeing how she was doing. But the truth was, it had never occurred to her to inquire about how Clea was holding up with having lost Gryph too. She just wanted to know what Clea knew.

"Sorry not to be in touch sooner."

"That's okay." Clea shrugged. "I know you don't like me. And I've been keeping up with the news, so I have an idea about what's going on. The appeal, for example."

"I'm sorry if I offended—"

"No, you're not." Clea narrowed her eyes. "You're not sorry. So skip it, and get to the real reason you're here." She fingered the whistle on a cord around her neck, eyes scanning her waterlogged charges.

"I'm hoping you might know what really happened that day."

"No. But I would tell you if I did." There was defiance in her eyes that elicited a sudden tug of shame in Phee. "Because I love Gryph, and I would do whatever I could to get him back, even if you think I'm just some slut who wants to hang off his arm for a while."

"I don't think that." But she did, or she had. Until right now. With Clea standing up for herself, here in her place of work where she so clearly had the respect of those around her, Phoenix could see a little of what Gryph saw in her. She could hear Oscar's minister voice intoning, "We are new wonders every day, each of us reborn with the sunrise ..."

"I am sorry." The words felt thick in her throat. "I am, Clea."

Clea's expression softened. "I didn't actually see it happen. I was there, like, seconds after. But I didn't see it happen. And the boys won't tell me anything."

It hit Phee like a kick to the gut. Clea might not have seen it happen, but she'd *been* there. Phee had known that, but it hadn't really sunk in until now what that truly meant. The fear, the horror. Seeing Gryph like that. Her boyfriend, for whatever that was worth. In all the time that had passed, Phee hadn't given Clea's feelings a single thought. Oscar would be ashamed of her. Hell, she was ashamed of herself.

"I'm so sorry, Clea. It must have been awful."

"It was." Her eyes teared up. "It was awful."

"I am so, so sorry that you saw him like that."

"Me too."

The girls said nothing for a moment, but then Phee pushed on, hoping Clea would let her.

"You've talked to them? The guys?"

"I've talked to Tariq," Clea said with a sigh. "He's the only one who'll get back to me. But I think that's because he won't let Huy or Neko speak for themselves. They're all locked up. Nothing in. Nothing out."

"I'm getting the same treatment, if it's any consolation."

Fawn bounded toward them, soaking wet and shivering. "Can I sit in the lifeguard chair? Just for a minute?"

"Sorry, Fawn. You know I can't let anyone up there unless they're a lifeguard."

"Please?"

"No," Clea repeated. "Why don't you go down the slide? But not headfirst this time or I have to give you a warning just like everyone else. Okay?"

"Okay." Fawn hurried off, careful not to break the no-running rule on the pool deck.

"You're good with her."

"You might notice I'm good at a couple of things, if you actually saw me as a person, and not some brainless slut."

"Ouch."

"Yeah, ouch."

Clea's boss called over from the concession stand and told her to get back to work, so she and Phee said goodbye. Phee felt antsy. She wanted to leave right away, but she'd promised Fawn a swim, so she made herself wait another half an hour before dragging a protesting Fawn into the change rooms and then home.

But being at home was worse. She still felt antsy. There was nothing to do, and that drove her mad. She wasn't meeting Marlin until later, and none of the other boys were returning her calls anymore, so she just had to wait. She lay down and tried to nap, but sleep would not come. She'd been up for two days and two nights now.

Phee was so tired at dinner that she could hardly keep her eyes open. She couldn't comprehend how Gryph could go out night after night and still function at all during the day, let alone win competition after competition. She excused herself early and shut herself in her room and tried again to sleep. She was going to meet Marlin later, and if she didn't get some sleep now, it would be a long time before she could hope for another chance at it. She set her alarm and shut her eyes, not very hopeful.

Thankfully, she did sleep. When her alarm went off, she woke with a start. She could've slept for days and days, but she had to go. The house was quiet when she padded down the stairs later. Riley whined as she passed, and she paused to give him a pat. Willis let her out the main gate with stern instructions to be back by five in the morning and not a moment later this time.

MARLIN MET HER at the benches again.

"What are you going to show me tonight?" Phee fell into step beside him as they headed off to the train station.

"A test-tube-baby factory where they make to-order babies for all those sad, desperate infertile couples with money to burn," Marlin said with a sardonic laugh. Then he did his best TV infomercial spokesperson impersonation. "And for only $19.99, pre-select the sex of up to four zygotes!"

"Not funny."

"We're going back to the lab," Marlin said. "You can help."

"What if I don't want to?" Phee stopped walking. "What if I wish you'd never shown me that place? What if I wish I never knew about it? What if I don't want to because I don't agree with you or your illegal reconning? What if I have my own opinions?"

"Do you? Agree?"

"I don't know. The world is set up the way it is for a reason. Good reasons, right?"

"You mean the tier system?" It had been like that, with doctors and business executives and politicians and lawyers being entitled to three recons, and then academics and accountants and pilots and such being allotted two recons, and then down the line through daycare workers and garbagemen and grocery clerks with their one each, and then everyone else, mostly jobless and destitute, not having rights to a single recon, ever. "That system was designed by the elite for the elite, Phee. Think about it. Is any one life more important than another?"

"Sure. Some crackhead from a no-per zone is not as important as my little sister." Phee remembered the ill-fated shuttle trip to the no-per zone. Those people were not as valuable as the people she loved. No way.

"Not to you, maybe." Marlin's tone was challenging. "But that 'crackhead' has a sister too. Who'd be just as upset if her sister died. In fact, more upset than you, because Fawn has three recons to her name. She'd come back."

"Not if Chrysalis doubted the circumstances around her death."

"Now you're talking about Gryph."

"Of course I'm talking about Gryph!" Phee had to remind herself to keep her voice down. They were waiting for the train, and while there was no one else around at the moment, who knew who might be nearby, and who knew what exactly was captured by the security cameras? "Who else would I be talking about?"

"It will all work out. With Gryph, I mean."

"Prove it. Tell me what really happened that night."

The train sighed to a stop and the two of them got on. The car was empty, but still Marlin whispered. "I will. When we get off the train."

TRUE TO HIS WORD, as they made their way to the warehouse, Marlin finally started talking about what really happened.

"If I tell you this, you have to promise not to talk to anyone about it. Not Nadia. Or Huy or Tariq or Neko. Definitely not Neko. Not a word."

"I promise."

"And I mean it about not telling Nadia. You can't ever tell her what I'm about to tell you."

"Tell me, already." Phee laughed, but it was a scared, nervous little bleat. She didn't like the way he was talking, and she couldn't help wondering if it was better in the long run that she didn't know. Part of her felt sick with unease, but the bigger part of her was a complete slave to her curiosity.

"I'm telling you because you've always been a good friend to me, and because I can see how much you're hurting not knowing what happened to your brother." Marlin stopped walking. He gripped Phoenix by her shoulders and waited until she met his eyes with her nervous gaze. "Gryph didn't kill himself, and it wasn't an accident."

They were in front of a boarded-up grocery store, long since abandoned, dark and ominous like a hulking, silent witness.

"I'm listening," Phee said, although her head pounded and her thoughts leaped ahead of her, making it difficult to focus on what he was saying. She tried to concentrate. That meant that it wasn't suicide! He'd be reconned! She glanced at her watch. It was just past midnight. Could she go to Chrysalis now? Surely there was someone there around the clock. Marlin would come with her, explain everything. Gryph could come home! But of course there was more. It was never simple.

"He was pushed."

"Who—" Phee blanched. "Not *you*? Is that why you disappeared?"

"No, it wasn't me."

"Tariq?"

Marlin shook his head, eyes downcast.

"A stranger!" Phee latched on to the notion with her relief like talons. "That's okay, then. Even if they do a lie detector test, right?

Doesn't matter who, so long as none of—" She caught herself. She wasn't that naive. If it had been a stranger, they would've said so all along. The boys were obviously covering up for one of their own. "Was it Huy?"

"No." Marlin took Phee's wrist, pulling her back to the present so that she could really hear what he was about to say. "It was Neko."

"No it wasn't!" Phee gasped. She pulled her arm away and hugged herself.

"It was Neko," Marlin said. "I saw the whole thing happen."

MARLIN EXPLAINED. The boys were on the platform, waiting for the train. They were teasing Neko, which was as normal for them as breathing. One of them always had to be the target, and it had been Neko's turn for a long while. Perhaps too long.

"You're a coward," Gryph said. "Why do you think we haven't initiated you yet?"

"I'm not a coward." Neko's cheeks blazed with sudden anger. He gave Gryph a shove, just to prove his point. Gryph didn't budge.

"You are so." This from Huy. "That's okay. You're just a little kid. You've got time to learn to do big-boy things." He lunged for Neko, making a grab for his pants. "Still got diapers under there?"

"Don't touch me, Huy."

"Why not?" Huy made another grab for his pants. "Afraid you'll catch my faggot cooties?"

"Shut up!" Neko's face went even redder, and his eyes flashed darker.

"Knock out the cameras, then," Gryph challenged. "I dare you."

The colour drained from his cheeks as fast as it had come. "What for?"

"Because," Tariq said, "he told you to."

"Yeah? Well, cowards do what they're told. Cowards are sheep," Neko said. "And I'm not a coward, so there. Knock out the cameras yourself."

But his bravado had gone too far. The resulting defiance did not go over well. Gryph got right up into his face, staring down at him, his nostrils flared with rage. Gryph narrowed his eyes. Spittle formed at the corners of his mouth. "Do it."

"Sure." Neko stammered out the word, aiming for nonchalance. "What do I care?"

Huy and the others stared at him, arms crossed across their chests, while Gryph still had him locked in his glare.

"So get going."

Once the cameras were disabled, it was only a matter of minutes before maintenance showed up to repair them. If the guys were still hanging around, there'd be no doubt who was to blame.

"Okay, okay." Neko sprinted down the stairs and was soon back with a handful of rocks. He aimed for the first one and missed. He missed again with the second.

Gryph took one of the rocks and threw it. With a quiet crack, the lens shattered. "You do the other one, or we're done. No more hanging out with us. You go your way, we go ours."

"Back to after-school care," Huy said with a laugh.

"Go easy on him, Gryph." This from Saul, who had mostly stayed out of this taunt session. "He's only little."

"I can take care of myself!" Neko aimed a rock at the other camera at their end of the station. He nailed it so hard that the camera lens shattered and the whole thing slouched in its casing.

"That's better." Gryph gave him a hard slap on the back. "Now, one last challenge for today."

"What do you want me to do?" Neko braced himself for it.

"You're going to push me in front of the train," Gryph said. The others eyed Gryph, not sure where he was going with this. You never knew with him. They'd play along, though. It usually made sense in the end, like the prank with the doors. Although that one had gone a little too far.

"What?"

Saul clapped a hand on Neko's shoulder. "You heard him." Out of sight of Neko, Saul raised his eyebrows at Gryph, questioning him silently.

"Yeah." Gryph grabbed hold of Neko and shoved him toward the edge of the platform. "There's a new program that stops the train before impact. Don't you watch the news?"

"You're making that up."

"Not at all." Gryph grinned at the other boys. "Am I making it up, guys?"

"No," Huy said at once.

"Nope," Saul and Tariq added reluctantly, not sure where Gryph was going with this particular prank. Saul glanced down at the people at the far end of the platform. No one was looking their way. He almost wished someone was, so Gryph's bravado might falter.

It was a Saturday, and this was the Industrial Sector, so not many people had reason to use this station. Just a handful, none of them wanting to share the platform with a group of unruly teenagers, even if one of them was Gryphon Nicholson-Lalonde. Gryph was wearing a baseball hat and sunglasses anyway, so none of the bystanders could tell who he was.

"Want to try it out?" Gryph gave Neko another little shove. "Want to try out this brilliant new technology?"

EVERYONE HAS A LIMIT, and Neko had reached his. He'd had enough of the teasing.

"You're full of shit." In a quick, instinctive move that drew on almost ten years of twice-weekly karate classes, Neko caught his leg behind Gryph's knee and spun him. Gryph teetered but didn't fall.

The train was coming.

With a hearty laugh, Gryph pushed himself forward and latched on to Neko.

"You think you're some kung-fu expert?"

The other boys came at Neko with karate chops and high-pitched *hee-yas*.

Neko slapped at them all. "Leave me alone!"

"Why?" Gryph said as he shoved him closer to the track. "Can't hack it? What're you going to do? Cry?"

The familiar ding-dong sounded, announcing the approaching train.

"Shut the fuck up, Gryphon!" Neko shoved him back, hard. Teeth gritted, eyes blazing, he locked arms with Gryph. "Shut up! You think you're such hot shit—"

"Neko!" Saul yelled, reaching out to grab the wrestling boys as the train drew closer.

"Little Neko," Gryph said, laughing, "trying so hard to be one of the big boys."

"Shut up!" Neko had one arm around Gryph's neck. "Shut up! Stop talking shit about me!" Gryph needed only a couple of seconds to twist out of his grip, but those precious seconds did not exist. With one angry shove, Neko let go of him. Gryph churned his arms in the air, trying to regain his balance as he teetered back, but his feet scrambled at the edge and he was falling.

"Gryph!" Tariq grabbed his friend's wrist, but Gryph's hand slipped free. As the train pulled into the station, the sensors detected that the boys were too close to the edge of the platform. The alarm sounded.

"No!" Neko screamed, regret shoving up his throat like bile. He lurched forward to pull Gryphon back, but Saul stopped him so he wouldn't fall too.

Saul and Neko stumbled back while Gryph fell forward onto the tracks just as Clea emerged from the bathroom behind them.

"Gryphon!" she screamed as the train slammed into him, kicking his crumpled body under, jamming him between the belly of the train and the rails.

"Gryph, no!" Huy screamed, lunging for the tracks. Saul had to hold him back too.

The train took excruciatingly long to finally come to a screeching stop.

The few people on the platform ran to see what all the commotion was about as Clea rushed to the edge of the platform. Thankfully, she couldn't see him. Tariq and Huy had already jumped down and were on their knees searching underneath the train for their friend.

They found Gryph halfway underneath the third car. He didn't make a sound. Not a scream. Not a whimper. Not a moan. One leg stuck out, his shoe kicked off with the impact. His socked foot made it seem as if he were taking a rest under there, as if he just wanted a nap. But his other foot ... that was what made Clea scream. His other foot had been severed with the impact—shoe, sock, and all—and had been launched into the air. It landed on the platform, in front of Clea. Like an offering.

She brought her hands to her mouth and screamed. Her shoulders shook, her knees trembled. Saul went to her, kicking the shoe and its gruesome contents over the ledge and taking hold of her. He held her as she screamed. Her voice grew hoarse, but she didn't stop screaming until the paramedics arrived and gave her a sedative. Then she collapsed in Saul's arms. He helped her onto the stretcher, and only after she was wheeled away did he turn his attention back to the boys.

Huy was crying, squatting beside the train, his whole body shaking with each sob. Beside him, Tariq sat back on his haunches, nodding at something the Crimcor agent looming over him was saying. Between the two boys, Gryph's socked foot and his leg remained motionless.

Neko stood on the platform, off to one side, pale and stunned, while the train was backed up to reveal Gryph's crushed body. Crimcor agents dragged Tariq and Huy back onto the platform, all the while drilling them with questions. The next time Saul glanced back at the tracks, someone had draped Gryph's body with a yellow tarp. Farther down the track, Gryph's severed foot was covered with another tarp.

"Clea told me she was there ..." Phee heard herself speak before the thought actually registered.

"She didn't see Neko push him."

"I know." Phoenix's fingers tingled, which made her realize that she'd been hyperventilating as Marlin told the story of what had happened. She felt light-headed, and made her way to the curb to sit down. She dropped her head into her hands. "She didn't say how awful it had been. She didn't say."

"Maybe she blocked it out?"

"And maybe she was kind enough to spare me."

Marlin sat beside her, his hand shoved between his knees. "It was only a joke," he said. "Gryph wasn't going to make Neko push him. It was only a joke. But then Neko snapped and pushed him before we could tell him not to."

"The boy who cried wolf," Phee said. "How was Neko supposed to know it wasn't real? You guys make up such shit."

"What's done is done, Phee." Marlin sighed. "The problem now is how to get Gryph back and not lose Neko."

CAUSE AND EFFECT

Neko.

Neko.

Nadia's little brother ... practically Phoenix's little brother.

"Is that why you took off and got reconned? To take the blame for it?"

"I wish it was that easy. But no. If that was the case, we'd have Gryph back by now. I thought about making a video of me confessing and sending it to Chrysalis. But they'd polygraph the guys, and they'd all fail, and then we'd all be in that much more trouble."

"Then why did you run away?"

"A Crimcor informant came to the house that afternoon, when I got home from being questioned. He told us that they were close to exposing my father. We had to go."

"Your dad?"

"He's our cryopreservation expert. He goes to jail, we lose our ability to recon entirely."

"Why?"

"We can only recon people who are banked with us, just like with Chrysalis. No bank, no recon."

"Your mom was making raisin-oatmeal cookies." Phee remembered her mission to his house. "And you had a roast-beef sandwich for lunch."

"How do you know that?"

Phee told him about hiding in his closet while Crimcor searched the house.

"So they were closer than we thought," Marlin said. "Thank God we left when we did. My mom tried to convince me and Dad that we were overreacting, that we had more time, but we didn't. And then they freaked after what happened with Gryph. They were sure my DNA would be tested at some point and blow our cover anyway. Maybe it would've, maybe not. Chrysalis took our prints and a facial scan, but that was it."

"Where are your parents now?"

"Doesn't matter."

"Will you go to them after?"

Marlin nodded.

"Why can't we say it was you?" Phee implored. "If you're going to take off anyway? Can't we try to get the guys to pass the poly?"

"Tariq could probably pass. And maybe even Huy. But Neko would blow it for everyone. I've been watching him. He's a mess. It won't work. And then he'd as good as give himself up."

"Don't you think that it's at least worth a try?"

"Not if the risk is getting Neko decommed." Marlin's eyes teared. "I'd never forgive myself if our prank ended up in his death."

"But Gryph's death is okay?"

"There's a chance they may still rule it an accident."

"You really believe that? You? When you're the one talking about stealing him and reconning him illegally? You think Chrysalis will just decide to recon him after all?"

"There's a better chance of that than of them forgiving Neko for pushing him."

"But it was an accident," Phee said. Just a teenage prank gone wrong. The guys can explain that."

"Accident or not, decomming him is the law."

BUT WOULD CHRYSALIS really decom someone for what was really just a misunderstanding? The first thing Phee did after she got home that night was look online for other cases. After two hours of searching, she was devastated with the conclusion. Anyone having anything to do with the resulting death of another person was decommissioned, without trial. No excuses, no exceptions. There was an appeal process, much like the one Gryph's recon was ensnared in right now, but it had only ever ruled on the side of decommissioning.

A news release from Chrysalis summarized the reality. Worse, the circumstances of that event were eerily similar. A group of teenagers had been camping, without parents or permission, at the park by the river. They had a bonfire and were horsing around. One kid pushed another kid as he was just about to jump over the fire. He stumbled into the flames and suffered burns all over his body by the time his friends pulled him out. They doused him with water and called for an ambulance, but he died the next day. Not only was his recon denied, but his friend who'd pushed him was decommissioned. What did Chrysalis have to say on the matter? Phee clicked on the image clip. There was that Hueson woman, brought to life on the lync screen, playing talking head for her employer.

"Chrysalis takes the responsibility of reconning our citizens very seriously, and so expects the same from those entitled to the privilege. Those who treat the sanctity of life with carelessness or apathy must understand that we cannot reward such behaviour by approving the recons of the people involved. It is our hope that our strict policies regarding this matter will result in fewer deaths, a safer world, and a better quality of life."

That was four years ago. She couldn't find another more recent incident like it. People—and three-pers especially—had a healthy respect for life and an understandable fear of the recon process and its limitations and potential complications. Oscar was right when he talked about three-pers being the last people who should be entitled to three recons. Three-pers lived in the safest, most medically and socially advanced communities. Most of the privileged never needed a recon. Ever.

She found plenty of media reports of murder and manslaughter among the one- and two-pers, and countless violent episodes in the no-per regions. But when it came to the three-pers, she was hard-pressed to find even a handful of wrongful deaths. Three-pers were polite, careful people. They just didn't die before their time.

Phee's eyes drooped, and the images on the lync monitor washed into a blur. The next thing she knew, she woke up slumped over in her chair, with Fawn peering at her, Bunny clutched in her arms.

"You were snoring. And your breath smells." With that, Fawn wandered off into the kitchen.

Phoenix sat up, feeling groggy. She could hear her parents moving around upstairs, so she wiped the drool from her chin and went about erasing the search history on the lync console. That done, she got up and stretched the kinks out and went to help Fawn get herself some cereal.

Fawn was chattering on about the day camp she was starting that morning, in the community hall of the Shores. Phee made appropriate sounds to indicate that she was listening, but she wasn't paying attention at all. She'd sworn herself to silence, promising Marlin that she wouldn't tell a soul. He trusted her, the same as he had with his other secret.

But this was different.

She couldn't see how she could get Gryph back without telling what Neko had done. Her heart pounded in protest. How could she choose? How could she sacrifice Neko to bring back her brother? She loved Neko as if he were her little brother, and Gryph because he *was* her brother. How could she do that to Nadia? Inflict the same pain that her family was going through now onto her dearest friend in the entire world? How could she sort this out and make it better? There had to be a way!

While she was racking her brain, an undercurrent derailed her thoughts. Was Gryph worth more? Because of his talents, and his tight-knit family? Because he got better grades than Neko? Because he was a leader whereas Neko was a follower? Because he was stronger and bolder and well rounded in a way that Neko wasn't?

Phee hated herself for setting two different values on two boys who held a similar place in her heart. She brought her hands to her head, trying to quell the confusion.

"Headache?" Her mother came into the kitchen, her eyes red from another rough night. She turned. "I'll go get you an aspirin."

"No, Mom." Phee grabbed her mother's hand and held it tight, wishing she could tell her the truth. "I'm okay. Just tired."

WHEN HER MOTHER came back from dropping off Fawn, she asked Phoenix to sit down with her and Oscar for a family meeting of sorts. Grandma came over from her house, Granddad in tow. He sat at the kitchen table with a grin on his face, happily picking at a piece of toast with butter and marmalade, a napkin tucked into his collar as if he were a toddler. Phoenix's mother stirred a couple of teaspoons of sugar into his tea and set it in front of him. He beamed up at her.

"Thank you, Mother."

"*Daughter*, Papa." This hardly fazed Eva, but it set Phoenix's heart down yet another steep curve of the emotional roller coaster she just could not get off these days.

"I'm your daughter," Eva said again, before turning her attention to her husband.

Phoenix sat on the long bench at the kitchen table, beside her father. He had his Bible in front of him. He placed one hand on it, the other on Phee's head. She rested her head on his shoulder, grateful for the warmth of his palm against her cheek, the steady rhythm of his heart.

"We have to start planning"—Oscar took a deep breath—"for the very real possibility that Gryphon might not be returned to us. The decision is today. And it will be final."

Eva and her mother shared a pained look. Phoenix resigned herself to yet another stiff drop of her heart.

"You mean a memorial service?" She looked up at her father, hardly able to get the words out.

"Yes."

Phoenix could not believe that this was happening to her. How had things gone so wrong?

"Oscar ..." Her mother's voice was drained. Flat. "How can we?"

"I know what—" Phoenix was going to tell them everything. She was going to tell her mother and father all that she knew. She was going to tell them with the certainty of her very next breath. But what about Neko? She would kill him! Or that's what it felt like anyway. She had to gulp it back to stop the confession. She couldn't tell. Not yet. Not without making a plan to save Neko. "I just ... you should—"

"I can't do this!" Eva moaned. "I cannot sit here and talk about such a thing!"

"Darling"—Phoenix's grandmother took Eva's hand in hers—"I know this is hard—"

"Yes, it's hard!" Eva turned to her mother. "And it's wrong! It's unjust!"

"It hasn't always been this way ..." Grandma's voice was calm, the way it was when she hushed Fawn to sleep. "Before, death was final. That was the way it had been since the dawn of time. And it is still final now, only now it is often postponed."

"For good reason!" Eva's cheeks were red, her eyes blinking anxiously. "We have the technology and so we should use it—"

"But, Eva," Oscar broke in. "There is still no denying a higher power at play here."

"Enough with your God talk!" Eva turned on him with a furious glare. "If I hear one more mention of God's will, I'll show you my will! My will will have me marching out of here with your children and never coming back. Do you hear me? Do you?"

"Mom!" Tears pushed at Phoenix's eyes. "Please ..."

But Eva was alight with grief and couldn't hear Phoenix for the roar of the fire. "Don't you tell me this is God's will! This is Chrysalis's doing! This is them proving a point! This is them judging him for not wanting to be their pawn anymore! You would sit there and allow them to play with his life like that? Would you?"

"Of course not," Oscar said.

"And it's not even true!" Eva bellowed. "I know that he didn't kill himself just to get out of his contract. It's a ludicrous suggestion. I know he didn't do it. I know it."

"But we are powerless against Chrysalis," Oscar said with a tired sigh. "You must know this too. We can only look to the scripture—"

"No!" Eva held up her hands. "I don't want your spiritual platitudes. I don't want your ministrations or your lousy, hypocritical God. And most of all, I do not want your weak indifference—"

"How can you say such a thing?" Oscar's hurt was audible in his voice. His eyes teared up. So did Phee's. She put her hands over her ears but could hear her father's tormented voice anyway. "I love our son!"

"Obviously not as much as I do! I want him back! I want him to come home! I want you to do something! Fix it, Oscar! I want you to fix it ..." Eva's bravado started to crumble. "I want him to come home to me. I want him here. I need my son back."

Eva's father stood up unsteadily and went to her side.

"Don't cry, pet." He drew her into a generous hug, surprising all of them with his timely lucid moment. "He'll come home. He will."

Phoenix fell into her father's lap and let loose the tears. She wept, her shoulders shaking, her face drenched. She wanted to tell them. She did. But she also wanted to do the right thing, and do what Gryph would want her to do, and she just wasn't sure what that was. As she cried, lost in confusion and fear and grief, her father cried too, quiet defeated tears streaking down his ruddy cheeks and into his beard.

Her family was ruined. They would never recover from this. Phoenix could see it now. Gryph would be cremated, and there would be a tension-filled service and then Eva would take Fawn and go to her parents and never come back. And Phoenix would stay with her father because as much as she loved her mother, Oscar needed her more. And she needed him. And that would be the new world order, post Gryphon. It was horrible to consider, and the awfulness of it made Phoenix cry all that much harder. And in that moment, with that glimpse of a terrible, inevitable future, Phoenix made her decision.

It was time to talk.

Her family—moreover, Gryph—*was* more important to her than Neko. She *could* sacrifice Neko for her family. The realization was a horrifying thought, and at the same time a cataclysmic relief.

"He didn't do it on purpose—" Phoenix lifted her head from her father's lap. "I know what happened."

Eva's eyes, still ablaze defiantly, turned to her. "What?"

"It was one of the boys." The words caught in her throat as if they were dragging each other back. "One of ... his friends ... pushed him."

"How do you know this?" Eva sat down. She reached for Phoenix's hand across the table. She gripped it hard. "Tell me."

"One of them told me."

"Who?"

But then Phee had a glimpse into another awful future: Neko's death. His home raided, his parents screaming as he's cuffed by Crimcor, dragged from his life, forced into the decom facility and gassed. And Nadia, blaming her. Hating her. For the rest of their lives.

There had to be another way.

"No." Phoenix started crying again. "I can't say!"

"You must, Phee." Oscar stroked her hair. "You have to tell us what you know."

Phoenix shook her head. "I can't."

"Can't?" Her mother spat the word at her. "You *can't?* Don't be stupid, Phoenix Elaine. Of course you have to tell us!"

"Eva, mind your words," Oscar admonished his wife as he put a gentle hand to Phee's flushed cheek. "She's clearly struggling in a very difficult place. God help her."

"Phoenix"—her mother's voice dropped low, menacing—"you must tell us what you know. You absolutely must! Your brother's life depends on it."

"I can't." Phoenix drew in a shaky breath. Her heart stung from her mother's harsh words, so it was easier to direct her refusal at Eva. Her mother had never said such hurtful things to her. Not ever. It was as if her mother had suddenly started speaking a terrible, alien tongue. "I just can't."

Eva glared at her. Phoenix couldn't bear it. She looked away, her mind betraying her by catapulting down into the darkest depths of bad ideas. Did their mother love Gryphon the most? Would she be as frantic if Phoenix died? She could hardly imagine it. But then her deaths had been simple. Straightforward. Or so she'd thought, until Gryph had admitted his part in her second death. She turned on her mother, suddenly gripped by spiteful jealousy.

"You think he's so perfect, don't you?"

"Don't you talk ill of him. He's—"

"—not nearly as golden as you think he is!" Phoenix felt anger take over her like a demon. "He pushed me into that river! He killed me!"

"He didn't." Eva's face paled. "You fell."

"He pushed me." Phoenix planted her hands on the table and leaned forward, fixing her eyes on her mother. "He told me himself. He pushed me! On purpose. Because he wanted to see what would happen. What coming back from the dead was like. He was curious."

"I cannot believe you're making this about you." Eva copied her daughter's pose, the two of them nose to nose across the table. "At a time like this, you still manage to make it all about you. You conceited little bitch."

"Oh!" Phoenix sucked in her breath, feeling every bit as if it were her last, but then a swell of rage pushed the next words out. "You know what, Mother? Fuck you."

Her mother lifted one trembling hand and slapped her hard across her face.

Phoenix reeled back into her father's arms. He tried to hold her, calm her, as Phee scrambled to get free. "She's upset, Phee. She didn't mean it."

"Let me go!"

"We're all upset. Please, sit. Everyone, please, let's just sit."

Shocked, Phoenix's grandmother put a hand to her mouth. Her granddad looked pained, as if someone had kicked him in the shin. They were the only reason she was sorry for cursing at her mother, but not enough to take it back.

She wrestled out of her father's grip and took off at a run, out the front door and across the green. She didn't know where she was going, but she had to get out of there.

"Phoenix, stop!" Eva was running after her, screaming. No apology for the slap, her mean words. Just begging her to stop and tell them what she knew. "Come back here! Tell us what happened!"

Phee kept running.

"You have to tell us!" Her mother's voice started to fade. Phee glanced back. Eva wasn't following her anymore. She had collapsed onto the grass in a defeated heap. "You can't do this. You can't!"

Phee slowed to a stop, her limbs suddenly sluggish as she took in the image of her mother like that. Helpless and devastated. She watched Oscar catch up and help her mother back onto her feet, and then Phee turned away and kept running. Away from it all. Away from everything.

RULING

Phee knew she was dreaming, but she couldn't pull herself out of it. The dream was so real that she had to convince herself it wasn't by focusing on the details. She was wearing the same dress she'd been wearing on the day Gryph died, but she'd left that dress in her laundry pile at the bottom of her closet. And she was barefoot. Which wouldn't be so odd, except that she was walking down the main corridor of the Chrysalis building. Alone, which also pointed out that it was a dream. But the rest was so real, and so much better than real life, that she didn't want to wake up.

There was Gryph, sitting on a bench, waiting to go home. He looked up when he heard her padding along the cool tile.

"Where are your shoes?" He grinned at her.

Phee shrugged. And then she ran to him and hugged him and he hugged her back.

"I thought you were going to be dead forever!"

"Here I am. New and improved. Just like you."

"It was awful, Gryph—" Phee was about to tell him about the past few weeks, but he stopped her.

"All that can wait." He stood. "Let's go home?"

"Yeah, let's." Phee followed him out into the sunshine, where they waited for a train. And then Phee reminded herself again that this was only a dream. She could do whatever she wanted.

"What should I do, Gryph?"

"Listen to me." In perfect dream-like fashion, he knew exactly what she was talking about. He turned to her and held her arms, giving her a little sobering shake. "Let me go. It wasn't Neko's fault. It was my fault."

"But you'll never come home!"

"Neko shouldn't be punished for it either."

Phee felt someone tapping her shoulder. It wasn't Gryphon. "I need more time."

"Wake up, Phoenix."

"You'll be okay, Phee." Gryph backed away from her, fading as he did.

"Wait, Gryph!"

"Phoenix!" Phee opened her eyes. The dream was gone. Marlin stood over her, the midday sun blazing behind him. Phee sat up. She'd fallen asleep on the bench, waiting for him.

"How could I sleep? At a time like this ..."

"I don't blame you."

Phee grabbed Marlin's wrist and looked at his watch. "There are only three hours left! What are we going to do?"

She told him about almost telling her parents. She told him about the dream too, how Gryph had told her to choose Neko's life over his. He nodded as she spoke.

"He would."

"But do I have to?"

"Can you live with yourself if you turn Neko in?" Phee's phone buzzed in her pocket. "I ... I don't know." The same exhaustion that had shoved her into sleep as she waited for Marlin pushed at her again now. She stifled a yawn. "I just don't know what I should do."

"It's time to get the boys together."

"I've tried that." Her phone buzzed again. She looked at the screen. Ten calls from home. Phee shut the phone off and slipped it back into her pocket. "I couldn't get them to talk. Not at all."

"With me this time." Marlin paled. "I'll talk to them."

"That's not safe. You said so."

"I'll handle it." Marlin shrugged. "It needs to be done. They had all this time to come up with a solution and they didn't. Now it's my turn."

PHEE WAS NOT AT ALL convinced that this was a good plan. And she was even less convinced that this was the best way to spend the last few hours before Chrysalis announced their ruling. On the other hand, she had to admit that she didn't have any better ideas. Her gut churned with anxiety as she and Marlin waited at the Steveston Pier Station, the place she'd arranged to meet the boys. She had not invited Nadia, because she and Marlin had both agreed that her presence would only complicate matters. He was going to tell them who he really was, and there was no guessing how Nadia would react, only that it wouldn't be pretty. There was no time for her to have a meltdown, so Phee had told Neko to be sure she didn't come with him.

So when Phee saw her best friend walking alongside her little brother, her heart sank. There wasn't the time.

"What are you doing here?"

"If you guys are getting together two hours before the ruling, it must be important." Nadia stepped forward to hug Phee, but Phee twisted away.

"You weren't supposed to come, Nadia."

"Why not? And anyway, my parents won't let Neko out unless I go with him. It was either him and me, or no Neko." Nadia noticed Marlin then, who was hanging back, but was clearly with Phee by the way he stood close to her. "Who's he?"

"He's ... a friend."

"Hi," Marlin said. He blinked hard, dug his nails into his palms.

It was obvious to Phee that he was forcing himself not to approach Nadia as he was accustomed to, with open arms and a kiss. He practically trembled from the effort it took to treat her as if he'd never seen her before.

"A *friend*?" Nadia laughed. Huy and Tariq got off the next train and made their way to them across the platform. Neko hadn't spoken yet. He fixed his eyes on the far end of the platform, where it had happened. "*We* are your friends. *He's* not your friend. What's going on, Phee?"

Marlin stepped forward. "My name is Marlin." He held out his hand for her to shake, but she just stared at him. "I'll explain everything, Nadia. I promise." There was a tremor in his voice. Phee wondered if he would start crying, but Nadia's sharpness broke the moment.

"Who is this guy? And why does he think he can talk to us like he knows us?"

Tariq joined them, having overheard Nadia's last words. "I think I know why."

Phee and Marlin both gawked at him. "You do?" Phee said.

Tariq nodded. "This is Saul. Right?"

"What?" Nadia's jaw dropped. Her eyes teared up, and her cheeks paled. "What's going on?"

"Nadia, babe ..." Marlin reached for her.

Nadia crossed herself and backed away. "Stay the hell away from me."

"How do you know, Tariq?" Phee turned to Marlin when Tariq's answer didn't come fast enough. "Did you tell him?"

"No," Marlin said. "I didn't."

And then Tariq spoke. "I've been following you, Phee."

"You what?"

"This is insane!" Nadia screamed. "Someone tell me what is going on!"

"And so I've seen him," Tariq continued, oblivious to Nadia's outburst. "I admit I'm making a leap, but I'm pretty sure that this guy is actually Saul. Am I right?"

"That's crazy!" Nadia exclaimed. "This is so messed up! He's not Saul."

"But you are," Tariq said to Marlin. "Aren't you? I got curious after seeing you with Phee and followed you back to Saul's house. You snuck in. Knew where everything was. And you blink super fast when you're nervous. Like right now. Just like Saul."

Marlin's eyes blinked quickly as he looked at Nadia.

"Please, Nadia." He held out his arms. "I can explain."

"No!" Nadia screamed. And then again. "No!" And then she turned on her heel and started running.

"Nadia!" Marlin called after her, but she didn't look back. "Go after her and explain!" he said to Phoenix. "Tell her I love her!"

Huy and Neko stared at the stranger, dumbfounded to hear him talk like that about Nadia, who as far as they knew he'd never met before today.

"There's no time, Marlin." Phee watched her friend sprint out of sight, down the stairs that led to the street.

"Go," Tariq said firmly. "Go after her, Phee."

Phee took a tentative step away from the small cluster of boys, still not sure if she should go after Nadia.

"Go, Phee!" Tariq yelled, startling her.

Phee ran along the platform and down the stairs. She found Nadia hugging herself, pacing in a tight circle. Nadia heard her coming and stopped. She looked up at Phee, and in that one glance Phee could see that this was not going to be easy.

"Nadia, let me explain ..." Phee waited for Nadia to break in, yell at her, do something Nadia-like, but Nadia was quiet, waiting. "Saul had to leave. His family is a one-per family living here illegally. His parents were involved in illegal recons." Again, she waited for Nadia to interrupt with a flurry of confusion, but she was still silent, staring at her. "Because they were about to be caught, they had to recon themselves so that they could go into hiding with new identities. But he still loves you. Very much."

Phee left it at that for the moment. She watched the information sink in. Nadia blinked, opened her mouth to say something, but nothing came out.

"That boy up there is Saul," Phee continued. "He's called Marlin now. He looks different, but it's him inside."

"Saul was a one-per?" Nadia whispered. She glanced around, making sure no one was within hearing distance. "All this time? He was lying to me?"

"Yes."

"He's one-per?" Nadia turned in another dazed little circle. "*My* Saul?"

Phee checked the time on her phone. One hour and forty-five minutes before the ruling. "Nadia, please listen to me." Nadia started her stunned pacing again. "Nadia!" Phee shook her hard. "We're running out of time. Listen to me!"

"I'm listening." Nadia started to cry. "I know what you're going to say. I know there's no time left. I know you have to go save Gryph, or try at least. Now I know why you didn't want me to come. I know that I have to just deal with this on my own right now. I get it, okay?"

"But—" Phee wanted Nadia to stay. Be a part of this. But she knew that wasn't going to happen.

"Go."

"You won't stay?"

"No. I can't. That's not Saul. And I can't be around somebody pretending to be him, true or not."

"It is Saul."

"It's not!" Nadia gave Phee a shove. "Now go. Just go. Okay?"

Phee moved to hug her, but Nadia held up her arms, refusing. "Not now."

"But—"

"Go, Phoenix. You have to go."

Phee checked her time on her phone again. She did have to go. Right now.

"You'll be okay? You won't do anything crazy?"

"I'll be fine." She let Phee hug her now. Phee clung to her best friend, and could feel that her whole being was vibrating with what she could only imagine was shock and confusion and fear. "You go."

"You won't come with me?"

Nadia shook her head.

"You can't stay here alone."

Nadia looked around. It was true. The Cannery was no place to hang out in the midst of a crisis.

"Come with me." Phee took her hand. "I'll put you on the train. You go home. Tell your parents that Neko is with me." At the mention of his name, fresh panic swept over Phee in a cold wave that nearly knocked her off her feet. She didn't know what was going to happen to Neko. She didn't know what was going to happen to any of them.

"One thing at a time," she said as much to herself as to Nadia. "One thing at a time, okay?"

Crying now, Nadia nodded. "I trust you, Phee. You'll fix it. You always fix things."

Phee didn't know what to say to that. She led her friend up the stairs. They waited as far away from the boys as possible. Phee glanced over at the small group, and shook her head when Marlin made as if to come to them. He stepped back, shoulders slumped.

The train came, and Phee ushered Nadia onto it with strict instructions to text her when she got home safely. She told her she'd come over as soon as she could.

"Don't hurry, Phee," Nadia said as the bell sounded, announcing that the train was seconds away from leaving. "You be with your family. Today is about Gryph."

But today wasn't just about Gryph. It was about Neko too. And Nadia had no idea.

"Love you, Nad." Phee waved as the doors closed.

"Love you, Phee." Nadia, still sobbing, waved as the train pulled away.

PHEE RAN BACK to the boys. They watched her approach, Tariq and Huy and Neko with steely gazes and in stony silence. Only Marlin spoke.

"What did she say?"

"Not much." Phee glanced at the silent threesome. "She needs time."

"And she's got time," Huy grumbled. "As much time as she wants. But Gryph doesn't. So what are we going to do about it?" He turned his attention to Neko, who looked as though he'd lost weight from his already skinny frame in the time since Gryphon's death. "What are we going to do about it, Neko?"

Neko paled. "I don't know."

"You begged us to give you time," Huy continued on, his tone cold. "There's no more time, Neko."

Clearly, Marlin had fully explained himself in Phee's absence, because the boys—in true male fashion—had moved away from the surprise and shock and straight to the business at hand. Gryph. Phee glanced at the clock above the elevator. An hour and ten minutes. Tariq looked at the clock too, then at Marlin.

"So?"

"So obviously I didn't pick today to tell you what happened to me because I wanted my old life back." Marlin cleared his throat. "I picked today because I think I have a way out of this for Neko. A way that will bring Gryphon back."

Neko lifted his red-rimmed eyes. "You do?"

Huy brightened. "What is it?"

Tariq turned to Phee. "You trust him?"

"I do." Phee moved closer to Marlin. "He's changed on the outside, but he's still Saul on the inside."

"What a crock of shit." Huy rolled his eyes. "You want that on a T-shirt, Phoenix? Because that's where a line like that belongs."

"We don't have time for this," Marlin said. "We really and truly don't. I'm sorry that I didn't come forward earlier, but I thought you guys would figure something out on your own."

Tariq and Huy and Neko shared a guilty look. They hadn't figured anything out. And with an hour left, they still had no clue how to get Gryphon back and keep Neko safe at the same time.

"But you didn't," Marlin said. "So here I am. Hate me, don't hate me. Trust me, don't trust me. It doesn't matter. You have no other option, do you?"

The three other boys shared that same look again, before Tariq spoke for all of them. "Okay. We'll go along with whatever you have in mind."

Huy aimed a sneer at Marlin. "But don't expect us to be all buddy-buddy with you, because at best ... at *best* ... you are a liar. You've lied to us since we were five years old. And at worst—"

"Guys!" Neko broke in. "The time," he whispered, pointing up to the clock. Exactly an hour left before Gryph's fate was decided once and for all. "Please, let's go."

MARLIN LED THEM down the stairs and out into the daylight. Phee was surprised that he was taking them in the direction of the illegal recon lab, but she didn't say anything. There was no time for questions. He led them past the CAPTAIN MURPHY'S FAMOUS FISH STICKS sign and right up to the very same door Phee had gone through not long ago, when all of this was as much a mystery to her as it was to the boys right now. But this time, Marlin opened the door and ushered them all in without a word about what they were about to see or had to keep secret. Phee hesitated, waiting for the boys to go in ahead of her. When she went inside, it took only a few seconds for her to register what she was seeing. Or not seeing. The lab had been dismantled. Not a trace of it remained. Except for Polly, who sat in a lone chair in the middle of what now was just a big, damp warehouse.

CONFESSION

The boys stood in a half circle around the chair while Marlin introduced Polly, not by name, though, only as his friend.

Polly nodded at Phee. "Good to see you again."

"Again?" Huy turned on her. "You know about this place?"

"Quiet," Tariq ordered. Huy crossed his arms and sulked while Polly began setting up a small camera and a smaller box with some sort of screen.

"What is all this?" Neko asked, his voice shaking. "Why are we here?"

"It'll be okay, Neko," Phee assured him, hoping that she was right. She trusted Marlin not to put Neko in harm's way, because of his love for Nadia, no matter how conflicted Nadia was about it all.

Marlin addressed the group. "Listen to me closely. This is how it's going to go—"

"Maybe," Huy interrupted. "If we agree to it."

Tariq shot Huy another harsh look.

"This is how it's going to go," Marlin began again. "Because there is no other way." He paused with a glance at Huy, waiting for his objections. None came this time. Marlin checked his watch.

"Thirty-five minutes until the ruling. We have that much time to make this happen."

Phee's heart pounded in her chest, objecting to all of this. It wasn't possible! Whatever Marlin had in mind, there wasn't time! Her heart thumped and thumped, as if saying *no way, no way, no way*. Phee strained to hear Marlin speak.

"Neko will confess, and we'll tape it. We'll send it to Chrysalis."

"No," Neko said. "I'm not doing it. I don't care who the fuck you say you are, Saul would never ask me to do that. Never!"

"I *am* asking you to do this. It's the only way to save you and Gryph."

"How the hell does that save me, huh?" Neko asked. "How?"

"You'll be reconned."

Huy's eyes widened. "What?"

"How?" Tariq asked.

"Where?" Phee looked around. "Clearly not here."

"You guys don't need to know any of that," Marlin said. "You just have to trust me."

"This is crazy." Neko started backing away, but he backed right into Tariq, who'd placed himself behind him, blocking the way to the door. "Let me go."

"Just listen, Neko." Tariq placed a firm hand on Neko's shoulder. "Don't worry about who he is or what his motivations are. Just listen."

"Please," Huy added. "For Gryphon."

Neko clamped his mouth shut and glared at Marlin.

"You will have a new identity. They'll never connect the new you to the old Neko. You can live the rest of your life without worrying that they'll find you."

"And I lose everything."

"You stay alive."

It could work. Phee's heart slowed with relief. It could really work! Neko might lose his family, his school, his friends. But that was better than losing his life! And Gryph would come home. "Would he go with you?" She directed the question to Marlin.

"Yes."

"Hell, I won't." Neko raised his eyebrows, arms crossed defiantly. "No one can make me do this. I'm sorry about what—" His words started to catch in his throat. He dropped his chin to his chest to regain composure. After a moment he looked up at Phee. "I'm so sorry, Phee. It was an accident. I never meant to hurt him like that."

"I know you're sorry." Phee offered him a small smile. "But it did happen. And you're the one Chrysalis will blame. You're the only one who can make this right. You're the only one who can bring him back, Neko."

"But what about my parents?" Tears streamed down his face. "What about Nadia?"

"They'll think you ran away," Marlin said. "To avoid being decommed. Tariq and Huy will tell them so. They'll think that you're healthy and safe. And that is far better than being dead. Isn't it?"

After another long moment, Neko nodded. "I get it."

"You'll do it?"

"I'll do it." With those few words, Neko grew up. Something in him shifted, and he was ready to do what was right.

"Twenty minutes," Polly broke in, camera in hand. "I'm ready when you are."

Marlin gripped Neko's other shoulder. "Ready to do this?"

"Yes."

"You're sure about this?" Tariq asked.

Neko shrugged. "Does it matter? We're doing it anyway. He's right. I don't have another option, unless Gryph stays dead. I don't want that."

Marlin steered Neko to the chair. Polly set the camera on a tripod before sliding the small screen in front of him.

"This is a bio lock," she explained as she slid a thin glove over one of his hands. "It guarantees that the next transmission sent from this camera is from you and no one else. It proves this isn't a fake, or doctored." She wrapped a slender band around each of his wrists. "And these tell them that you're telling the truth." She pointed to the small screen, where Neko's heart rhythm was now dancing in irregular waves. "You have to calm down, son."

"I'll try." He took a deep breath and let it out slowly through his mouth.

Phee took Neko's hand. "Thank you, Neko."

"I just hope it works."

"Thank you." Phee hugged him, and the thought was not lost on her that this was probably his last day as Neko Balkashan. After this, he would be forever changed. But he would be alive. And Gryph too. That's what mattered. Both boys would live.

THE ONLY SOUND in the warehouse was the cooing of the pigeons roosting in the rafters, and Neko trying to steady his breathing. Polly set up the camera, checked the bio locks, and stepped back. She nodded. Neko stared at the camera, at the devices on his wrist like handcuffs. He dropped his gaze to the floor.

Phee stood to the side with the others. Would he go through with it? Was he changing his mind now? Phee checked her phone for the time, ignoring the twelve messages, all from her parents. Eleven minutes until the ruling. They all shuffled silently, not wanting their voices on the tape. Phee willed Neko to look up, to start speaking. To get this over with.

Finally, with nine minutes left before Chrysalis announced Gryph's fate, Neko lifted his head and started talking, his voice trembling, his eyes damp.

"This is an important message for the Chrysalis Corporation. My name is Neko Balkashan and I am making this tape of my own free will. This is my confession. I caused the death of Gryphon Nicholson-Lalonde. I did it. I pushed him off the train platform. I won't make excuses because I know—" Neko gritted his teeth against tears. "Because I *know* what happens to people like me.

You'll kill me no matter what I say, no matter how remorseful I am. You'll kill me and call it 'decommissioning' and it'll be the news for a couple of days and then it'll be everything back to normal. If my death even makes the news."

Phee glanced at Marlin. This wasn't exactly what Phee was thinking of when it came to an official confession. But then Neko spoke the magic words again in an angry rush.

"I did it," Neko said. "I pushed him. He didn't jump. Do you assholes hear me? He did not jump. And you're all complete idiots if you think he would. So there it is. Blame me. Hunt me down. I'm your bad guy. Just let Gryphon go home to his family." This time Neko couldn't help the tears. "Let him live."

Polly switched the camera off remotely. Neko leaped up from the chair and started to pull off the bio locks.

"Not yet," Polly ordered. "After we send the transmission." Neko slumped back onto the chair as Huy and Tariq gathered around him.

"You did the right thing." Huy bent to hug him, but Neko shrugged him off.

"Don't touch me."

Marlin clapped a hand on Neko's back. "It'll be okay, Neko."

"I said don't fucking touch me! None of you." Neko pointed a finger at each of the boys and then at Phee too. "Don't come near me."

Polly looked up from the small console. "It's sent."

With that, Neko ripped off the glove and wristbands and threw them to the floor. "Happy? Everyone happy now that my life is ruined?"

"It's not ruined," Polly said. As she tried to calm Neko, Marlin told Phee to call Chrysalis.

"Tell them who you are and that you have to speak to Nora Hueson immediately," he whispered as Phee fumbled to find the number online. "Hurry!"

Five minutes left. She made the call, and then waited while the receptionist put her on hold.

Huy surfed on his phone for a live news feed from Chrysalis. He stared at the screen. "They're already talking!" He waved his phone for everyone to see. Phee rushed over. There on the tiny screen was Nora Hueson, standing at a podium on the front steps of Chrysalis, the blue sky behind her. The camera panned to the left, where Phee's family sat in the front row. Oscar and Eva sat erect, not touching. Phee started to cry, her own phone still to her ear.

The sound from Huy's phone was tinny, but they could make out what Hueson was saying. "It is with heavy hearts that we make today's ruling in the recon case regarding Gryphon Nicholson-Lalonde." And then Shapiro was suddenly at Hueson's side, cupping her hand to Hueson's ear to whisper something to her. Hueson nodded, and then addressed the crowd. "If you will excuse me for just one moment."

The news camera followed her offstage where she took the phone from Shapiro. All of a sudden Phee heard Hueson's voice in her own ear.

"Phoenix?"

"Ms. Hueson." Phee had almost forgotten what she was supposed to be doing. "Wait, wait. I have some important information," she stammered. Beside her, Marlin nodded, encouraging her. "Chrysalis has just been sent a confession from the boy who pushed Gryphon."

"Now, Phoenix, I know you're upset about the ruling—"

"It's real!" Phoenix yelled into the phone. "With bio locks and everything! That's proof!"

Hueson paused before speaking again. Phee could only hope that she was telling Shapiro to check the lync for the transmission. Phee glanced at Huy's phone. The camera was trained on her family. Oscar and Eva were talking. Fawn leaned against her mother, Bunny clutched in her arms. Phee was supposed to have been there. She should have been there. She prayed that this would work, because if it didn't she'd never forgive herself for abandoning her family at such an awful time. The camera panned left, to an empty chair beside her father. Phee started crying. She should have been there.

"Phoenix?" Hueson was back on the line. "Are you with this boy right now?" She'd watched the video! She believed it!

"No."

"Where are you?"

"Nowhere."

"Tell me where you are, Phoenix. If you have that boy with you, you must turn him in. Do you understand me?"

"I'm not with him."

"Then why aren't you here with your family?" Hueson's tone was patronizing. She was trying to get Phee to talk. On Huy's small screen, Phee watched Shapiro usher her family into the building, and then she took the podium, announcing that the news confer-ence was cancelled. Indefinitely.

"You'll recon him?" Phee asked. "He's going to be okay?"

"Where are you, Phoenix?"

Marlin grabbed the phone and ended the call. "They're tracking you." He took Huy's too, powering them both off. Tariq did the same to his. Neko too. Polly powered down the camera equipment so they couldn't trace that either. The small group stood for a moment in the middle of the old warehouse, and then Marlin spoke.

"We have to go. Tariq and Huy, you go with Phoenix. Get her to her parents." Marlin turned to Neko, who was pale, his eyes still wet with tears. "I'll take Neko. Polly, you do as we planned." And with that, he took Neko by the arm and made for the door. "Now! They might've already traced you here, Phee. Go!"

But she couldn't move. She could only stand there and watch her best friend's little brother leave. She'd never see him again. Nadia and her parents would never see him again. This was it!

"Neko!" She ran to him and hugged him. "Thank you. Thank you."

He stiffened in her arms. She pulled away a little and looked up at him.

"Be strong, okay? I'll take care of Nadia. Marlin will take good care of you."

"I don't need anyone to take care of me." He wrestled free of her grip. She caught a glimpse of him when he was six and had fallen off his bike when the three of them were on the way to the corner store for ice cream. He'd run to Phee, crying. She'd sat on the grass with him in her lap. He'd flung his arms around her neck and bawled while Nadia knocked on the door of the nearest house to ask for a bandage. He was still that little boy to her, so all this seemed impossible. Unreal.

"Phoenix!" Marlin yelled from where he held the door open, the sunlight slicing in, reminding them all of the world outside. "We have to go now!"

"This isn't the end, Neko." Phee grabbed Neko again, and this time when he tried to break away, she hugged him again and held on for dear life, just as he had when he was six. "It's the beginning of an enormous adventure. You've always been up for adventure. I know you can do this."

"I don't know if I can," he said as Marlin physically hauled him out the door. "But I'll give it a shot. Take care of Nadia, okay?"

"I will."

"Tell Gryph that I'm sorry!"

And then he was gone.

Phee followed the boys outside. Marlin and Neko were already halfway down the block, heading north at a dead run. Tariq and Huy were waiting for her on the sidewalk.

"Come on," Huy called.

Phee jogged over to join them, and then the three of them hurried back to the train platform, all of them keeping an eye out for Crimcor.

HOME

Phoenix's entire family went to Chrysalis to pick up Gryphon on the day he was due to come home. They got there early and were ushered in through the back, because the front courtyard was already abuzz with media and Gryph's fans. Phee was a little surprised about the fans; Gryph could never officially compete again. His career was over. The best he could ever do now was compete with the Recon Athletic Association, which he'd always said was no better than being in the Special Olympics. That's what the old Gryph said anyway. Phee wondered what he'd think about it now that he was reconned himself.

She held Fawn's hand as they waited in the same little room where they'd received so much bad news. Fawn clutched Bunny to her and leaned against Phee's leg, excited but wary.

"You think he'll remember me?" she asked with wide eyes, pressing Bunny's paw to her cheek the way she always did when she was anxious.

"Of course." Phee kissed Fawn's forehead and drew her onto her lap. "He's got all his memory. He's as good as new."

When Phee found out that Gryph had come out of the recon with his memory intact, she was surprised at her initial reaction.

She was disappointed. It was only a fleeting regret, but it lasted long enough for her to feel a chill of guilt. She was happy for him, of course. Of course she was! She didn't even want to think about what it would've been like if he'd lost it all. But still, a small part of her wished he could truly understand what it was like. What he'd done to her so many years ago.

"Phoenix?" Her father stood over her, the others gathered at the door behind him. "It's time."

Phee trailed behind the others. Oscar and Eva walked at the front, Fawn between them. Then her grandma, holding her granddad's hand. Then her auntie and uncle, each with a twin by the hand. And then Phee. To think that her family, in various formations, had done this walk twice already, for her.

They were led into a room of windows, the sunlight streaming in from all sides. It felt hallowed, and therefore gimmicky in Phee's mind. As if Chrysalis was trying to evoke something biblical. Behold the resurrection, or some such drivel.

There was a white leather couch along one wall, but only Phee's granddad sat. The twins slid under it, playing hide-and-seek. The others just stood, nervously waiting. Silky drapes slid open on the opposite wall, revealing a polished silver door. It opened too, and there was Gryph, dressed in the slacks and button-down shirt Eva had brought down for him the day before.

He grinned at them all, then plucked at the tailored shirt. "Who picked this ugly thing?"

"I did." Eva, shaking with silent tears, rushed to him and covered his cheek in kisses. She hugged him and petted his hair and finally rested her hands on his broad shoulders. "You look handsome."

"I look like I just stepped out of a catalogue for a prep school."

"Gryphon"—Oscar opened his arms—"thank God you've come back to us." Father and son hugged. Oscar wiped away tears when he finally let Gryph go. "Thank God."

For some reason, Gryph was avoiding Phee. And she him. She hung back, letting him greet everyone else. When he was done,

Fawn happily situated on his back, her arms around his neck, Bunny mashed between them, Phee caught his eye.

"Hey."

"Hey, yourself." He gripped Fawn with one arm and embraced Phee in an awkward hug with the other. More like what she was used to from Uncle Liam. Not her brother.

And as if they'd agreed on it beforehand, the two of them left it at that. The rest could wait. Her questions, Gryph's questions. Neko. Marlin. All of it would wait.

THE STUFFED ANIMALS that Fawn had set out to welcome Gryph home weeks ago were still in their places on the front steps, though a little more sun bleached and dirty. Fawn, who would not let go of Gryph and was now gripping his hand as they walked home from the station, pointed them out when they turned the last corner.

"They're for you," Fawn said. "We're having a party!"

"Thanks, Fawn." He bent to hug her and let her climb onto his shoulders while he was crouched. "Where's the cake?"

"Not out here, silly. Inside!" Fawn laughed. "I helped make it and I decorated it all by myself. It's chocolate with the gooey stuff inside."

"My favourite!"

Riley heard the family coming up the walk and managed to arrange himself on all stiff fours and make his way to the door to greet them. He was so excited to see Gryph that he jumped up, putting his front paws on Gryph's chest.

"You've been reconned too, buddy?" Gryph scratched Riley's ears before the dog's burst of energy was spent and he started to sag. Gryph helped him down, and then set Fawn back on her feet too.

"Gryph!" Clea emerged from the kitchen where she was waiting with Tariq and Huy to surprise him.

"Clea." Gryph pulled her into his arms and gave her a long, serious kiss.

"Gross!" Fawn made a face and covered her eyes.

"The guys are in the kitchen." Clea took his hand. "They're dying to see you." She slapped her forehead. "Oh God, that was the wrong thing to say."

"Clea"—Gryph kissed her again—"don't worry about it."

"I'm just so glad you're here." Clea took his face in her hands. "I thought you were gone."

"I'm here." Gryph pulled away. "But I need a few minutes with the guys. Alone. Okay?"

"Yeah," Clea said, clearly wounded. "Yeah. Of course."

No one had explained to Gryph what had happened to Saul and Neko, so the family gave the boys some space to tell Gryph. Of course, Oscar and Eva had no idea what had really happened to Saul and Neko, so they had no idea what Tariq and Huy were telling Gryph.

Everyone waited in the living room, and when nearly an hour had gone by, Fawn couldn't contain herself any longer. She was done playing with the twins and wanted to get on with the party.

"What about the cake?" she pestered Eva. "We have to have cake."

"Give them a little more time, honey."

"They've had enough time!" Fawn dashed out of the room and banged on the closed kitchen door. "Open up, it's Fawn."

With a pleading glance from her mother, Phee went after Fawn. The kitchen door opened, and Huy let Fawn in with a dramatic sweep of his arm. "Miss Fawn, you may enter."

Phee followed her little sister into the kitchen. Tariq and Gryph leaned against the counter in the very same pose, arms crossed, eyes not giving away the truths that had recently flown about the room. Huy stood in the middle of the room, a fake smile plastered on his face.

"Time for cake?"

"Cake! Cake!" Fawn ran to the fridge and lifted it out, struggling to hold it steady.

"Guys?" Phee took the cake from her as it angled dangerously toward the floor. "Everything okay?"

"Fine," Gryph snapped.

Tariq nodded.

"We're good for now," Huy added. Whatever that meant.

CLEA AND THE REST of the family trailed into the kitchen, cake was served, and for all appearances it looked like a great party. But Phee knew better. Gryph's smile was forced, and she could tell by the distant look in his eyes that he was upset about Neko and Saul.

Finally, her aunt and uncle took the twins home, and Eva walked her parents across the green to their house. The boys left, with Clea, who did not want to leave and had, in fact, cried until Gryph promised to see her the very next day. Everyone gone, Oscar ushered a reluctant Fawn upstairs for her bath.

"But I don't want to!" she screamed. "I want to stay up with Gryphon!"

"He'll be here in the morning," Oscar said. Then he turned to Gryph. "You will, right, kiddo?"

"I'm not going anywhere, Dad."

"Good to hear." Oscar picked up a thrashing Fawn and made his way up the stairs.

Gryph and Phee sat at the kitchen table amid the detritus of the party and stared at each other for what seemed like a year. Finally, Gryph broke the silence.

"Where's Nadia?"

"I don't know." The words caught in Phoenix's throat. "She won't talk to me."

Gryph hardened his expression. "Do you blame her?"

"Do you blame *us*? For doing what we did?"

"No," he replied. "I'd be lying if I said I did. I just ..." He ran his hands through his hair and sighed. "I just wish there was a better way. I just wish that I could go back and do it differently."

"You're alive. Neko's alive. Saul is safe."

"But that's not good enough. Neko's gone. Forever."

"Maybe not." Phee shrugged. And then she grinned. "Maybe he'll show up someday and surprise us all. Maybe he'll be short and fat and freckly."

Gryph laughed. "I doubt it." Another long moment of silence. Again, Gryph was the one to break it. "You want me to talk to Nadia?"

"No," Phee said.

Silence fell over them again. The clock above the doorway ticked away the seconds. This time it was Phoenix who spoke first.

"I'm glad you're home, Gryphon. I missed you."

Gryph nodded. "I'm glad I'm home too."

The back door opened with its customary creak and Eva swept in, still riding on the joy that had fuelled her since finding out that Gryph would be reconned. She spotted the two of them sitting at the table and laughed.

"Hang on." She backed outside and pulled the door shut. A few seconds passed and the door swung open again. "I will never get tired of that, seeing you where you belong, Gryph. At home. With us. Safe and sound."

WITH FAWN FINALLY ASLEEP, Oscar joined them all downstairs in the living room, where the four of them sat around, not sure what to do with themselves.

"We played Snakes and Ladders when I came home," Phee said. "Remember?"

"I hate Snakes and Ladders," Gryph said.

"At least you remember the rules."

"How about a game of chess, Phee?" Gryph pulled out the board and set it up. Eva and Oscar watched them for a while, then excused themselves and went off to bed.

Gryph was going to win, as usual.

"You haven't lost that skill," Phee said as he collected her queen, placing her alongside a legion of her pieces that he'd already captured.

"I'm sorry, Phoenix," Gryph said out of nowhere.

"About what?"

"About everything." He silently knocked over her king, ending the game. "I'm sorry that I pushed you in the river. I'm sorry that I've been such an asshole. I'm sorry for how awful the last few weeks must've been for you."

"It's okay, Gryph. Really."

"But most of all, I'm sorry about what happened with Neko. And that I cost you your best friend."

Phee felt her throat swelling, and she knew she was going to cry. She didn't want to. She'd cried so much over Nadia that she genuinely thought she didn't have a tear left.

EPILOGUE

Life eventually settled into what would have to suffice for the new normal, what with Saul and Neko gone.

And Nadia.

She had as good as vanished from Phee's life too. She felt adrift without Nadia.

She dreaded the first day of school so intensely that she threw up twice before she even got out the door. She couldn't understand how Gryph could be so calm about it. The whole school would rehash what had happened to him until they were tired of it, which would take who knew how long.

"It'll be okay," Gryph said as they got on the train. Sure enough, within seconds he was swept into a crowd of school-mates full of questions. He wrestled his way out to check on Phee as the train pulled into the school. "Want me to walk you in?"

"No thanks," she said. "Tariq is meeting me."

"Ah, boyfriend trumps brother."

"In this case, yes." Phee offered him what she hoped was a smile. "I can do without the fanfare you attract."

Clea, his biggest fan, was waiting with Huy on the front steps. After a quick hello, Phee excused herself and went around back, where Tariq was going to meet her.

"Hey." He greeted her with a kiss. "I'm surprised you came."

"My parents forced me to. Get back on the horse, it'll blow over, blah, blah, blah."

"It will." Tariq took her hand and steered her to a bench, where they sat for a while, watching kids stream into the building with their new clothes and bulging backpacks. They'd probably all had very ordinary summers. How gladly Phee would have traded with any one of them.

"I used to love the first day of school," she said. "Nadia and I always took the same train. The eight-ten. After we'd spent most of the night before texting each other about what to wear. Or not wear."

"Speak of the devil," Tariq said, pointing. "Look."

Nadia was walking across the field, heading straight for her.

Phee turned to Tariq. "Did you talk to her?"

"Nope."

"Gryph or Huy?"

"Not that I know of."

"Not Clea?"

"I doubt it."

"No one put her up to this? Promise?"

"Promise." He stood, bending to kiss her lightly on the lips. "I'll let you girls work it out."

Phee felt a smile stretch across her face, even though she doubted Nadia was coming over to be pleasant. She was probably going to lay down the law and tell her not to talk to her, not to eat lunch near her, not to come up to her in the hallway. No matter, though, Phee couldn't get rid of her grin.

"Nadia!" Phee leaped up.

Nadia hesitated, then sloughed off her backpack and gave Phee the fiercest hug ever.

"I can't do it anymore." Nadia cried on her shoulder. "I can't lose you too."

"Me either."

"For now, though"—she pulled away and gave Phee a serious look—"I don't want to talk about it. I mean it. Okay?"

"Whatever you say."

"But I will tell you something." Nadia cupped a hand to Phee's ear. "I heard from Neko and Saul ... Marlin, whoever," she whispered.

"You did?" Phee glanced around to make sure no one was near.

"They're okay." Nadia grinned. "They're on the East Coast with his parents. I don't know where exactly, but they're okay. Neko's even in school."

Phee was so relieved. All this time she tried not to think about Neko and Marlin and where they were, or what they were doing. The first bell rang.

"Come on." Nadia grabbed her hand and pulled her up. "Let's go. We're going to be late. And you have to tell me what's going on between you and Tariq."

ACKNOWLEDGMENTS

Thanks be to the sharp and critical minds of Jake Powrie, Morgan Roff, Eleanor Roberts, Emily Harris, Geneva Haughton, Emanuelle Lyons, and especially Christianne Hayward, who brings together all the adolescent brilliance on a regular basis. It is always a pleasure and an honour to stand in front of such a talented young firing squad.